JACOB BUNN

Legacy of an Illinois Industrial Pioneer

JACOB BUNN
Legacy of an Illinois Industrial Pioneer

Andrew Taylor Call

BRUNSWICK PUBLISHING
LAWRENCEVILLE, VIRGINIA

Copyright © 2005 by Andrew Taylor Call

All rights reserved under International and Pan-American Copyright Conventions. No part of this book may be reproduced in any form or by any means, electronic or mechanical, including photocopying or by any informational storage or retrieval systems, without written permission from the author and the publisher, except by a reviewer who may quote brief passages in a review.

Library of Congress Cataloging-in-Publication Data

Call, Andrew Taylor, 1981–
    Jacob Bunn : legacy of an Illinois industrial pioneer / Andrew Taylor Call.
        p. cm.
    Includes bibliographical references and index.
    ISBN 1-55618-209-0 (alk. paper)
    1. Bunn, Jacob, 1814–1897. 2. Businessmen—Illinois—Biography. 3. Business and politics—Illinois—History—19th century. 4. Illinois—Economic conditions—19th century. I. Title

CT275.B78518C35 2005
977.3'03'092—dc22
[B]

ISBN 10: 1-55618-209-0
ISBN 13: 978-1-55618-209-9

Cover Design by Elizabeth T. Greer and Melinda Williams
Photo of author by Duane Willie and Better Image Photography

First Edition
Published in the United States of America by

Brunswick Publishing Corporation
1386 Lawrenceville Plank Road • Lawrenceville, Virginia 23868
434-848-3865 • http://www.brunswickbooks.com
http://www.bunnlegacy.com

"Westward the course of empire takes its way. . . ."[1]
— George Berkeley

This book is dedicated to my grandfathers, who embodied the highest ethical standards in business leadership, the greatest generosity in civic benefaction, and the sincerest respect for individual vision and integrity in commerce and in society.

•

Henry Stryker Taylor, 1908-1994
William Frederick Call, 1912-1973

•

This work is also dedicated to my great-uncles who were and will always remain a great source of inspiration to me.

•

Willard Bunn, Jr., 1913-2002
George Regan Bunn, 1915-2002

Brief Bunn Family History

Jacob and Elizabeth Jane Ferguson Bunn (who died in 1886) had the following children:

    William Ferguson b. 1852 never married

    Mary b. 1854 died

    Sarah Irwin b. 1856 married Frank Hatch Jones

    Henry b. 1858 never married

    George Wallace b. 1861 married Ada Willard Richardson

    Jacob, Jr., b. 1864 married Mildred Jeffress

    Alice Edwards b. 1867 never married

In New Jersey, Jacob Bunn, b. 1736, married a Mary Elizabeth _____; their son Henry Bunn, b. 1772 married Mary Sigler, b. c. 1787, and had sons Jacob, b. 1814 and John Whitfield, b. 1831 (among many other children who stayed in the East); then Jacob in Illinois married Elizabeth and had Henry b. 1858 and Jacob, Jr., b. 1864 (as well as the other children listed); this Henry never married. Except for the very beginning of the book, all the Henry Bunn references are to the son of Jacob Bunn in Illinois.

Note: Sarah Irwin Bunn married lawyer Frank Hatch Jones in the early 1880s; she died in 1892; when her husband remarried, he married Nellie Grant Sartoris, daughter of Ulysses S. Grant (all are buried in the Bunn plot at Oak Ridge Cemetery in Springfield).

George Wallace Bunn married Ada Willard Richardson in 1886; they had Willard Bunn who married Ruth Regan, and George "Gib" Wallace Bunn, Jr., who married Melinda Jones.

Table of Contents

TABLE OF ILLUSTRATIONS AND PHOTOGRAPHS xi

ACKNOWLEDGEMENTS xv

INTRODUCTION 1

CHAPTER I
    The Genealogy and Family History of Jacob Bunn 9

CHAPTER II
    From Hunterdon to Sangamon 13

CHAPTER III
    The J. Bunn Grocery Company: Academy
    for Young Business Visionaries 19

CHAPTER IV
    Visions for Utility, Infrastructure, and the
    Birth of a City 34

CHAPTER V
    The Bunn-Lincoln Machine: Network of
    Integrity and Promotion 70

CHAPTER VI
    A Friend for the Friendless 87

CHAPTER VII
    Steel Rails and Sugar Beets 96

CHAPTER VIII
    Twilight of the Springfield Banker 160

Chapter IX
The Timepiece Savior 180

Chapter X
Echoes of Industry and Reflections of Integrity 227

Appendix

I. General Chronology of the Mechanical Innovations of the Sangamo Electric Company 249

II. Some Key Institutional Components of the Sangamo Electric Company Corporate Family 253

III. General Table of Executives and Various Positions Occupied 256

Notes 261

Bibliography 275

Index 283

Table of Illustrations and Photographs

1. Jacob Bunn. 42
2. John Whitfield Bunn as a young businessman in Illinois, and a protégé of Jacob Bunn. 43
3. John W. Bunn & Company: wholesale building and principal offices. 44
4. The J. Bunn Grocery Company. 45
5. Bunn Capitol Grocery Company coffee coupon. 46
6. An artist's interpretation of the Southwest corner of the Springfield Town Square. 46
7. "Wishbone Coffee" label, on an original Bunn Capitol Grocery Company coffee tin. 47
8. "Bunn Capitol Grocery Company" business label, on same original "Wishbone Coffee" tin. 47
9. Elizabeth Jane Ferguson, the wife of Jacob Bunn. 48
10. Illinois Watch Company series portrait of Abraham Lincoln. 49
11. Close-up view of the John W. Bunn and Company building and office, in Springfield. 50
12. First Presbyterian Church, Springfield, Illinois. 51
13. The Springfield Home for the Friendless. 52
14. Richard Yates. 53
15. Lucretia (Wheeler) Johns Douglas. 54
16. Betsey Elizabeth (Johns) Richardson. 55
17. Lucy (Willard) Richardson. 56
18. Illinois State Capitol. 57
19. Ada Willard Richardson as a young girl. 58
20. Original photograph of George Wallace Bunn. 59
21. John Whitfield Bunn in middle age. 60
22. William Douglas Richardson as a young businessman. .. 61
23. William Douglas Richardson in middle age. 62

24. Stock certificate of the Springfield Iron Company. 63
25. Advertisement for the Springfield Iron Company. 64
26. La Fayette Smith. 65
27. An artist's rendering of the Springfield Iron
    Company factory complex. 66
28. Up-close image of Springfield Iron Company
    buildings. 66
29. Group photograph taken of several Springfield Iron
    Company employees. 67
30. Group photograph taken of several Springfield Iron
    Company employees. 67
31. The Lincoln Monument, in Oak Ridge Cemetery,
    Springfield, Illinois. 68
32. The Illinois State Capitol, with street railway tracks
    converging in the distance. 69
33. Orlin H. Miner. 140
34. Shelby Moore Cullom. 140
35. Charles Henry Rosenstiel as an older man. 141

THE FREEPORT TRIUMVIRATE
36. Jacob Bunn. 142
37. Charles Henry Rosenstiel. 142
38. Jerome Increase Case. 142

39. Jerome Increase Case and the "Big Four" of the
    agricultural machinery industry. 143
40. Charles Richardson. 144
41. The Leland Hotel of Springfield, Illinois. 145
42. The Chicago and Alton Railroad Company
    train depot in Springfield. 146
43. Morris Selz and his son J. Harry Selz of Chicago. 147
44. Charles H. Schwab. 148
45. John Villiers Farwell. 149
46. Charles Benjamin Farwell. 149
47. Portrait of John Whitfield Bunn. 150
48. The Springfield Marine Bank, originally known as the
    Springfield Marine and Fire Insurance Company. 151
49. The Lincoln Library. 152
50. Benjamin Hamilton Ferguson. 153
51. Portrait of Antrim Campbell. 153

52. Portrait of Robert Irwin. 153
53. The facade and entrance to the Springfield
    Marine Bank. 154
54. An artist's rendition of the Springfield Marine Bank. 155
55. F. K. Whittemore. 156
56. The Springfield Marine Bank in the late 20th
    century during some renovation. 157
57. Judge Christopher C. Brown. 158
58. An original check written on an account at the
    J. Bunn Bank. 159
59. An unused notebook bearing the corporate seal
    of the Springfield Marine Bank. 159
60. John C. Adams. 201
61. John Todd Stuart, Esq. 201
62. John Willliams. 201
63. Jacob Bunn and Jacob Bunn, Jr. 202
64. Factory and principal offices of the Illinois
    Watch Company. 203
65. A detailed illustration of the Illinois Watch
    Company campus. 203
66. The interior label of an Abraham Lincoln
    Essay Contest Award medal case. 204
67. A Lincoln Essay medal. 204
68. The reverse side of the Lincoln Essay medal. 204
69. Color postcard of Illinois Watch Company. 205
70. Reverse side of color postcard of Illinois Watch
    Company. 205
71. Color collage postcard promoting Illinois
    Watch Company. 206
72. Reverse of collage postcard promoting Illinois
    Watch Company. 206
73. Stock certificate of Springfield Watch Company. 207
74. Illinois Springfield Watch Company wooden box. 207
75. Landscaped entrance to Illinois Watch Company. 208
76. Photograph of Illinois Watch Company. 208
77. Advertisement for Illinois Watch Company wrist
    watches. 209
78. Illinois Watch Company advertisement. 210
79. Another wrist watch advertisement for the Illinois
    Watch Company. 211

80. Another wrist watch advertisement for the Illinois Watch Company. 212
81. Photograph of Illinois Watch Company employee and executive party. 213
82. Photograph of one of the Illinois Watch Company Women's Clubs. 214
83. Large group photograph of employees of Illinois Watch Company. 214
84. Another employee gathering at the Illinois Watch Company. 215
85. Illinois Watch Company employees working. 215
86. Worker administering radio transmissions at Illinois Watch Company. 216
87. Another photograph of the production process at the Illinois Watch factory. 217
88. The Illinois Watch Company and campus after a severe ice storm. 217
89. John Whitfield Bunn as an elderly man. 218
90. Pocket watch that belonged to a great-grandson of Jacob Bunn. 219
91. Wrist watch that belonged to Ruth (Regan) Bunn. 219
92. An Elgin Watch Company pocket watch. 220
93. An Illinois Watch Company pocket watch. 220
94. Another Illinois Watch Company pocket watch. 220
95. "Bunn Special" Railroad pocket watch. 221
96. Closed-faced Illinois Watch Company pocket watch. 221
97. Open-faced Illinois Watch Company pocket watch. 221
98. Robert Carr Lanphier. 222
99. Jacob Bunn, Jr. 223
100. Sangamo Electric Company factory poster and advertisement. 224
101. Photograph of Springfield factory and campus of Sangamo Electric Company. 224
102. Advertisement for the Sangamo Electric clock. 225
103. Sangamo tachograph. 226

Acknowledgements

The author wishes to acknowledge with sincerest gratitude and highest respect the following people and institutions (in alphabetical order), whose inspiration, assistance and counsel made this biography possible:

- Alderman Library of the University of Virginia and all of its staff and librarians.
- Brenda Anderson, Administrative Assistant, Bank One Springfield.
- Kim Bauer, Lincoln Curator, Abraham Lincoln Presidential Library (formerly the Illinois State Historical Library).
- David Bunn Boynton, a great-great-grandson of Jacob Bunn.
- Robert H. Bunn, President, Bunn Capitol, Inc., and a great-great-grandson of Jacob Bunn.
- Willard Bunn, III, a great-great-grandson of Jacob Bunn.
- Connie Butts, Manuscripts Cataloger, Abraham Lincoln Presidential Library (formerly the Illinois State Historical Library).
- Matthew Baldwin Call, my father, a retired History, German, and Russian teacher, and my friend and advisor.
- Bruce Alexander Campbell, author of *The Sangamon Saga*.
- Bob Cavanagh, Reference Assistant, Abraham Lincoln Presidential Library (formerly the Illinois State Historical Library).
- Jim Cohlmeyer, Archivist II, Inventory Control Section, Illinois State Archives.
- Dr. Evan Davis, Visiting Assistant Professor of English and Rhetoric, Hampden-Sydney College.

- Katherine Sankey Davis, a descendant of George W. Chatterton and Virgil Hickox.
- Earl Gregg Swem Library, College of William and Mary, Williamsburg, Virginia, and especially Debra Weiss, Reference Librarian, and Hope Yelich, Cathy Reed, Christie Arntz.
- Jane Ehrenhart, Supervisor, Reference and Technical Services, Abraham Lincoln Presidential Library (formerly the Illinois State Historical Library).
- Susan Enlow, great-great-granddaughter of Jacob Bunn.
- Family of George Regan Bunn for their encouragement throughout this project.
- Family of Willard Bunn, Jr., for their encouragement, support and assistance throughout this project.
- Fred Friedberg, Esq., Senior Vice President and General Counsel, Toshiba Medical Supply, Inc., and author of *The Illinois Watch: The Life and Times of a Great American Watch Company*. 2004.
- William Furry, Acting Assistant Executive Director, Illinois State Historical Society.
- Farrell Gay, for his generous contributions of Illinois Watch Co. and Sangamo Electric Co. memorabilia.
- Linda Garvert.
- Dave Grabarek of the Library of Virginia.
- Elizabeth Taylor Greer, my mother and editor, publisher of *Blue Ridge Traditions* magazine, owner of the Blue Lady Bookshop, and a great-great-granddaughter of Jacob Bunn.
- T. Keister Greer, my step-father, a retired attorney, and author of the legal history, *The Great Moonshine Conspiracy Trial of 1935*. 2003.
- Kathryn M. Harris, Division Manager, Library Services, Abraham Lincoln Presidential Library (formerly the Illinois State Historical Library).
- Dr. Richard P. Hattwick, Chairman, National Business Hall of Fame.

- Dr. John Hoffmann, Librarian, Illinois Historical Survey, University of Illinois Library, Urbana-Champaign.
- Dr. Kurt Hohenstein, Esq., Associate Professor of History, University of Virginia (2003).
- Barry Houmes, Farm Manager, Farm Department, Bank One Springfield.
- The Illinois State Historical Library and specifically its Director Kathryn M. Harris and its librarians Jane Ehrenhart, Connie Butts, Jan Perone, and Bob Cavanagh.
- Gerald Karwowski and the Oak Clearing Museum of Union Grove, Wisconsin.
- Dr. Joseph F. Kett, Corcoran Professor of History, University of Virginia (my advisor and friend).
- David Lee, MyFamily.com, Inc.
- Anthony J. Leone, Jr., and the George Pasfield House.
- The Lexington Genealogical & Historical Society, Inc., Lexington, Illinois, and specifically its researcher and historian Dennis Hieronymus.
- The Library of Virginia (Richmond, Virginia) and its Staff and Librarians.
- Barry J. Locher, Editor, *The State Journal Register*, Springfield, Illinois.
- Curtis Mann.
- The National Association of Watch and Clock Collectors, Columbia, Pennsylvania.
- Linda Oelheim, Reference Associate, Abraham Lincoln Presidential Library (formerly the Illinois State Historical Library).
- Jan Perone, Newspaper Librarian, Abraham Lincoln Presidential Library (formerly the Illinois State Historical Library).
- Ted Polk of the Library of Virginia.
- The Prairie Archives, Springfield, Illinois.
- Walter J. and Marianne S. Raymond, Publishers.
- John Reinhardt, Supervisor, Inventory Control Section, Illinois State Archives.

- Joe Rosenstiel of Rochester, New York, great-great-grandson of Charles Henry Rosenstiel, Illinois agribusiness and industrial visionary.
- Matt Rutherford, Reference Librarian, Local and Family History, The Newberry Library.
- Edward J. Russo.
- The Sangamon County Historical Society.
- The Sangamon Valley Collection of the Lincoln Library and specifically its historians Curtis Mann, Linda Garvert and Edward J. Russo.
- Christopher Schnell, Assistant Editor, Papers of Abraham Lincoln.
- Cheryl Schnirring, Manuscripts Manager, Abraham Lincoln Presidential Library (formerly the Illinois State Historical Library).
- Stacey Skeeters, Operations Associate, Inventory Control Section, Illinois State Archives.
- Ruth Solomon, great-granddaughter of Charles Richardson, for her very generous contribution of family photographs.
- The Stephenson County Genealogical Society, Freeport, Illinois, and The Freeport Public Library.
- Julia Stewart, Night Assistant and Circulation Librarian, Carrier Library of James Madison University.
- Elizabeth Bunn Taylor, my maternal grandmother, and a great-granddaughter of Jacob Bunn.
- Dr. Mark Thomas, Professor of History, University of Virginia.
- Debra Weiss, Reference Librarian, Earl Gregg Swem Library, College of William & Mary.
- Melinda Williams of Melinda's Computer Graphics.

Introduction

This book celebrates and examines an Illinois industrial pioneer, Jacob Bunn (1814-1897). It is simultaneously a biographical sketch, a career study, and a brief treatise on the economic maturation of a frontier region. It is a study in entrepreneurship, an examination of nascent industry, a study in business strategy, and a display of multifarious legacies left by the achievements of many people. The work is, moreover, an illustration of the highest forms of business integrity, of civic benefaction, and of personal commitment to success.

The setting of this work is Springfield, Sangamon County, Illinois, and other regions of the state. The period is the 19th century. Many of the achievements discussed begin by having impact upon nothing more than local communities; some of these achievements culminate in exerting influence upon nothing less than the world.

An important chapter in the annals of Illinois history is the career of Jacob Bunn, a 19th century pioneer, businessman, and industrialist whose experience encompassed much of the historical development of the City of Springfield, the County of Sangamon, and the State of Illinois.

Jacob Bunn was the founder or co-founder of more than fourteen business enterprises; many of these were small concerns, yet some attained massive proportions, and also led to later corporations of international note. All were monuments to his business abilities. An initial inventory of the themes that course through this historical treatise is appropriate. At no point is one theme separate from the others; each exists in a mutual collaboration with the others to represent a coherent system of social action that should serve as a model for individuals who are engaged in business and philanthropy. Throughout this paper are interwoven the themes of personal vision for success, dedication, perseverance, honor, integrity, altruism, civic benefaction, legacy, and the discernment and successful exploitation of economic opportunities. Bunn represents the social phenomenon described by Robert D. Putnam as the "social capitalist," one who understands how to orchestrate the human and material resources of a region to the benefit of all people involved.

In Robert D. Putnam's sociological treatise, *Bowling Alone,* Putnam articulates the characteristics of "social capital." The benefits of social capital include the ability of citizens to resolve collective problems with greater ease and the power of the individual and the collective to generate societal advancement through communities of trust and dependability. Social capital gives one a valuable perspective on the fates of other people and the circumstances of one's environment, the formation of valuable communication networks, and psychological and even biological improvements in individuals' lives.[2]

Jacob Bunn helped to bring about vast amounts of social capital in 19th century Springfield. He worked with other civic and business leaders to perpetuate a myriad of social benefits, ranging from food distribution and municipal utilities to improvements in the banking and manufacturing sectors of central Illinois. Bunn and the others with whom he collaborated upon so many endeavors should serve as examples to the business and civic leaders of the communities of today.

Wherever there exists a drought of social capital there exists simultaneously a wealth of opportunities for the "social capitalist" to instigate a capital recuperation in the area where the reservoir is becoming arid. The life of Jacob Bunn exemplifies the traits of the successful social capitalist, and illustrates brilliantly the achievements that the accomplished social capitalist can have through a lifetime of work, dedication, vision, and honor. Edward Russo states in his book *Jacob Bunn and His Descendants,*

> Historian Don Harrison Doyle speaks of the central theme of 'individual opportunity' which became a great part of the folklore of early Illinois and the West;
>
> 'The chances for underprivileged but hard-working young men to succeed in an open society were continually celebrated in newspapers, literature, and political rhetoric. The model was a young man who left his family and secure environment in the East in order to build a career in a wonderfully open western society—who built their careers and fortunes out of nothing more than their own talent and sheer determination.'[3]

This statement characterizes the life of Jacob Bunn with indisputable precision. Jacob Bunn was engaged in business for approximately sixty years consecutively, from about 1836/1837 to the autumn of 1897. Throughout that period, he was engaged as a grocer, commissioner, utility promulgator, bank founder, bank director, sales agent, financier, Republican campaign manager, entertainment entrepreneur, coal entrepreneur, securities capitalist, newspaperman, land speculator, manufacturer, hotel owner, railroad promoter, railroad director, agriculturalist, civic leader, and comprehensive business visionary.

An examination of his life attempts to provide as detailed an account as possible of each of the aspects of Bunn's business career. Due, however, to the varying availability of germane historical documents, certain phases are explained and described in greater detail than others. This book is an assemblage of numerous and diverse historical documents, among which are both primary and secondary sources, recent and antique documents, detailed and general accounts. Each document, however, serves a purpose, and each possesses value either as a direct view or as a mirror of the complex and varied sociopolitical and industrial natures of the state of Illinois in the 19th century.

For the purpose of devoting more specialized attention to the patterns of the entrepreneurial achievements of Jacob Bunn and of the business leaders with whom he was associated, the contents have been arranged according to a thematic scheme, and not a strictly chronological one. Such a plan will better enable a more complete account of the development of each phase of the careers examined in the following pages. A general career chronology has been assembled at the end of this chapter for the purpose of assisting the reader with a precise placement of numerous key events, and can be referred to as a legend.

This work is meant to celebrate the unique achievements of many of the leading business and industrial visionaries of Springfield, and the individuals with whom they collaborated to help raise the state of Illinois from a pioneer region to one of the leading commercial centers in the United States. Although this commercial "saga" is told primarily from the perspective of Jacob Bunn, it is meant to recognize and honor the achievements of all who are mentioned here. The story of Bunn's achievements and legacy is also meant to recognize all who have followed the examples of integrity, vision, an undying determination to overcome obstacles, and a commitment to influencing family, community and society in positive ways. Although this book could not possibly provide a comprehensive enumeration of the business and civic achievements of all such people who lived and operated during the 19th century in Illinois, it should nonetheless be viewed as a commemoration of these unnamed people.

It is the intention of this study to depict the strong character of Illinois businessmen of the 19th century and the character of those who have followed them. Let us hope that the younger generations of the present will seek to emulate the qualities of the business and civic leaders that are set forth in the following chapters. The examples of the men and women in this book should serve as models for business and civic endeavor. Furthermore, these examples of vision and integrity are both timeless and essential to the survival of business communities and to the survival of communities as a whole. It is hoped that this book will serve in some capacity to help rekindle a renaissance of business integrity at all levels of operation.

May this study serve as a source of inspiration to business people of all ages. Let there come about an "integrity revolution" in American business communities, so that a widespread recuperation of image can be enjoyed by the business communities of the present time. Let the true essentials of commercial enterprise—integrity, vision, determination, and a solid concept of business as a phenomenon inextricably connected to the communities that surround it—be rediscovered and preserved, not as incidental lessons of little effect, but as the primary guiding principles of action in the commercial arts.

A General Chronology of the Business Careers of Jacob Bunn

- 1836-1840: Organizes at least one local grocery business, in Beardstown and in Naples, Illinois.

- 1840: Co-founds McConnel, Bunn & Van Syckel, on July 1 of that year.

- 1841/1842: Becomes sole proprietor of the grocery business, having purchased the interests of partners McConnel and Van Syckel; alters business name to "J. Bunn Grocery Company" [1934–present, named Bunn Capital Grocery Company].

- 1845: Organizes the Springfield Rope Company.

- 1848: Assists with the financing and establishment of the Springfield Telegraph.

- 1851: Incorporates with other investors the Springfield Marine and Fire Insurance Company.

- 1857: Incorporates with other investors the Springfield Waterworks Company.
- 1858: Incorporates with other investors the Springfield & Pana Railroad Company.
- 1858: Organizes the J. Bunn Bank in Springfield
- 1850s: Supports Abraham Lincoln financially and socially in his presidential campaign.
- 1861: Incorporates with other investors the Springfield City Railway Company.

  Serves as one of the commissioners and founders of the Chicago and Alton Railroad Company.

  The Civil War begins.
- 1865: Incorporates with other investors the Pana, Springfield and Northwestern Railroad Company.

  Incorporates with other investors the Chicago Republican Newspaper Company.

  Incorporates with other investors the Germania Sugar Company in Chatsworth, Illinois.

  The Civil War ends.
- 1868/1869: Obtains exclusive proprietorship of Western Coal & Mining Company, the Sangamon Distilling Company, Riverton house lots, hotel, and extensive acreage of land with coal rights.
- 1869: Promotes, along with other businessmen, the Springfield Board of Trade.

- 1871: The Great Fire of Chicago.
- 1871/1872: Co-organizes Rosenstiel, Bunn & Case, a partnership established for the purpose of manufacturing sugar from beets.
- 1873: Panic of 1873 commences in September.
- 1877/1878: Reorganizes the Illinois Springfield Watch Company, changing the corporate name to "Illinois Watch Company."

    Commences process of liquidation of personal assets.
- 1878: J. Bunn Bank closes officially due to financial failure caused by The Panic of 1873.
- 1878-1897: Serves as president of the Illinois Watch Company and as Chairman of the Board of Directors of the Company, on numerous occasions.
- 1890: Final liquidation of Jacob Bunn's personal assets is completed by Judge Christopher C. Brown in July.
- 1897: Dies in an office of the Illinois Watch Company on October 16.

I

The Genealogy and Family History of Jacob Bunn

Tracing the genealogy of this particular Bunn family has been a source of frustration to the most ambitious genealogists. Nonetheless, researchers have successfully located a considerable body of definitive data on the immediate ancestry of Jacob Bunn, and research has generated solid and educated theories as to the identities of his more distant progenitors. Although only two generations of paternal ancestors have been documented definitively beyond Jacob Bunn, it is possible that the ultimate paternal ancestor in America was an Edward Bunn, a native of England who settled in Massachusetts.

A record dating from 1642 indicates that Edward was already 50 years old in that year. There exists also a record of a Matthew Bunn, a son of Edward Bunn, who moved to New Jersey in 1670.[4] A Jacob Bunn who was born in or about 1736, and who is the proven paternal grandfather of the Jacob Bunn who is the subject of this treatise lived in Hunterdon County, New Jersey, during the 18th century.

The family was Presbyterian. They attended the Presbyterian church located near their farmstead in the village of Alexandria. In this church existed the baptismal records of Jacob's and his wife's ten children. Among these offspring was a son, Henry, who was born in 1772. Henry's youth was spent becoming accustomed to the occupations of farming and stock-raising.⁵ He married a Pennsylvania native by the name of Mary Sigler, in approximately 1808, and relocated to a farm near the farm belonging to his parents. Mary Sigler Bunn died at the age of forty-five in July of 1833. Their third child, and firstborn son, Jacob, the subject of this paper, was named for his grandfather.⁶

>Jacob Bunn (b. 1736) = Mary Elizabeth _____
>|
>Henry Bunn (b. 19 October 1772; d. 1859)
>= Mary Sigler (b. ca. 1787; d. 1833)
>|
>Jacob Bunn (b. 18 March 1814; d. 16 October 1897)

Jacob Bunn was born 18 March 1814 in Hunterdon County, New Jersey.⁷ His year of birth placed him in a period of United States history that predates by over a decade the dawn of the era of large railroad companies, which would begin with the chartering of the Baltimore and Ohio Railroad Company in February of 1827. Consequently, the lives of pioneer businessmen such as Jacob Bunn evolved in an era that was largely connected with the development of the railroad industry in America. As railroad companies were chartered, and as these companies began to construct increasingly extensive networks of transportation and commerce, they helped to bring about the birth of new towns and cities, thereby creating new zones and centers of commerce. Exactly these types of regions, with a prospect of prosperity, were the quintessential socioeconomic forums for individual vision, integrity, achievement, and legacy.

Little is definitively known of the early boyhood or adolescence of Jacob Bunn. It is certain, however, that for the first twenty-two years of life he would have been constantly engaged in assisting his father and siblings in maintaining an agricultural livelihood. This would have been true particularly after the death of his mother in 1833, which occurred when Jacob was nineteen years of age. "For a young boy facing the perplexities of coming manhood, the sudden assumption of family responsibility must have weighed heavily indeed."[8]

It would have seemed that he would inherit the New Jersey agricultural life that had served as the occupation of his ancestors and siblings. Such an inheritance would never take place, however, as Bunn would be the first of his family to abandon the agrarian lifestyle of western New Jersey, and the first of the family to pioneer westward to the prairie and river towns of the more distant regions of what had been referred to as the Old Northwest. In his day our Midwest was still considered the frontier, the "West."

Bunn's life was exemplary of the "rags to riches" story that the lives of so many entrepreneurs of the late 18th century and 19th century also illustrated. The story of this life and legacy began with the decision to travel westward with the hope shared by so many people of his time for success and fortune. "The great West, with opportunity for all, was <u>the</u> major fascination for countless Americans in the 19th century and especially for the inhabitants of New Jersey."[9] Bunn, like many of his compeers, discerned the opportunities available in the West, and decided to partake of the promise of fortune that they offered so vividly.

His decision to leave New Jersey and to travel westward can be viewed as the commencement of his first venture. The remark made by John Babsone Lane Soule, "Go West, young man, and grow up with the country," which was immortalized by Horace Greeley's editorial in the *New York Tribune*,[10] characterizes the contents of the following chapters of Jacob Bunn's life with sterling precision.

Jacob Bunn did not only grow up with the country, but he and all others like him were also an inseparable part of what helped to grow the country, thereby drawing other nascent visionaries from eastern states or foreign countries. All such individuals ultimately assumed prominent seats within the set of American pioneers who built the industrial Midwest of the United States. Midwestern businessmen, lawyers, educators, medical professionals, artists, authors, laborers, and farmers must all be viewed as builders of American frontier society. Illinois has been one of the most dynamic theaters of commercial vision and industrial power in the American experience, and its leaders have much to teach the business communities of the present day.

II

From Hunterdon to Sangamon

At the age of twenty-two, Jacob Bunn left New Jersey for Illinois, having been made aware of the "fertility of the Illinois country."[11] He arrived for the first time in Springfield, Illinois, in May of 1836. Springfield at this time possessed a population of 1,951, and "seemed to hold little promise for greatness," due largely to an absence of navigable waterways during an age when the steamboat was a dominant mode of transportation.[12] At this time, Vandalia was the capital of the state of Illinois,[13] which had attained official statehood on 3 December 1818,[14] having theretofore enjoyed territorial status since statutory declaration on 1 March 1809.[15]

Bunn traveled onwards toward the western towns of Illinois, on the Illinois River, a major regional artery of commerce which connected its numerous port centers to the Mississippi River, and therefore to the commercial centers of the globe. He settled in Naples, Morgan County, Illinois. Naples was a town of six hundred permanent residents, with ample boat landings and river traffic of three hundred steamboat arrivals and departures each year.[16] The locale provided ideal circumstances for commercial initiative, and it would be small river villages like Naples that would be the site of Bunn's first undertaking in business.

It was in the commercial centers of Naples and Beardstown, Illinois, where Bunn established himself in business for the first time. He entered business as a wholesale grocer. The precise date when Bunn established his initial business is unknown. Moreover, the wherewithal he utilized in doing so is also not known.[17] His establishment of the business would in all likelihood have been sometime in early 1837.

In building up the grocery business of which he had been founder he traveled by boat to cities such as New Orleans, in order to procure the goods necessary for a healthy grocery enterprise.[18] It is likely that St. Louis would also have been among his more frequent ports of call, as it was a leading center of commerce and travel. The grocery business and the travels that were required to operate successfully in this sector of the frontier economy quickly transformed Bunn into a cosmopolitan merchant who was abundantly aware of the possibilities for fruitful commercial ventures in towns situated on rivers of the magnitude of the Mississippi.

One should take immediate notice of the devotion that Bunn exhibited in organizing and tending to the small wholesale grocery business in which he was engaged, which, as far as has been ascertained thus far, was his first entrepreneurial activity. This business would remain a permanent component of his subsequent business undertakings, as would the characteristic unwavering devotion to all business endeavor, which he exhibited always. Despite the apparent success that Bunn experienced in the Illinois River villages of Naples and Beardstown, he would not remain in Morgan County for very long. Nonetheless, Morgan County would always remain the authentic beginning of the commercial career of Jacob Bunn.

At the end of the third decade of the 19th century news arrived that the locus of the state capital was being transferred from Vandalia to Springfield. In December of 1839, the seat of government was officially transferred to Springfield.[19] Acting again as a visionary, and discerning the potential benefits of relocating to the new state capital, Bunn decided to move to Springfield for the purpose of establishing business operations in the new state capital. He certainly would have made this decision on an intuition that a new capital city would provide a location to successfully initiate and develop a business enterprise. From this point in time onward, Springfield would remain the new matrix of state legislative and economic decision-making power, and as a result, would be a strategically advantageous location for any entrepreneur, in any line of business. Prior to becoming the state capital, Springfield had existed as a settlement for many years.

Elisha Kelley, a North Carolinian, had settled in the area that later became the township of Springfield. It was the Kelley family that originated the name "Springfield." Their cabin had been situated in a field with trees and a spring. Elisha Kelley had initially visited the soon to be created State of Illinois in the spring of 1818.[20] While Kelley was among the patriarchs of initial settlement in the region, the founder of the Sangamon County business community was arguably Elijah Iles.

Elijah Iles was a Kentucky native, who through his

mother's family, was related to "Davy" Crockett. He had herded cattle for many years. Abandoning this livelihood, Iles traveled west, becoming a land agent for eastern speculators. He decided that Missouri was too distant from pertinent markets, and moved to Springfield, where he opened the first storehouse in June of the year 1821. His business dealt in wrought iron, pot metal, and dry goods. He developed an extensive trade with the Indians and other settlers, and the geographical scope of his enterprise was considerable, extending from the Illinois River in the west to Champaign County in the east, and from Tazewell County in the north to Macoupin County in the south.[21] Iles was among the pioneer merchants whose contributions to the success of the maturing economies of central Illinois helped to lay the foundations upon which later business pioneers, such as Jacob Bunn, could build. The diversity of business occupations in Sangamon County flowered as the number of settlers increased.

Other first generation Springfield businessmen included Jacob Roll, a storekeeper, Jacob Carman, a tavern keeper, Robert Pulliam, the first licensed tavern keeper in Sangamon County, and Archer Herndon, the owner of the Indian Queen Tavern.[22]

Other individuals who were instrumental in the founding of the business sectors of Springfield and Sangamon County were Hooper Warren, founder and printer of the *Sangamo Spectator* in 1826, the first newspaper in Sangamon County; Thomas Cox, a distiller; Thomas Strawbridge, the county's first saddler; William G. Cantrall, a cotton pioneer; Jacob Ellis, a blacksmith; James and Joseph Sheppard, proprietors of grist mills; Benjamin McElwain, who operated a carding machine; Jabez Capps, a shoemaker; John Evey, a pot manufacturer; and H. M. Armstrong, a hat manufacturer. John Dryer set up the first woolen mills along with H. M. Armstrong, in 1834. Asa and George Eastman were the establishers of a steam mill at Springfield. Other pioneering concerns included Hurst & Taylor, merchants, and Jonathan Roland Diller and Dr. William S. Wallace, both of whom were engaged in the druggists' business.[23]

The town of Springfield was incorporated 2 April 1832, with its present name having been declared official upon its incorporation. Among the various proposals for the city's name were included "Sangamo," and "Calhoun." Matters of civic development quickly came to the surface. Immediately subsequent to the city's incorporation the Board of Trustees established a Board of Health, to tend to issues of sanitation. The Trustees also enacted numerous ordinances for the purpose of introducing a greater degree of civic order than there had been prior to these regulations. Among these were prohibitive levies exacted on acts of public nuisance and regulations regarding people's custody of animals.[24]

Among Springfield's pioneer social and artistic developments was the inception of a choral society, which began in the Second Presbyterian Church in 1835. Forming the "nucleus of the first musical society in the city…It was known as the Springfield Harmonic Society and was formed for the purpose of cultivating sacred music."[25]

Among the very first business phenomena of the newly incorporated municipality was the opening of a general store on the State House Square by George Pasfield, an English-born American merchant of Springfield.[26] In 1840, Jacob

Bunn, in collaboration with two partners, would further complement the growing business community of Springfield by establishing a grocery store at the southwest corner of Fifth and Adams Streets.[27]

III

The J. Bunn Grocery Company: Academy for Young Business Visionaries

Arriving in the capital city in 1839, Jacob Bunn brought with him almost four years of experience in the grocery trade. He came to Springfield with sufficient knowledge of the business to enter into partnership in another grocery concern with two other pioneer business leaders. The firm resulting from this collaboration would be the beginning of the Springfield legacy of Jacob Bunn, and would constitute the ultimate foundation for all that he would accomplish throughout the 19th century. For he found his start in Springfield and in Illinois business on the floor of the retail and wholesale house of McConnel, Bunn & Van Syckel. Although Jacob Bunn had undertaken business enterprise prior to 1840, it was in the summer of 1840 when he became established permanently in the business community of Springfield. It would be from this city that he would act as a patriarch of local, state, and national industry.

Bunn commenced business in the new state capital in partnership with Murray McConnel, who had held previously the offices of Illinois State Senator and auditor of the Federal Treasury, among other public positions, and another partner by the name of Van Syckel. The partners organized the firm of "McConnel, Bunn & Van Syckel," a grocery company that dealt in wholesale and retail goods, in July of 1840.[28]

Though the partnership enjoyed instant financial success, it would be short lived. In July of 1842 news came that Bunn had dissolved the partnership. There was apparently no animosity in this dissolution. In all probability, the dissolution took place, instead, as a result of Bunn's ambition to be a prime mover in the world of commerce, and an entrepreneur who operated second to nobody.[29] After completing the purchase of the McConnel and Van Syckel interests in the grocery concern, Bunn altered the name of the business to "J. Bunn," to reflect the change in the partnership.[30]

The two-year partnership experience, however, undoubtedly played an important role in seasoning the young Jacob Bunn, in that he would have become acquainted with the partnership as both an organizational form and as a business strategy. Operating in the capacity of a business partner served him well, as he would subsequently participate as an active force in the organization and perpetuation of numerous business enterprises with numerous individuals as partners.

The new J. Bunn Grocery Company offered an increasingly wide array of commodities. The business dealt in glass, queensware, nails, wines, liquors, sugars, coffees, teas, molasses, tobacco, fish, turpentine, fruits, meats, and paints and oils of great diversity, including vermillion, Spanish brown, yellow ochre, chrome yellow, and Venetian red.[31] His expertise regarding merchandise had obviously achieved the highest level, and he gradually developed a reputation among companies that were based in distant areas. Undoubtedly due to the success of the J. Bunn Grocery Company, Bunn became involved as a commercial agent for at least one company that was located in another state. In 1848 he served as the Springfield representative of the New York Canton Tea Company.[32] This association is illustrative of his growing reputation in the sectors of wholesale and retail commerce. Although it is not definitively known from historical documents, Bunn could have traveled to New York City, as he had traveled to New Orleans in previous years, to investigate and acquire new store inventory. It would seem that his connection with the New York Canton Tea Company might have necessitated such business travels. Bunn traveled extensively, and apparently made abundant observations of each place he visited, as would be the ideal manner for a merchant. On one occasion, on 10 May 1850, a brief notice appeared in the *Daily Journal*, stating:

> Mr. Bunn returned from New Orleans last night. He represents that the weather has been very cold below. No Cholera at New Orleans. There had been a forced sale of 40,000 bags of coffee at 8, 8 1-2 and 8 3-8 cents. Regular rates of coffee, 8 3-8 [and] 9 cents. The coffee market was nearly bare; and the impression was that the rates would settle down to about 10 cents. There was a crevase [sic] some 60 miles above New Orleans which had destroyed many plantations.
>
> A vast number of emigrants were arriving at New Orleans.[33]

Bunn's leadership capabilities were evident in the rapid expansion of the grocery business. In fewer than ten years

Jacob Bunn had built a company that was a major commercial institution not only in Springfield, but also in central Illinois. A newspaper article in 1849 provided ample evidence of the high esteem that the J. Bunn Grocery Company had earned in the region.

> J. BUNN, Wholesale and Retail Dealer in Groceries and Glass and Queensware, south of the Capitol. We have heard it said that his business will reach one hundred thousand dollars the present year. Merchants of Mason, Christian, Piatt, Moultrie, and Logan, purchase goods extensively of him. The completion of the Rail Road will add greatly to the wholesale business of Springfield, and seems to be operating to give a start to other branches of business. Mr. Bunn usually purchases pork largely, which he puts up here—a business which will be greatly increased.[34]

The newspaper article above provides in addition to a positive summary of the J. Bunn Grocery inventory an interesting remark concerning the nature of the creative catalyst of the railroad industry. The railroad industry is largely responsible for the success of wholesale and retail houses such as the J. Bunn Grocery Company. By connecting such commercial houses to urban areas and to river ports, railroad networks simultaneously provided commercial institutions with opportunities for expansion. The article also refers to the pork purchasing that the J. Bunn Grocery Company undertook. With the advent of the railroads, such a business could join together networks of commercial institutions, spanning many regions and many states.

Springfield was still a young capital city, and Jacob Bunn was contributing handsomely to its development. Spreading as quickly as this economic development was his reputation.

His business reputation was spreading throughout middle Illinois and in the last months of 1849 the *Globe* newspaper, from as far away as Charleston, Illinois, reported in glowing terms on the successful young Jacob Bunn, one of the 'merchant princes' of Springfield.[35]

His establishment [the J. Bunn Grocery Company] is, unquestionably, one of the most thoroughly complete within the bounds of the whole state... there is nothing you can name, belonging to his line of business, that he has not on hand. Just such merchants as Bunn we like to see flourishing everywhere.[36]

Additionally, his reputation as a successful merchant with a seemingly inexhaustible line of merchandise was coextensive with his reputation as an honest businessman. "But in the last years of the 1840s Springfield knew Jacob Bunn only as a quiet, reserved, fanatically honest businessman."[37] His unwavering sense of integrity would characterize all of his business and civic undertakings throughout the entirety of his career and life. He had built up the largest grocery company in the city.[38] He employed in the grocery business his younger brother John Whitfield Bunn, as a clerk, T. K. Babcock, bookkeeper, James Canfield, clerk, Elisha Drummond, assistant bookkeeper, Benjamin Hamilton Ferguson, clerk, John H. Merriweather, clerk, and John Moran, a porter.[39] The grocery industry had been the sector of activity in which Bunn had made his entrance into the world of business and commerce, and it would remain forever among the most prominent facets of his legacy to the business community of Springfield and to the commercial vitality of central Illinois.

The J. Bunn Grocery Company underwent several alterations in its corporate name and organization over the decades, but ultimately assumed the name, "Bunn Capitol Grocery Company," and continues today as one of the leading food service corporations in the Midwest and in the United States. The first change in business name occurred in 1858, when John Whitfield Bunn became a full partner in his brother's firm; to reflect the change in partnership, the name was changed to "J. and J. W. Bunn Company."[40]

On 21 September 1928, the officers of the John W. Bunn and Company and the J. F. Humphreys Company initiated the legal proceedings whereby the two corporations would merge to form one. The resolution of merger read in part as follows:

> RESOLVED: That the said John W. Bunn & Co. a corporation with its principal place of business at Springfield, Illinois, and J. F. Humphreys & Co. a corporation with its principal place of business at Bloomington, Illinois, are hereby consolidated into a single corporation upon the terms and conditions hereinafter set forth, which conditions are as follows:
>
> - The name of such consolidated corporation is Bunn and Humphreys, Inc.
> - The object for which it is formed is 'To manufacture, buy or otherwise acquire, own, mortgage, sell, assign, consign, transfer or otherwise dispose of, trade and deal in and with goods, wares and merchandise, including food products and other articles of commerce, and to do all and everything necessary or convenient for the accomplishment of any of the purposes or objects and powers above mentioned or incident thereto.'
> - The duration of the corporation is ninety-nine years.
> - The location of the principal office is 411 S. Main Street, Bloomington, County of McLean State of Illinois.[41]

The first board of directors of the Bunn and Humphreys Company consisted of George W. Bunn, Sr. and Willard Bunn of Springfield, the son and grandson, respectively, of Jacob Bunn; Howard Humphreys, Rogers Humphreys, John E. Hall, A. C. Flood, and O. W. Johnson, all of Bloomington, Illinois. The final legal action of merger was accomplished in October of 1928. The Articles of Merger read in part as follows:

> Whereas, from a certificate duly signed and verified under oath filed in the Office of the Secretary of State on the 22nd day of October A.D. 1928 it appears that at a meeting of the stockholders of the
> JOHN W. BUNN AND COMPANY
> J. F. HUMPHREYS AND CO.
> duly convened a resolution was passed to consolidate in accordance with the provisions of an Act entitled 'AN ACT IN RELATION TO CORPORATIONS FOR PECUNIARY PROFIT' approved June 28, 1919, in force July 1, 1919, and all acts amendatory thereof, a copy of which certificate is hereto attached;
>
> Now Therefore, I, LOUIS L. EMMERSON, Secretary of State of the State of Illinois, by virtue of the powers vested in me by law, do hereby certify that JOHN W. BUNN AND COMPANY AND J. F. HUMPHREYS AND CO. have legally consolidated into and formed BUNN AND HUMPHREYS, INC. as provided in the aforesaid Act.[42]

The principal office continued to be held in Bloomington, Illinois, until legal process was initiated in the winter of 1930 to relocate to Springfield. The articles of change in location read in part as follows:

> Whereas, from a certificate duly signed and verified under oath filed in the Office of the Secretary of State, on the 20th day of February A.D. 1930 it appears that at a

meeting of the stockholders of the BUNN & HUMPHREYS, INC. duly convened a resolution was passed to change location of principal business office in accordance with the provisions of an Act entitled 'AN ACT IN RELATION TO CORPORATIONS FOR PECUNIARY PROFIT' approved June 28, 1919, and acts amendatory thereof, a copy of which certificate is hereby attached;

NOW THEREFORE, I, WILLIAM J. STRATTON, Secretary of State of the State of Illinois, by virtue of the powers vested in me by law, do hereby certify that BUNN & HUMPHREYS, INC. has legally changed location of principal business office from 407-411 South Main Street, Bloomington, Illinois to 927 East Adams Street, Springfield, Illinois as provided in the aforesaid Act.[43]

In January of 1934 Bunn and Humphreys, Inc. altered its corporate name to Bunn Capitol Grocery Company. This corporate name has been retained by the company for more than seventy years. The resolution for this purpose read in part as follows:

BE IT RESOLVED, That the name of this Company be changed from Bunn and Humphreys, Inc. to Bunn Capitol Grocery Company, and that the Articles of Incorporation of this Company be amended accordingly.[44]

After the corporate name had been changed officially in 1934, other changes soon followed. The Bunn Capitol Grocery Company merged with the Capitol Grocery Company. The merger was completed 30 June 1937, and this marked the end of the Capitol Grocery Company, which had surrendered its assets entirely to the Bunn Capitol Grocery Company.[45] Among the better known products of the Bunn Capitol Grocery Company were the "Bunny Brand" of sweet peas, the "J. W. B." salad and pie sliced apples, and "Wishbone" coffees.

What is especially important about the J. Bunn Grocery Company is that it not only served the communities of central Illinois, and acted as a pacesetter in the wholesale and retail sectors of the economy, but that it also provided opportunities for others to begin their careers in Illinois business. John Whitfield Bunn and Benjamin Hamilton Ferguson, brother and brother-in-law respectively to Jacob Bunn, began their careers in the J. Bunn Grocery Company, and it was from the floor of this business that these men built their own unique legacies to the State of Illinois. Jacob Bunn, however, was their mentor, and he helped bring them forth as civic and commercial leaders. While the well-known Bunn Capitol Company icons such as the "J. W. B.," "Bunny Brand," and "Golden Age" labels were associated with some of the company's most famous products, men such as John Whitfield Bunn and Benjamin Hamilton Ferguson were associated with some of the most important commercial and municipal developments in Springfield and in all of Illinois.

As a business organization that has survived the Panics and Depressions of 1857, 1873, 1883, 1893, 1907, 1920, and 1929, the Bunn Capitol Company qualifies as a genuine veteran of the numerous periods of tumult in the economic history of the United States. It has exhibited success since its infancy in the early 1840s.

The Bunn Capitol Company remains today a monument both to Jacob Bunn's first Springfield commercial venture and to his first success in business. In many respects, the Bunn Capitol Company has served the city of Springfield and the regions of central Illinois, and is still operated by a member of the Bunn family: Robert Hatcher Bunn, a great-great-grandson of Jacob Bunn. The Bunn Capitol Company retains its principal offices in Springfield, the city where it was organized over 164 years ago. Additionally, the Bunn Capitol Company is the only surviving company that was originally founded by Jacob Bunn. All of the other Jacob and John W. Bunn enterprises have either collapsed over time or have been absorbed into other concerns. Consequently, the Bunn Capitol Company remains the first and the last of the enterprises founded by the patriarch of the Bunn family in Illinois.

As business continued to prosper in the new state capital, the need for infrastructural improvements became increasingly apparent. Jacob Bunn would have been aware of the constantly changing needs, as transportation and communication technology developed. He therefore concerned himself prominently with such internal improvements for urban development and promotion. Jacob Bunn would serve as one of the leading forces in the development of numerous civic improvement projects.

One of the most important facets of the Jacob Bunn legacy was his interest in promoting individuals who were willing to work hard for success. Two careers that truly sprang from the Jacob Bunn legacy were those of John Whitfield Bunn and Benjamin Hamilton Ferguson.

John Whitfield Bunn was born 21 June 1831 in Hunterdon County, New Jersey,[46] on the family farm which Jacob had left in 1836. John was only five years old when his brother left for Illinois, but his brother would eventually come back to visit, and that visit would change John's life forever. The April, 1920 issue of the *Journal of the Illinois State Historical Society* included a commemorative tribute to John W. Bunn, who had died that year.

> Jacob Bunn had returned to Milford [a location near the Bunn farmstead in New Jersey] on a visit, and took with him wonderful stories of the rolling prairies and fruitful fields of Illinois... and of the very fine place it was in which to live. John, with all of a young boy's adventurous longing to see something of the world himself, and not just through another's eyes, heard these stories with secret hopes of some day striking the westward trail and feasting his own eyes on the wonders it unfolded. One day during his brother's visit John was out in a field near his farm home busy at the necessary but uninteresting task of picking up stones from the field and loading them into a wheelbarrow. This was done in order to clear the ground for cultivation and also to get the stones for fence making. Every one who has ever been in the East knows the rock-piled fences of that section, vine woven, charming, picturesque, inviting one to climb over and explore the other side, to wander away from their confines and down grassy glades—grassy, that is between the boulders and outcropping stones—or up little mountains that have strayed away from the greater ranges. It is certain that John Bunn had no eye however for the picturesque qualities of the fence those stones he was picking up should build. He had only a young boy's dislike of the irksome, tedious, uninviting task. What boy wants to pick up stones when there are fields and hills to wander through, or streams in which to fish? 'What would you think,' Jacob suddenly said to his brother, 'if I should tell you that out where I live we have field after field, with acres upon acres where you couldn't get enough stones to fill a wheel barrow?' John looked at his older brother for a moment, then replied, 'I would say that I'd like to go out there to live. I'd like to get out of doing work like this. I'd like to see a different country.'[47]

The conversation between the two brothers should be referred to as the "Wheelbarrow Dialogue," as it would be that dialogue that would be the watershed in the life of John Whitfield Bunn, who would later that year join his brother in Springfield, Illinois, and would there embark upon a career in business that would span more than seventy years.

> His brother promised then to bring him out west to live. He did not make the return trip with Jacob at that time, but some months latter [sic] when three men from Springfield who had come from the same section of New Jersey went back there to visit, Jacob Bunn sent for his brother to come out with them.
> That journey was possibly the most eventful John Bunn ever took in his life.[48]

Over the course of the decade that he spent in the employment of his brother's grocery company, John Whitfield Bunn learned the commercial arts from his brother Jacob who was seventeen years his senior and would eventually become one of the most prominent civic and commercial leaders of the Midwest. Although the two brothers' careers were distinct, neither Jacob nor John can ever be viewed as being truly separate in their careers. The Jacob Bunn Legacy consisted not merely of corporations, but also of the type of mentoring and inspiration that would motivate young men such as John W. Bunn to begin a new life.

From the stony fields of western New Jersey to the fertile plains of Illinois, John Whitfield Bunn rose from filling wheelbarrows with stones to serving as the first treasurer of the University of Illinois, the treasurer of the Board of Commissioners of the 1893 Chicago World's Fair, as the

Commissioner of Pensions of the State of Illinois during the Civil War period, and as the founder and co-founder with his brother of more than twenty business enterprises. Jacob Bunn was a man of vision, and he had a vision for his younger brother. From the New Jersey farm to the Springfield wholesale floor to the Chicago World's Fair, John W. Bunn was the beneficiary of his brother's goodwill, vision, mentoring, and care.

Benjamin Hamilton Ferguson was the younger brother of Elizabeth Jane Ferguson, who married Jacob Bunn in 1851. He served as a soldier during the Civil War. He recruited Company B, 114th Illinois Infantry, and not long afterwards was chosen to serve as the Company's Captain. Ferguson participated in several battles, including Vicksburg and the Battle of Jackson. He was a member of the Grand Army of the Republic, serving with Stephenson Post.[49] Benjamin H. Ferguson, like John W. Bunn, effectively learned the arts of business and trade from his experiences as an employee of the J. Bunn Grocery Company. Beginning his career in business as a clerk and bookkeeper in the employ of the J. Bunn Grocery Company, Ferguson would rise from the wholesale house floor to executive positions with the Springfield Marine Bank and the Illinois Watch Company. As can be seen, the Ferguson and Bunn families were not only connected by the marriage of Elizabeth Jane Ferguson to Jacob Bunn, but by the friendships that existed among the members of both families.

Benjamin H. Ferguson worked as a cashier for the Springfield Marine Bank, an institution of which Jacob Bunn was a founder in January of 1851. Ferguson eventually became a president of the bank. He was additionally engaged in the crockery business and enjoyed immense success therein.⁵⁰ Ferguson also served as the vice-chairman of the board of directors of the Illinois Watch Company, serving the company with both Jacob and John W. Bunn as director. The name of the Ferguson crockery business was the Bon-Ton China Shop. It was located on the southwest corner of Springfield's Fifth and Monroe Streets.⁵¹ The successes that Ferguson enjoyed were undoubtedly due largely to the tutelage that he received while in the employ of Jacob Bunn, who served as his business mentor.

Of interest is that Elizabeth Jane (Ferguson) Bunn and Benjamin H. Ferguson had a brother named William Ferguson, an attorney who had traveled to California and who was active within political forums in San Francisco. In 1856 William Ferguson was elected to the United States Senate from California, but tragically was shot and mortally wounded shortly thereafter by an acquaintance, George Penn Johnson, who had disagreed with Ferguson over a political matter, and had challenged Senator Ferguson to a duel to settle the disagreement. Johnson had been an editor of a political newspaper and a U. S. Court clerk.⁵² Had this chain of events transpired differently, Senator Ferguson might have left an enduring legacy in the annals of California political history. Despite his tragically brief career in California, Ferguson was nonetheless illustrative of the same individual entrepreneurship that characterized Jacob and John W. Bunn, and should not be forgotten.

Although the original structure that housed the J. Bunn Grocery Company no longer stands, the legacy of the business that once stood on that corner continues today. While the business dealt in groceries and in dry goods, it also offered career futures to the young men who were willing to dedicate themselves to integrity and to building the economies and commercial zones of Illinois. The employees of the J. Bunn Grocery Company must also be viewed as students of commerce, for they learned both from their personal experiences as employees and from the teachings of seasoned entrepreneurs such as Jacob Bunn, who in turn had learned from superiors in his own time, years before.

From the southwest corner of the Old Capitol Square in Springfield came the business which served as the ultimate parent of the initiative, experience, expertise, and success that helped to fuel the development of 19th century Illinois. That business was the J. Bunn Grocery Company.

Consequently, to refer to the original J. Bunn Grocery Company merely as a grocery company would be historically insufficient, as the institution served effectively as an academy for those who would have been considered to be students of business at the time. Retrospectively, therefore, it would seem the J. Bunn business sign should have read: "J. Bunn Grocery Company: Wholesale House, Retail Store and Academy for Aspiring Visionary Entrepreneurs."

IV

Vision for Utility, Infrastructure, and the Birth of a City

Among the crucial features of burgeoning urban regions are infrastructure and utilities. Wholly aside from his involvement in the grocery business, Jacob Bunn played a role in early municipal development, which would include improvements in communications, city transportation, and water circulation, among other measures. John Whitfield Bunn also contributed handsomely to civic and urban development endeavors.

The need for the establishment of a municipal water facility led to opportunities both for entrepreneurship and for civic vision. "Agitation began in 1857 for a better water supply, since no progress had been made when four years earlier, a chain pump had been installed at the southwest corner of the square."[53] The desire for an improved water supply stemmed largely from the fundamental notion that a high-quality water system is a prerequisite for the success of industrial growth.

In the April 6 issue of the *Illinois State Register* there appeared an editorial comment:

> The greatest drawback upon our city thus far has been an insufficiency of water. If we had the necessary supply of water, we might occupy a front rank amongst manufacturing cities. [54]

The Springfield Waterworks Company, which was established in 1857, signified another important event in the annals of Springfield's municipal progress. "This company was incorporated at the last session of the Legislature with the following Directors: John T. Stuart, William B. Fondey, N. H. Ridgely, John W. Priest, Charles R. Hurst, John Williams and Jacob Bunn."[55] Having served as a member of the company's first board of directors, Jacob Bunn participated actively in its birth. John W. Priest was made President and William E. Keefer was appointed Secretary.

Subsequent to a resolution that increased the capital stock to $20,000, the company's subscription books were opened at the Banking House of N. H. Ridgely, the Banking Office of J. Bunn, the office of Stuart and Edwards, the office of the Sangamo Insurance Company, the Mayor's office, and at the store of John Williams. The Mayor was given the authority to summon a meeting of the Waterworks Board whenever "it [was] thought necessary for further action under the charter...."[56]

A prevailing confidence in artesian well-drilling as the *modus operandi* for tapping water supplies had clearly been aired in the *Illinois State Register* at the time of the enactment of the Waterworks charter. "The subject of artesian wells has recently excited some degree of interest in our city. There is no kind of doubt but that water can be obtained by artesian wells in this city at a very small expense."[57] A company resolution authorizing the Secretary to advertise for proposals for "sinking an Artesian well..." was ratified,[58] setting in motion the initial stages of the company's institutional mission. Despite extensive drilling attempts, however, the Waterworks Company failed to locate any water wells.

> The Springfield Waterworks Company, organized to furnish the city with water, went ahead with the artesian well digging for two years... they found no water, although they did strike a vein of coal. This digging was done on Washington Street, near the eastern limits of the city at that time.[59]

By serving the Waterworks concern in a directorial capacity, in addition to having been a general promoter of that utility, Bunn had played an important role in a fundamental infrastructure of Springfield.

Even though the well-drilling efforts yielded no water, they did afford a greater knowledge of the fossil fuel wealth that would be used in the 1870s. The accidental discovery of coal deposits beneath the city by the well digging endeavors of the Waterworks Company provided a fortuitous foreshadowing for Bunn, as he would eventually become eminently affiliated with the coal industry of Sangamon County.

Another aspect of Bunn's involvement with the establishment of Springfield utilities was his vital connection with the setting up of the city's first telegraph. The communications system in Springfield was to undergo a critical transformation with the advent of the city's first telegraph. Jointly with Springfield merchant John Williams, who was another important force in Springfield's commercial growth, Bunn was the instrumental force in the construction of the city's first telegraph line in 1848. Together, they facilitated the financing of the project. "[Jacob Bunn], jointly with John Williams, another prominent merchant, sold all of the necessary stock needed to build Springfield's first telegraph line in 1848."[60] These two men had enabled in Springfield the institution of what was not only a developing technology, but what was a successful commercial venture that enabled and improved the regional communications industry.

John Williams was another important pioneer Springfield merchant. Williams' initial business experience in Springfield was that of a clerk in the store of Elijah Iles. He was later one of the subscribers of the Springfield Marine and Fire Insurance Company, and the founder and president of the First National Bank, which was chartered on 12 December 1863, which although not the oldest bank in Illinois, was the first to be organized "...expressly for banking purposes..."[61]

Until the arrival of the telegraph in Springfield, the city received news of "current events" from old newspapers and from itinerant visitors who were traveling through the city by means of stagecoach. The Illinois and Mississippi Telegraph Company strung a telegraph wire through Springfield in 1848. On 1 January 1849, the *Illinois State Register* commenced the printing of telegraph dispatches. In the summer of 1849, the Illinois & Pacific Telegraph Company established a telegraph office, situated above the Chatterton Jewelry Store on the west side of the city square. It was this office that carried the first message of the nomination of Abraham Lincoln for the presidency.[62]

The telegraph system enjoyed immense success in

Springfield. The assertion that "no city in Illinois, except Chicago, does a larger business with telegraph companies than Springfield," which appeared in a special newspaper report forty-five years after the telegraph's inception,[63] illustrated the swiftness and scale of success that Springfield's telegraph industry had experienced.

A compatriot industry to the communications sector was the transportation industry, and Bunn was among the numerous Springfield businessmen who assumed a central role in the development of this industry. On 18 February 1861, the legislature of the State of Illinois enacted a statute containing the articles of incorporation of the Springfield City Railway Company. The founders were enumerated in the articles of incorporation, and included were Jacob Bunn, John T. Stuart, Stephen T. Logan, Benjamin S. Edwards, Christopher C. Brown, Thomas S. Mather, and George Carpenter.[64]

> Section 1   Be it enacted by the people of the State of Illinois represented in the General Assembly That Jacob Bunn, John T. Stuart, Stephen T. Logan, Benjamin S. Edwards, Christopher C. Brown, Thomas S. Mather and George Carpenter, and their successors be and they are hereby created a body corporate and politic by the name of the Springfield City Railway Company for the term of fifty years with all the powers and authority...for the purposes hereinafter mentioned.
>
> Section 2   The said corporation is hereby authorized and empowered to construct, maintain, and operate a single or double track railway with all necessary, and convenient track for turnouts, sidetrack and appendages in the City of Springfield, and in, on, over, and along such street or streets, highway or highways within the present or future limits of the City of Springfield.

Section 3   The capital stock of said corporation shall be fifty thousand dollars and may be increased from time to time at the pleasure of said corporation, it shall be divided into shares of fifty dollars each and be issued and transferred in such manner and upon such conditions as the board of Directors of said Corporation may direct.

Section 4   All the corporate powers of said corporation shall be vested in and exercised by a board of directors and such officers and agents as said board of directors shall appoint. The first board of directors shall consist of Jacob Bunn, John T. Stuart, Stephen T. Logan, Benjamin S. Edwards, Christopher C. Brown, Thomas S. Mather and George Carpenter, and Thereafter of not less than three nor more than seven stockholders, who shall be chosen each and every year by the stockholders, at such time and in such manner as the said corporation shall by its laws prescribe. The said directors shall hold their office until their successors are elected and qualified, and may fill any vacancies which may happen in the board of directors by death resignation or otherwise—they may also adopt such bylaws rules and regulations for the government of said corporation and the management of its affairs and business as they may think proper, not inconsistent with the laws of this state.[65]

The corporation held its principal offices variously at 823 East Monroe Street, at 331 South Fifth Street and at the corner of Third Street and Adams Street, in Springfield.[66]

The newly established Springfield City Railway Company served as a nucleus of urban transportational infrastructure and eased the intra-municipal travel of both city residents and visitors. Additionally, the new transit system facilitated people's access to recreational areas such as the local twelve-acre park, located next to the Oak Ridge Cemetery.[67] Bunn was a force in the establishment of a city transportation service that promoted local recreation among Springfield residents, newcomers, and visitors. Consequently, the Springfield City Railway Company played a prominent role in increasing the ease with which visitors to Springfield could explore the area and its attractions.

Demands for useful materials, such as rope, also occupied Bunn's time, and further illustrated his interest in profiting by supplying useful materials as well as his desire to expand the scope of the city's business by successfully discerning every new economic demand. "Already his frenetic energy and quest for city development was apparent."[68] He saw new markets for new products. And, in addition to having been affiliated with the (attempted) development of water, communications, and transit systems of the city, Bunn successfully capitalized on the demand for industrial materials, such as rope, twine and other similar items that could serve multiple purposes. Thus, he organized the Springfield Rope Company. This business dealt in hemp cordage, embracing broom twine, seine twine, bed cords, plow lines, and tarred rope, among other related materials.[69]

For him, there was no enterprise either too large or too minute for him to promote with the utmost dedication. He would continue to aggrandize this personal commitment to economic success by being an instrumental force in the establishment of an important public institution of commercial activities, the Springfield Board of Trade. Formed in 1869, the Springfield Board of Trade existed to assist the development of local industry. "Its function was as a *'promoter of industry,'* and it performed this well." The body was backed by Jacob Bunn, Samuel Rosenwald, who later contributed to the founding of Sears & Roebuck,

Benjamin Ferguson, and Clinton Conkling. The Board of Trade contributed to the organization of the Springfield Watch Company, the Springfield Woolen Mills, and the Alexander Corn Products factory.[70]

Both Jacob and John Bunn were able to use their financial enterprises and civic activities to build their city's infrastructure and its importance in the nation. A startling and novel discovery, from examining all of Jacob Bunn's many visions and successes in the business community of the young capital, is his personal and corporate support of someone so identified by history with Springfield that he is synonymous with Springfield: Abraham Lincoln. Jacob Bunn was for Lincoln a financier, a close friend, and an advocate.

1. Jacob Bunn. Illinois industrial pioneer, visionary, and patriarch of the Bunn family of Springfield, Illinois. This photograph of Bunn is one of the only photographs known to have been taken of him. (Photo courtesy of the Sangamon Valley Collection at the Lincoln Library, Springfield, Illinois.)

2. John Whitfield Bunn as a young businessman in Illinois, and a protégé of Jacob Bunn. (Photo courtesy of *Men of Illinois*, Chicago: Halliday Witherspoon, 1902.)

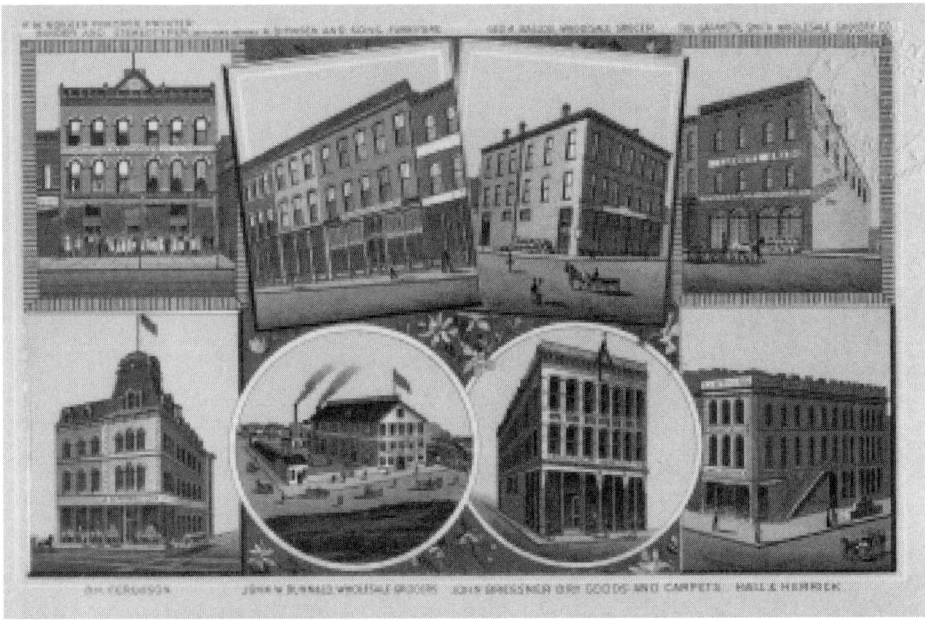

3. John W. Bunn & Company: Wholesale Grocers. See picture second from lower left. (Photo courtesy of the Sangamon Valley Collection at the Lincoln Library, Springfield, Illinois.)

4. The J. Bunn Grocery Company: See corner of building in lower right portion of photograph. The man standing by the window of the J. Bunn Grocery Company, wearing the black business suit, and with left arm extended, is thought to be Jacob Bunn. (Courtesy of the Sangamon Valley Collection at the Lincoln Library, Springfield, Illinois.)

5. Bunn Capitol Grocery Company Coffee Coupon. Note that the company at the time when this coupon was issued operated corporate offices in both Springfield and Bloomington, Illinois. (Author's personal collection.)

6. An artist's interpretation of the Southwest corner of the Springfield Town Square. Notice the J. Bunn Grocery Company, and the business sign that reads "J. Bunn." (*Historical Encyclopedia of Illinois and History of Sangamon County,* Vol. II, Newton Bateman and Paul Selby, Eds., Chicago: Munsell Publishing Company, 1912.)

7. *"Wishbone Coffee" label, on an original Bunn Capitol Grocery Company coffee tin.* (Coffee tin contributed by Robert H. Bunn to author's personal collection.)

8. *"Bunn Capitol Grocery Company" business label, on same original "Wishbone Coffee" tin.* (Author's personal collection.)

9. Elizabeth Jane (Ferguson) Bunn, the wife of Jacob Bunn. She was the daughter of Benjamin and Sarah (Irwin) Ferguson of Pennsylvania. (Photo courtesy of the Sangamon Valley Collection at the Lincoln Library, Springfield, Illinois.)

10. Illinois Watch Company series Portrait of Abraham Lincoln. Although barely visible in this image, there appears at the lower right corner of the portrait the corporate seal of the Illinois Watch Company, whose administration consisted of many men who had been personal friends and associates of Mr. Lincoln's. (Author's personal collection.)

11. Close-up view of the John W. Bunn and Company building and office, in Springfield. (Photo courtesy of the Sangamon Valley Collection at the Lincoln Library, Springfield, Illinois.)

FIRST PRESBYTERIAN CHURCH, SPRINGFIELD

12. *First Presbyterian Church, Springfield, Illinois. Jacob and Elizabeth Ferguson Bunn, John Whitfield Bunn, Sarah Irwin Ferguson (mother of Elizabeth Ferguson), and Jacob and Elizabeth's children all attended this church, which still exists today.* (Photo courtesy of *Historical Encyclopedia of Illinois and History of Sangamon County,* Vol. II. Newton Bateman and Paul Selby, Eds. Chicago: Munsell Publishing Company, 1912.)

HOME OF THE FRIENDLESS, SPRINGFIELD

13. *The Springfield Home for the Friendless. This institution served to assist women and children whose husbands and fathers had been lost or killed in battle during the Civil War. The Home provided shelter, food, and employment opportunities for its residents. It was one of Springfield's most important charitable institutions, and embodied the visionary philanthropy of Illinois business and civic leaders.* (Photo courtesy of *Historical Encyclopedia of Illinois and History of Sangamon County*, Vol. II. Newton Bateman and Paul Selby, Eds. Chicago: Munsell Publishing Company, 1912.)

14. Richard Yates. Prairie attorney, Illinois General Assemblyman, United States Congressman, Illinois Civil War Governor, United States Senator, Republican Party leader, and member of the Bunn-Lincoln Machine. (Photo courtesy of *Historical Encyclopedia of Illinois and History of Sangamon County*, Vol. II. Newton Bateman and Paul Selby, Eds. Chicago: Munsell Publishing Company, 1912.)

15. Lucretia (Wheeler) Johns Douglas. She was the maternal grandmother of William Douglas Richardson, and the great-grandmother of Ada Willard Richardson, who married Jacob Bunn's son George Wallace Bunn. (Author's personal collection.)

16. Betsey Elizabeth (Johns) Richardson. She was the mother of William Douglas Richardson, and the paternal grandmother of Ada Willard Richardson. Her husband, Henry Earle Richardson, of Connecticut, was a farmer and a tavern and inn proprietor. She lived with her son William in Springfield in her later years. (Author's personal collection.)

17. Lucy (Willard) Richardson. She was the wife of William Douglas Richardson and the mother of Ada Willard Richardson. Her father, Alexander Perry Willard, of Oneida County, New York, was a descendant of Major Simon Willard, who had emigrated from Horsmonden, England to Cambridge, Massachusetts Bay Colony, in 1634, becoming an important civic and commercial figure in New England. After relocating to Springfield, Illinois, Alexander Perry Willard founded, with Robert Zimmerman, also originally of New York, the company of Willard & Zimmerman, a premier and pioneering paint and wallpaper company in the new state capital. (Author's personal collection.)

18. Illinois State Capitol. Much of the construction of this building had been completed by William Douglas Richardson. The construction costs totaled, in 1807, approximately $4 million. (Photo and historical data courtesy of Souvenir of Springfield, Portland: L. H. Nelson Company, [year unknown]).

19. Ada Willard Richardson as a young girl. Ada was the daughter of William Douglas Richardson and Lucy Willard. Ada married George Wallace Bunn. (Author's personal collection.)

20. Original photograph of George Wallace Bunn. George was the third son of Jacob Bunn and Elizabeth (Ferguson) Bunn. He attended the Lawrenceville School in New Jersey. Inheriting his father's sense of vision and dedication to business, George served as the president of the Bunn Capitol Grocery Company, as president of the Springfield Marine Bank, was an important Illinois Republican Party supporter, and served for many years as a member of the board of directors of the Illinois Watch Company. He married Ada Willard Richardson. (Author's personal collection.)

21. John Whitfield Bunn in middle age. (Photo courtesy of the Sangamon Valley Collection at the Lincoln Library, Springfield, Illinois.)

22. William Douglas Richardson as a young businessman. In 1866, at 29 years of age, Richardson was already a partner in a Springfield-based real estate and insurance company, which was known as "Richardson & Latham." (Author's personal collection.)

23. *William Douglas Richardson in middle age. Richardson had been a railroad clerk, a real estate and insurance entrepreneur, and was the founder of the Richardson Construction Company which had received a contract for a major portion of the construction of the new State Capitol. He also was a founder of the Springfield Iron Company, and was a member of the first board of directors of the Springfield Iron Company, which became a pacesetter in the steel and iron industries of the United States. William married Lucy Willard.* (Author's personal collection.)

24. Stock Certificate of the Springfield Iron Company. William Douglas Richardson and John Whitfield Bunn were among the founders of this corporation, and both served as members of the first board of directors of the concern. John Whitfield Bunn also served as vice president of the corporation. (Photo courtesy of the Sangamon Valley Collection at the Lincoln Library, Springfield, Illinois.)

25. Poor's Railroad Manual – Advertisement for the Springfield Iron Company. (Photo courtesy of *Poor's Railroad Manual*, 1890.)

26. La Fayette Smith. A founder of the Springfield Iron Company. (Photo courtesy of *Men of Illinois*, Chicago: Halliday Witherspoon, 1902.)

27. An artist's rendering of the Springfield Iron Company factory complex. (Photo courtesy of the Sangamon Valley Collection at the Lincoln Library, Springfield, Illinois.)

28. Up-close image of Springfield Iron Company buildings. The building situated to the right was the company store for the employees of the Springfield Iron Company. (Photo courtesy of the Sangamon Valley Collection at the Lincoln Library, Springfield, Illinois.)

29. Group photograph taken of several Springfield Iron Company employees. (Photo courtesy of the Sangamon Valley Collection at the Lincoln Library, Springfield, Illinois.)

30. Group photograph taken of several Springfield Iron Company employees. (Photo courtesy of the Sangamon Valley Collection at the Lincoln Library, Springfield, Illinois.)

31. The Lincoln Monument, in Oak Ridge Cemetery, Springfield, Illinois. William Douglas Richardson was the contractor for the memorial. Jacob, John W., and many members of the Bunn family are buried in Oak Ridge. (Photo courtesy of Souvenir of Springfield, Portland: L. H. Nelson Company [year unknown].)

32. The Illinois State Capitol, with street railway tracks converging in the distance. (Photo courtesy of the Sangamon Valley Collection at the Lincoln Library, Springfield, Illinois.)

V

The Bunn-Lincoln Machine: Network of Integrity and Promotion

It would be insufficient to state merely that Jacob Bunn was an important factor in the political career of Abraham Lincoln. Jacob had become personally acquainted with Lincoln early on in his career in Illinois, and years later he would introduce his brother John to Lincoln. A strong friendship developed among the three men that would last throughout the remainder of Lincoln's life. Lincoln shared many responsibilities with the Bunn brothers in numerous civic and commercial activities. Lincoln's personal bank account is on display in a glass case in the lobby of what was the Springfield Marine Bank, and can still be viewed today.

The involvement of the Bunn brothers with Abraham Lincoln was a multifaceted relationship of support, cooperation, collaboration, and vision, and always must be understood within the context of a sincere friendship. Jacob Bunn and Lincoln were railroad promoters, actively engaged in the support of local and regional railroad interests. And Lincoln introduced John Bunn to the realms of public office when he assisted and promoted John in Springfield officialdom.

The Bunn-Lincoln friendship can be examined from a variety of historical vantage points. Among the most conspicuous aspects of the friendship was the commitment that Jacob and John W. Bunn exhibited with respect to the political promotion of their close friend and associate.

Lincoln's political career can be viewed as the first instance in the history of the United States of large-scale corporate interests successfully supporting a Republican candidate for the presidency. As a result, Jacob and John W. Bunn and their associates constituted what might be termed the first instance of the federal Republican Party corporate-political "machine" in the history of the United States. This instance should be referred to as the "Bunn-Lincoln Machine." The term "machine" is employed here in a neutral manner, however, and is in no way intended to imply any of the negative connotations that so frequently attend the word in both current and historical political parlance. Perhaps one might simply refer to the association as the Bunn-Lincoln Association, but the term "association" as used in this context fails to convey the commitment, loyalty, and personal friendship that fully characterized the Bunn-Lincoln acquaintanceship. Furthermore, the term "machine" efficaciously denotes the strong nature and purpose of the acquaintanceship.

The Bunn-Lincoln Machine was a stronghold of friendship, integrity, and vision for community, state and country. It was an association which was characterized by honesty, and not by corruption. The Machine included more than just Jacob and John W. Bunn, however, and involved many other members of the Springfield community who shared not only the Bunn brothers' political sentiments, but also an association and friendship with Abraham Lincoln.

The Bunn family provided Lincoln with substantial financial support, powerful media venues, ample social opportunities for further support for the candidate, and the sincerest personal friendship throughout the presidential campaign process.

> As leaders in so many public projects, it was inevitable that they should also become involved with the political fortunes of their long-time friend Abraham Lincoln in his successful bid for presidency of the United States. The Bunns solicited for and managed Lincoln's $10,000 campaign fund.[71]

The fact that the Bunn brothers were involved with the management of Lincoln's campaign fund is not surprising, when one considers the combined experience that Jacob and John W. Bunn had had in the management of capital resources. Their experience and expertise made them ideally suited to the task of campaign finance management. The support which the Bunn family provided for Lincoln was not, however, restricted to a mere financial backing. "Jacob and Lizzie Bunn [Elizabeth Jane Ferguson, wife of Jacob Bunn] contributed not only financially, but opened their house for the many entertainments required of an aspiring candidate."[72]

The diversity of the Bunn family's active and dedicated involvement with Lincoln's campaign was demonstrated again and assumed yet another form when it involved the news media. Jacob had provided the funds that enabled Lincoln's discreet acquisition of a printing press that allowed both Lincoln and the Republican Party to expand their support from among the German population of the United States. "Jacob also provided the money which enabled Lincoln to quietly purchase a printing press and German type with which he published a German language newspaper promoting the Republican Party platform."[73]

Indeed, Jacob and Elizabeth Bunn and John W. Bunn continued to support Lincoln, his political ideologies, and the Union during the Civil War period. Jacob Bunn and other Springfield bankers contributed financially to the war efforts of the State of Illinois during the Civil War. This involvement is discussed in detail in Chapter VIII, "Twilight of the Springfield Banker."

John W. Bunn became a major beneficiary of Lincoln's political insight and wisdom, and could be said to have learned the arts of politics and statesmanship from this mentor. Judge Isaac N. Phillips of Bloomington, Illinois, solicited and compiled a series of letters written by several men who had known Abraham Lincoln. In a letter written for Judge Phillips in recollection of Abraham Lincoln and his personal association with him, John W. Bunn discussed in considerable detail various experiences and dialogues with Lincoln. The introductory statement of the letter is itself evidence of the friendship that existed among Lincoln and the Bunn brothers.

> MY DEAR SIR: Your request that I should give you, in a letter, some of my personal recollections of Mr. Lincoln and my estimate of him, both in a social way and as a politician, is before me. My answer shall be made wholly from my personal knowledge and observation of the man. I shall, of course, not try to exhaust the subject, but will give you a little of Lincoln as I saw him and as I knew him.

> If, in doing this, it should appear that I put in a good deal about myself, I must plead as an excuse that I could not write my recollections of Lincoln without, to some extent, writing about myself....[74]

An interesting characteristic of the Bunn-Lincoln Machine is the fact that Lincoln not only was the beneficiary, but was also himself a benefactor. Specifically, while Jacob and John W. Bunn contributed money, opportunities and, undoubtedly, some counsel and advice to Lincoln, Lincoln himself effectively assumed the role of political mentor to John W. Bunn. John Bunn continued,

> My early contact with Mr. Lincoln was brought about by the fact that he was my brother's regular attorney. Almost immediately after coming to Illinois I began to know Lincoln in such a way as a boy knows a prominent man whom he often sees and talks with. In the year 1853, I remember that Judge Douglas made a great political speech in the State House. Lincoln was present and heard him, and gave notice that he would answer Douglas, one evening very soon, from the same platform. It was a way Lincoln had to talk with people and find out the views they took of current events, but he seldom or never asked anybody's advice. Accordingly, the next day after Douglas had made his speech Lincoln came along and stopped to talk with me upon the sidewalk in front of my brother's store. He said to me, 'Did you hear the speech of Judge Douglas last night?' I answered that I had heard the speech, and he said, 'What do you think of it?' I replied, 'Mr. Lincoln, I think it was a very able speech, and you will have a good deal of trouble to answer it.' To this he replied, 'I will answer that speech without any trouble, because Judge Douglas made two misstatements of fact, and upon these two misstatements he built his whole argument. I can show that his facts are not facts, and that will refute his speech.' I was present and

heard the reply which Mr. Lincoln made to Judge Douglas' speech, and to my mind he did disprove Douglas' facts, and, as I thought, completely answered his arguments.[75]

Lincoln was twenty-two years older than John W. Bunn, old enough to have been his father, and arguably served, with Jacob Bunn, as the most important mentor that John Bunn ever had. Jacob Bunn and Lincoln were far closer in age. While learning the ways of commerce from his older brother, John Bunn was also learning the ways and methods of political processes from Mr. Lincoln.

> Between 1850 and 1861, I saw Mr. Lincoln very often. I am proud to say that I was one of his junior political agents. Like very many others, I was always glad to do for him anything that I could do. I was often present at political gatherings, held for the purpose of consultation, and I thus came to know pretty well the workings of his mind, so far as they could be learned from close personal contact and observation…
>
> In the year 1857 Mr. Lincoln asked me one day if I did not wish to run for city treasurer of Springfield. The city was then an almost hopelessly Democratic city, and the proposition rather startled me. He, however, gave me encouragement to believe that I could be elected, if I would go about the matter in the right way. My brother, Jacob Bunn, who was present at the time, said to Mr. Lincoln, 'John will run if you want him to.' The candidate of the Democrats was Mr. Charles Ridgely. I confess I was pleased with the idea, and, when the Republican city convention met, I was an interested auditor of the proceedings…The convention was nearly over, and I began to think the matter of my nomination had been forgotten. In a city so Democratic as Springfield, Republican nominations were regarded at best as rather formal and perfunctory matters. Near the close of the convention a young man—a lawyer

who was an inmate of Lincoln's office—addressed the chairman, and said he would like to make a nomination for the office of city treasurer, but that if the suggestion he should make did not meet with the favor of every delegate present, he would withdraw the name. He then put my name in nomination, but again said, 'If there is any delegate on this floor opposed to the candidacy of Mr. Bunn, I do not wish his name to be voted upon or to go on the ticket.' No one objected and I was nominated by acclamation.

When I saw who was nominating me and knew that he was an inmate of Mr. Lincoln's office, I, of course, knew very well that he was acting under Mr. Lincoln's orders. The result of the election was that I was chosen for treasurer, and, I may say, I was again chosen in 1858, in 1859 and in 1860. In all these campaigns I was, so to speak, 'under the political wing' of Mr. Lincoln.[76]

John W. Bunn was twenty-six years old when he entered politics. He had lived in Springfield at that time for ten years. One should note here again that when Jacob Bunn offered his brother an opportunity for a new existence, in Illinois, he ignited in his brother an engine of vision and achievement that would take him from the New Jersey farm field to prominent elected offices in the State of Illinois. While John W. Bunn was experiencing the nature of the political campaign process, he again was the beneficiary of Lincoln's political tutelage.

A day or two after my first nomination for city treasurer I was going up town and saw Mr. Lincoln ahead of me. He waited until I caught up and said to me, 'How are you running?' I told him I didn't know how I was running. Then he said, 'Have you asked anybody to vote for you?' I said I had not. 'Well,' said he, 'if you don't think enough of your success to ask anybody to vote for you, it is probable they will not do it, and that you will not be elected.' I said to him, 'Shall I ask Democrats to vote for me?' He said, 'Yes, ask everybody to vote for you.' Just then a well known Democrat by the name of Ragsdale was coming up the sidewalk. Lincoln said, 'Now, you drop back there and ask Mr. Ragsdale to vote for you.' I turned and fell in with Mr. Ragsdale, told him of my candidacy, and said I hoped he would support me. To my astonishment, he promised me that he would. Mr. Lincoln walked slowly along and fell in with me again, and said, 'Well, what did Ragsdale say?' 'Will he vote for you?' I said, 'Yes, he told me he would.' 'Well then,' said Lincoln, 'you are sure of two votes at the election, mine and Ragsdale's.' This was my first lesson in practical politics, and I received it from a high source.

In the year 1861, when it was about time to nominate a treasurer again, I had a conversation with Mr. Lincoln. He asked me if I was going to run again for treasurer. I said, 'Mr. Lincoln, do you not think that men frequently run for office too often for their own good?' He replied, 'Yes, they very often do.' I gathered from this that he probably thought I had better not run again, and so I dropped out of the race.[77]

Evident in this recollection of John W. Bunn of his associations with Lincoln is a strong sense of brotherhood. Jacob and John W. Bunn were actual brothers, but were also, with Lincoln and with many other Illinois civic and business leaders, brothers in vision, in values, and in the endeavors necessary for the achievement and implementation of these social values and sentiments.

Also evident in the Bunn-Lincoln Machine was the sense of integrity that characterized the outlook and values of John W. Bunn. The fact that he withdrew from the race for Springfield city treasurer signified that he had developed sufficient political acumen to discern that running for a fifth term might generate the notion in the Springfield community that Bunn was ambitious. Instead, Bunn understood that he had served the city for four successful consecutive years in the treasury, and was content to retire from this public office with a sense of positive accomplishment, and to allow for new candidates, with new ideas and aspirations, to assume the office which he had held with honor and competence. As John Bunn became a more seasoned participant in political affairs, he began to develop an acute judgment regarding the personal character of other politicians. John Bunn continues,

> I may here relate a little incident which is characteristic of Lincoln. During the time between the election of Lincoln and his departure from Springfield to go to Washington, he had his office in the old State House—a building which still stands on the public square, though it has been repaired and a good deal changed. I was, of course, very greatly interested in the campaign in which the Republicans had succeeded in electing Lincoln. I was on a local committee which had charge of matters in Springfield and Sangamon county and was treasurer of the committee. One day, after the election had resulted successfully, I went up to Mr. Lincoln's room in the State House, and as I went up the stairs I met Salmon P. Chase of Ohio just coming away. When I entered the room I said to Mr. Lincoln, rather abruptly, 'You don't want to put that man in your cabinet.' It was an impertinent remark on my part, but Mr. Lincoln received it kindly and replied to me in a characteristic way, by saying, 'Why do you say that?' 'Because,' I said, 'he thinks he is a great deal bigger than you are.' 'Well,' said Lincoln, 'do you know of any other men who think they are bigger than I am?' I replied, 'I do not know that I do, but why do you ask me that?' 'Because,' said Mr. Lincoln, 'I want to put them all in my cabinet.' This is, perhaps, unimportant talk, but I think it shows a real characteristic of Lincoln

and shows that he was not afraid to match himself against other men, however prominent they might be.[78]

This dialogue served as another lesson in practical politics for John W. Bunn. The Bunn-Lincoln Machine not only assisted John Bunn in being elected to four terms as the Springfield city treasurer, but, after helping to elect Lincoln to the presidency, also sent John Bunn to state-level office in Illinois. John W. Bunn managed the Civil War pensions for the State of Illinois during the Civil War, and the dialogue by which he achieved this office is of significant historical interest, as it illustrates the network of friendship and promotion which characterized the Bunn-Lincoln Machine.

> I always had a deep admiration and reverence for Mr. Lincoln and, of course, was very active, in my way, in forwarding his candidacy in the campaign of 1860. After the campaign was over and had been successful, I was once in Lincoln's office in the State House, when some question came up about my having spent a great deal of time in and about the canvass locally. Lincoln asked me some questions which brought out the fact that I had spent a good deal of my own money in the canvass—a thousand dollars, or more. Mr. Lincoln said to me that I was not able to lose that money. He spoke very seriously. I replied, 'Yes, Mr. Lincoln, I am able to lose it, because when you go to Washington you are going to give me an office.' This statement seemed to almost startle him. The look on his face grew very serious. He said to me that he had not promised me any office whatever. I replied, 'No, Mr. Lincoln, you have not promised me anything, but you are going to give me an office just the same.' 'What office do you think I am going to give you?' asked Mr. Lincoln. I said, 'The office of pension agent here in Illinois. During Isaac B. Curran's term as pension agent under Buchanan I have done all the work in

the office, in order to get the deposits in my brother's bank. The salary amounts to $1,000 a year, and when you go to Washington you are going to give me that office.' To this he made no word of reply. He did not say that he would give me the office, or that he would not, but on the 7th of March, 1861, I was appointed to the office of pension agent of Illinois by Caleb B. Smith, Secretary of the Interior.

I do not believe that anything on earth could have extracted a promise from Mr. Lincoln to give me that office, nor do I think he would have bargained to give any man an administrative office before or after his election. It is probable that he had selected the members of his cabinet, and that he had advised them of the fact before they were appointed, but, outside of his cabinet officers, I do not believe he promised anybody an office before the day of his inauguration, and yet the incident I have above related shows that he was not by any means insensible to ordinary political considerations.

Lincoln was the leading lawyer in central Illinois before his election to the presidency. He was universally respected for his purity and his uprightness and for the rigid integrity that he never failed to exhibit in all the relations of life. He received from all who came in contact with him the high respect and consideration which was due to his position and to his great ability and character.

Very truly yours,

John W. Bunn[79]

In examining each Republican presidential candidate throughout United States history, one will notice that there is a network of capital resources that attends the candidate's campaign. In many respects, Jacob and John W. Bunn were among the apostles of corporate support for the Republican Party and its candidates at the Federal level. The Bunn brothers laid foundations for later Republican Party supporters.

Jacob Bunn was almost an exact model for a well-known later 19th century industrialist and Republican Party presidential supporter in Ohio. The Bunn brothers' business associations and their involvement with the Lincoln election campaign were strikingly similar to those of this later businessman who exhibited similar patterns of entrepreneurship and political involvement: Marcus Hanna. A most vivid parallel exists between Marcus Hanna and Jacob Bunn.

The career path of Marcus Hanna was so strikingly similar to that of Jacob Bunn that reasonable speculation might arise as to whether the two men had actually known each other, or at least had known of each other. Given Hanna's prominence in the media, Bunn would have had to have been familiar with Hanna at least by name. But could Hanna have known Jacob Bunn, or have known of him? Whether Hanna did or did not, his career in business and industry mirrored that of Jacob Bunn, and the parallels are compelling.

Bunn's involvement with Lincoln in many ways set the stage for future instances of business support for the Republican Party, like the Hanna-McKinley Machine. The Hanna-McKinley Political Machine mirrored in many respects the pattern of the "Bunn-Lincoln Machine," which predated it by thirty-seven years. Evident in even a cursory comparison of the careers of Jacob Bunn and Marcus Hanna are conspicuous parallels in business activity, as well as in patterns of industrial promotion. Hanna continues to mirror Bunn with respect to political association, but not the manner of public demeanor. Regardless of their career parallels, Bunn and Hanna possessed remarkably different outlooks on publicity. Both Bunn and Hanna were "kingmakers," but the former was a man who harbored a profound aversion to publicity, while the latter was a man who enjoyed a pronounced and widespread public presence.

A comparison between Jacob Bunn and Marcus Hanna betrays an interesting historical paradox. The two were engaged on numerous occasions in identical industries. Even the chronologies of their respective business undertakings mirrored one another. Both, for instance, commenced business as grocers and commissioners. But the two could not have subscribed to more different principles of public image.

Marcus Hanna was born 24 September 1837 in New Lisbon, Ohio. He entered the grocery and commission business, in Cleveland, Ohio, and thereafter became interested in the coal and iron industries in that city. Moreover, Hanna was an instrumental force in the establishment of the Union National Bank, and was the proprietor of the Cleveland Opera House, as well as of the *Cleveland Herald*. He was also a predominant figure in the birth and growth of the Cleveland street railway system.[80] His active promotion of the Ohio politician William McKinley led to McKinley's success. "At once the McKinley boom was launched, Hanna's protégé being heralded as the 'advance agent of prosperity.' "[81]

Jacob Bunn entered the grocery and commission business, became affiliated with the iron and coal industries of his region and state, and was the founder of the J. Bunn Bank, a private bank, in addition to having been a co-founder of the Springfield Marine and Fire Insurance Company. Additionally, Bunn became the proprietor of

Rudolph's Opera House of Springfield, which later became known as the Old Chatterton,[82] and was the co-owner and later sole proprietor of the newspaper known as the *Chicago Republican*.[83] He also contributed to the birth of the Springfield street railway system, as has been discussed already. One might reasonably adapt the statement about McKinley being Hanna's protégé as follows: "At once the Lincoln boom was launched, Bunn's protégé being heralded as 'the advance agent of union and industry.'"

The nature of Hanna's image as a supporter of Republican politics, however, varied vastly from that of Bunn's. Jacob Bunn was the epitome of the discreet magnate, the elusive financier who could provide vast support for a candidate, such as Lincoln, and remain perpetually beyond the scope of limelight publicity. He employed what might be termed the tactic of quiet support, contributing to the cause of a particular political campaign, but remaining an unseen force in the mechanics of the entire processes of the campaign and the election. Unlike his brother, John W. Bunn, who successfully campaigned for the office of Springfield City Treasurer,[84] Jacob refrained from pursuing public office.

No known item of historiography indicates that Jacob Bunn ever requested of Lincoln any type of political benefit, once Lincoln had been elected President. Instead, Bunn's "gain" would have been Lincoln's promulgation of his "free-soil" political ideologies, which Bunn shared completely. During a time in United States history when the railroad industry was accumulating immense industrial momentum, people who possessed political connections often discerned the opportunities for financial gain through ambitiously promoting their interests to the federal legislature via their respective candidates. Instead, Bunn remained primarily a regional businessman, occupied predominantly with the perpetuation of local business interests. Hanna, on the other hand, did quite the opposite.

> In the new scheme of things business and politics were natural allies and men like Hanna, assuming that individual and social profits are indistinguishable, generally did not scruple to use the government to advance their own personal and economic interests.[85]

Hanna was an ambitious Republican supporter. Subscribing to the notion of economic protectionism, by means of tariff enactments, Hanna became an ardent supporter of William McKinley because of their shared protectionist attitudes, which became abundantly obvious with the passage of the McKinley Tariff Act, which was enacted into law 1 October 1890.[86] At the time of the statute's enactment, McKinley, the official sponsor of the act, was chairman of the Ways and Means committee. Opposition to the tariff measure tarnished McKinley's image sufficiently to prevent him from being reelected to the House. Hanna adopted McKinley as his political pawn, and "...promptly brought out McKinley for governor and solicited contributions in his behalf even from Chicago and Pittsburgh manufacturers who were urged to save the cause of protection from another disaster."[87] If Hanna had been contacting businessmen in Chicago for support of [his candidate] McKinley, it is quite possible that Hanna had contacted personally, or even became acquainted with John W. Bunn, who was prominent in Chicago industry and in Republican Party activities.

Hanna was not only McKinley's most powerful financial advocate, but he also was an agent of the convalescence of McKinley's political image.

It is not known whether Marcus Hanna was acquainted with, or even knew of, Jacob Bunn, but the two were contemporaries during the later 19th century. And since both subscribed to and supported the Republican Party, they might have known of each other. According to existing accounts, Jacob fervently shunned publicity. Quietly and with much discretion and deliberate avoidance of publicity, the Bunn family offered their support of various concerns, unlike the very public manner of involvement exhibited by Hanna, in connection with McKinley. A consequence of Jacob Bunn's general aversion to publicity was that the Bunn-Lincoln Machine has remained largely unknown, until now. Consequently, the Bunn legacy of Republican Party support, while the founding instance, chronologically, of business and Republican Party politics at the federal level, is not the 19 century's most notorious business and political collaboration.

After Abraham Lincoln's death, Jacob Bunn remained a close friend and associate of the Lincoln family. He was one of the pallbearers at Lincoln's funeral, along with Jesse K. Dubois, Stephen T. Logan, John T. Stuart, James N. Brown, Governor Gustavus Koerner, Judge Samuel H. Treat, Col. John Williams, James L. Lamb, Erastus Wright, and Charles W. Matheny.[88] He furthermore was chosen to be on the executive committee formed to oversee the construction of the Lincoln Monument, in 1869. The committee consisted of Jacob Bunn, John T. Stuart, and John Williams.[89] The primary contractor hired to construct the Lincoln

Monument in Oak Ridge Cemetery was William Douglas Richardson,[90] who became an in-law of Jacob and John W. Bunn, when his daughter Ada Willard Richardson married Jacob's son, George Wallace Bunn, in 1886.

The Bunn-Lincoln Machine was the prototype for successful large corporate sponsorship of a Republican Party presidential candidate. Jacob Bunn, John Whitfield Bunn, Abraham Lincoln and the others who were associated with the Lincoln electoral campaign were among the apostles of the corporate political machine model for candidate sponsorship. From the days of their association with the Alton and Springfield Railroad to the day when he introduced his brother John to Lincoln, to the days of the 1860 presidential campaign, Jacob Bunn had been for Lincoln a commercial associate, a legal client, a political ally, a kingmaker, and a friend.

VI

A Friend for the Friendless

In addition to supporting political campaigns, urban infrastructure, and business enterprises, Jacob Bunn donated generously to philanthropic causes, and was among the leading philanthropists of Springfield. He had discerned in civic benefaction a high art of humanity to which all should aspire. Furthermore, it was to his having been a visionary benefactor that Springfield owed many of its distinguished institutions. Bunn greatly assisted in the formation and development of numerous and diverse civic enterprises that were the foundations upon which many current Springfield organizations have been built.

In 1856, the first library association of Springfield was organized. Seven hundred dollars were contributed by the city's residents. Jacob Bunn served as the organization's first treasurer. J. T. Carter was the Association's first president, and Thomas Mather and William H. Herndon were its first secretaries.[91]

Bunn also helped in the founding of another institution of education. He was among the founding trustees of the Bettie Stuart Institute, which was a school established to provide girls with a genteel education. The school offered instruction in chemistry, literature, astronomy, botany, moral philosophy, Latin, and history, among other subjects.⁹² Jacob Bunn, John A. Chestnut, John T. Stuart, Christopher Brown, M. [sic] [Norman] M. Broadwell, and A. W. French comprised the school's first board of trustees. The school was named in honor of Bettie Stuart Brown, the wife of Christopher Brown. After the death of his wife, Christopher Brown donated the land upon which the school building was constructed.⁹³ Interestingly, Christopher Brown would serve as the legal counsel administering the liquidation of Jacob Bunn's assets, at the end of the 19th century.

While the need for educational facilities such as schools and library organizations presented several clear opportunities for civic vision of local consequence, the social and economic ramifications of the Civil War generated a plethora of local and statewide emergencies, which in turn presented further opportunities for civic leadership. Jacob Bunn was one of the public benefactors who provided excellent vision and guidance both to civic and to political concerns that sought to maintain and perpetuate the welfare of the State of Illinois and its people, during the years of the Civil War.

Bunn partook of the decision-making body formed by Springfield citizens to serve as an ancillary to the State of Illinois in the war effort. On 17 April 1861, a public meeting was summoned in Springfield, for the purpose of addressing locally the issues of assisting the State of Illinois in the war effort. Jacob Bunn, Charles H. Lanphier, Edward L. Baker, Charles A. Keyes, N. W. Matheny, H. G. Reynolds, E. B. Hawley, B. A. Watson, C. L. Morrison, and T. J. V. Owen were appointed to serve as a committee on resolutions.⁹⁴

Bunn also contributed support through the J. Bunn Bank. From one perspective, he could be viewed as a businessman. From another, he could be viewed as an altruist. "The outbreak of the Civil War in 1861, though long rumored, found Illinois unprepared with supplies and properly trained troops. Springfield banks, led by J. Bunn, immediately offered Governor Richard Yates $100,000 for this purpose."[95] A letter of gratitude from Governor Richard Yates, a Republican governor who served in that official capacity from 1861 to 1865,[96] further elucidated the conditions of the loans issued by Springfield banking institutions:

> Executive Office,
> Springfield, Ill, April 18, 1861.
>
> To Messrs. J. Bunn, N. H. Ridgely and President of the Marine Fire Insurance Company:
>
> Gentlemen:—Your communication of the 1 inst., tendering to me, and, through me, to the State of Illinois, the sum of one hundred thousand dollars, as a loan to facilitate necessary preparations for the organizing and collecting of the State troops to put down resistance to the laws and open rebellion, has been duly received. Your generous offer is gratefully accepted....[97]

Although it was certainly possible that Governor Richard Yates' Republican political persuasion made him, in Bunn's estimation, a desirable beneficiary of financial assistance and support, a more probable conjecture would be that Bunn was motivated by a sense of commitment to the wellbeing of Illinois and the whole country.

As Jacob Bunn was an important participant in the

financial support of Illinois during the Civil War, proving, with all of his associates, the spirit of civic commitment that the citizens of Springfield possessed, Jacob's brother, John Whitfield Bunn, also came to the aid of the Illinois war effort. John W. Bunn facilitated the logistical component of the Illinois war strategy, by serving as a wartime messenger, delivering messages containing instructions of great importance to key military leaders. During 1861, John W. Bunn, as Special Messenger, delivered no fewer than three such messages. In a message addressed to General R. K. Swift, dated 20 April 1861, John W. Bunn relayed the following information from Governor Richard Yates:

> CHICAGO, April 20, 1861.
>
> Gen. R. K. SWIFT:
>
> I am instructed by Governor Yates to inform you to raise the largest force possible, including artillery, and take possession of Cairo at the earliest moment. The utmost secrecy is required. Have your expedition start as if going to Springfield via Illinois Central Railroad.
>
> (Signed) John W. Bunn, Special Messenger from the Commander-in-Chief, Governor Yates[98]

This message reflected the concern that Springfield had for the southern regions of the state, which were vulnerable to Confederate attack. Cairo was located at the southernmost section of Illinois, and was an important regional center, because of its location on a major commercial waterway. The attention of the Yates administration was captured and held in no small part by the fact that the geographical proximity of southern Illinois municipalities, residents, and institutions to the Confederacy was tantamount to an undisputed and indefinitely long period of vulnerability to Confederate strategic military and vigilante maneuvers. John W. Bunn was further instructed to relay messages regarding the secret strategic defenses of southern Illinois, particularly Cairo and its vicinity.

> CHICAGO, April 20, 1861.
>
> I am directed by the Commander-in-Chief to say that it is hoped that the utmost expedition will be made as well as secrecy observed in the destination of the troops. It is intended that your paymaster and quartermaster shall report to the proper officers at Springfield. We want to concentrate all information at this point as to the condition and position of our forces, and you will please see that a proper communication, and as frequently as possible, is made to Springfield. Perhaps the state of feeling in Southern Illinois may require the utmost dispatch and secrecy, without regard to other considerations, but there are others of great importance.
>
> By order of the Commander-in-Chief.
> (Signed) JOHN W. BUNN, Special Messenger.[99]

John W. Bunn relayed additional messages, regarding matters such as the joining of forces and the appointment of officials.

> I would here say that Roger Fowler has been appointed commissary, and J. D. Webster paymaster, to the expedition.
>
> (Signed.) JOHN W. BUNN, Special Messenger.[100]
>
> CHICAGO, April 20, 1861.

GEN. R. K. SWIFT:

DEAR SIR:
  I am directed by the Commander-in-Chief to say that Captain John Pope, U.S. Army, will join your expedition at some point.
By order of the Commander-in-Chief.
(Signed.) JOHN W. BUNN[101]

The example set by the Springfield banking establishment incited similar action by other Illinois banks. "Banks in Chicago and other cities soon followed suit."[102] While Jacob Bunn was heavily occupied with providing state financial support, Elizabeth Ferguson Bunn, his wife, had discerned another symptom of wartime that was afflicting Springfield, namely, the need for refuge for war victims.

Because of the Civil War, Springfield had an influx of women and children seeking refuge from the wartime turmoil of their regions. Springfield's enterprising and philanthropic citizens responded to this influx of people in need of care. As husbands and fathers left to serve in the military, they left wives and children behind, with the hope of someday being able to return to them. "The years of 1862 and 3 were full of anxiety and sadness. Daily young men were marching away to war."[103] As these men went to war, their families were immediately cast into a state of uncertainty. Seeking refuge became one of the predominant occupations of wives who were left alone to care for children, and whose own safety was imperiled indefinitely by the war conditions. Many of the families who resided in the borderlands sought refuge from the perpetual proximity with the fighting, and as a result fled to locations farther to the north. "Trainloads of war victims began to arrive in the city. Mostly women and children, these homeless sought safety in Illinois to escape the border warfare in which their farms had been destroyed."[104]

Farms were not the only property casualties of border warfare. Francis Springer, a Lutheran minister and an important educator in the Springfield community noted the specific types of tragedy that afflicted women and children in the border regions. "In Arkansas he encountered women and children in the utmost misery, suffering from a border warfare, their homes burned, robbed of horses and stock, widowed and orphaned in a night and driven into the Union lines by hunger and anguish."[105] Springfield, Illinois, was both an important point of reception for many of the wartime émigrés, and a bastion, even a symbol, of the safety and care that was so desperately needed by the war-torn families of the border regions.

"[Francis Springer's wife, Mary Springer] remembers how happy [the women and children] were to reach Springfield, the goal that promised relief from their miseries."[106] Springfield was not prepared to accommodate sufficiently the numbers of people who were seeking refuge there. *Ad hoc* philanthropy was evident, as when the merchant John Williams adapted his store for the assumption of war charity functions, serving to collect any money, items of clothing and food that any person might deposit there, and then serving as a repository for these necessities, providing them for the indigent war refugees.[107] The need for an organized charitable institution, specifically one that was designed to provide wartime charity, was becoming rapidly apparent to the citizens of Springfield, and this growing necessity presented a great opportunity for philanthropy, because as one source articulated the condition of the time, "Care for these refugees was unorganized and erratic."[108]

Charity intended to combat the conditions of hunger of the refugee children was evident when numerous Springfield benefactors assumed the duties of caring for the children themselves. "Mrs. Hay, Mrs. Bunn [wife of Jacob Bunn], Mrs. Matheny, who had taken starving little children home for Sunday dinner, had been talking to their husbands... and had urged that something be done."[109] The response to the growing need for organized care was the establishment of the Springfield Home For The Friendless. It should be noted that the ladies of Springfield contributed greatly to both the conceptual development and the bringing to fruition of charitable institutions that would assist wartime victims. Elizabeth Jane Ferguson Bunn was one such lady.

The Springfield Home For The Friendless was incorporated 12 February 1863, by a special act of the Illinois legislature. Among the signatories of the charter was Elizabeth Ferguson Bunn. The Home was intended to provide temporary shelter for its occupants, until good homes could be secured for them.[110]

The Springfield Home For The Friendless was a dynamic social force in the community, as it provided its occupants with much more than just shelter. The Home served to procure employment for those of its residents who were of appropriate ages. The Home furthermore could assume legal guardianship of a child, should the father be unable to care for a child, or should both parents of a child be unable to provide adequate care. The management of the Home consisted of Judge Treat, president, George Pasfield, vice-president, G. P. Bowen, secretary, and Jacob Bunn, treasurer.[111]

Jacob Bunn also served as a member of a committee appointed to investigate the financial feasibility of acquiring the "Franklin House" property, which was being offered by P. C. Canedy for six thousand dollars. After a thorough examination of the property, the committee reported that they believed the property not to be capable of furnishing adequate space. "...The committee reported on Canedy's offer 'that they had examined the premises, and owing to insufficiency of grounds connected therewith deem it inexpeditious to purchase the same.' "[112]

The Springfield Home For The Friendless successfully aided many war refugees. It was the precursor to the Family Center of Sangamon County. In addition to serving in official capacities, Jacob and Elizabeth Bunn had frequently held Home board meetings at their residence.[113]

The Bunn family had been actively engaged in the establishment of the Home, and had participated in its formation, development, and success, and therefore had helped provide shelter, food, employment, and comfort to the women and children who had turned to Springfield as their haven from Civil War.

VII

Steel Rails and Sugar Beets

Jacob Bunn was engaged in a variety of local civic and business concerns. Even his support for Lincoln could be viewed as having been "regional," in that his affiliations with Lincoln and the Republican Party were primarily confined to Illinois.

In each of the business and civic enterprises he sought to bolster from within the economic and cultural maturation of Springfield. Vision for the development of a specific locale, however, frequently necessitated endeavor at more far-reaching levels. Jacob Bunn envisioned the greatness and commercial success of Springfield and of central Illinois as phenomena emanating not only from sources located within the capital city boundaries, but also from sources situated beyond its immediate vicinity. Of all of the industries of the age, the railroad industry presented the greatest number of efficacious venues for commercial development on a multiregional scale. The regionally blossoming railroad industry represented a wealth of opportunities for local municipal, industrial, and commercial developments. As a result, the railroad industry galvanized the visionary energy of Jacob Bunn, and of so many others who sought to promote the growth of an Illinois commercial network.

"Railroads were responsible for much of Springfield's phenomenal wealth in the early 19th century. Jacob Bunn was much interested in their development."[114] John W. Bunn, as well, was a prominent participant in the rapidly growing industrial capacity of Illinois.

A dedicated and multi-faceted involvement with the promotion of regional railroading would remain a prominent aspect of Jacob Bunn's business interests throughout the entire duration of his business career, from 1840 until his death in 1897. His interests in the railroad industry manifested themselves in diverse fashions. Interestingly, Bunn would be involved in the railroad industry directly, through promotion of railroad corporations, in the earlier years of his career, and indirectly involved with the industry later on, through the organization and direction of corporations whose commercial purposes centered upon various aspects of the railroad industry. The success of the central Illinois railroad industry would be due largely to his services.

By playing an active role in the growth of the railroad industry in the vicinity of Springfield, Bunn magnified the scope of his business activity and vision. His interest in the success of regional railroad networks would have consisted partly of a desire to connect the grocery business to the rails, and therefore to a larger commercial network. As an article in the *Illinois State Journal* stated, "The completion of the railroad will add greatly to the wholesale business of Springfield, and seems to be operating to give a start to other branches of business."[115] The railroad would have added to the vitality of the wholesale industry and to other industries as well.

Among the earliest instances of Jacob Bunn's local promotion of the expanding railroad industry in the Springfield area was his service as a commercial representative of the Northern Cross Railroad, in the year 1844.[116] The Illinois legislature authorized on 26 February 1841 the expenditure of $100,000 for the purpose of completing the Northern Cross Railroad. The road had already connected Meredosia, a point located on the Illinois River, to Jacksonville, Morgan County, Illinois. Only the grading of the section extending from Jacksonville to Springfield had been completed at that time. By 15 February 1842 the Northern Cross had reached Springfield, connecting it to the Illinois River, at Meredosia. Northern Cross trains left Springfield every Monday, Wednesday, and Friday. On the other days of the week, the trains departed from the Meredosia station. The company was eventually sold to Nicholas Ridgely and to Thomas Mather, both of Springfield, and to James Dunlap of Jacksonville. The enterprise was rebuilt, and was renamed the Sangamon and Morgan Railroad. The new company opened a route in 1849 between Springfield and Naples, Illinois, with two trains per day operating on the line.[117] Interestingly, Naples was one of the towns where Jacob Bunn had entered the grocer's trade, in the 1830s.

A similar instance of his dedication to industrial growth, through strategic railroading, was his assistance with the initial promotion of the Alton and Springfield Railroad. On 6 July 1847, a notice appeared in the *Illinois State Journal* informing residents of Springfield and its vicinity of plans for a new railroad company, to be known as the Alton and Springfield Railroad, which would connect Springfield to the Mississippi River, at the town of Alton, Illinois, which is located on the Mississippi River and quite near St. Louis. The members of the committee that spearheaded this project were Jacob Bunn, Abraham Lincoln, John Williams, John T. Stuart, John Calhoun, B. C. Webster, J. N. Brown, P. P. Enos, William Pickrell, and S. B. Opdycke.[118] As early as 1847 it was evident that Bunn and Lincoln shared an interest in promoting the railroad industry, and the two men would remain in an ideological brotherhood with respect to the promotion of business and industry, particularly the railroads.

In 1850 Jacob Bunn and John Williams were published correspondents on the subject of the organization of a railroad company whose road would connect Springfield with Terre Haute, Indiana. The correspondence addressed primarily the subject of constructing the most efficient route, in the best interests of a healthy and efficient system.

Sullivan, Ill., Jan. 10, 1850

John Williams, Esq.

Sir: Our object in addressing you is to ascertain the views of the citizens of Springfield in regard to a road from that place to Terre Haute, Indiana.

There is a strong effort making to organize a company to construct a road from Alton to Terre Haute. But as you will have a road from Springfield to Alton, and also one to Quincy, and having already completed the road on the section from Springfield to Naples;—we are of opinion that a road from Terre Haute to Springfield, would be more advantageous, and meet the approbation of capitalists more than one to Alton.

Should you feel an interest in the subject, (which we have no doubt you do,) any movement made by you upon it, will be responded to here; and we think under existing circumstances it requires immediate action.

Let us hear from you on the subject.

    Your's, &c.   R. B. Ewing
                              W. B. Duffield[119]

In response to the Ewing-Duffield letter, Jacob Bunn, Virgil Hickox, Pascal P. Enos and John Williams replied. Their response demonstrates some of their concepts of strategic planning for the financing of railroad development.

                                          Springfield, Jan. 15th, 1850

Messrs. R. B. Ewing and W. B. Duffield;

    Gentlemen:—We have placed before us, your letter to Col. John Williams, of this City, relative to a projected railroad, from this point to Terre Haute, and assure you that the citizens of this place are quite alive to its importance and willing to co-operate in any plan that may be tho't advisable for ensuring its construction. The certainty of the early completion of the road connecting Springfield with the *Mississippi*, at Alton, and the extension of the Sangamon and Morgan railroad to the *Mississippi*, at Quincy, offer great inducement to Eastern enterprise in its efforts to reach that great channel of Western commerce, through a continuous line of railroads, by connecting with them, at this point—thus securing two great feeders to the road, from the Upper and Lower Mississippi. Philadelphia and Baltimore are now in their rivalry for Western trade—each constructing (the one by Pittsburgh, the other by Wheeling,) railroads; one of which will be pushed on through the central portions of Ohio, Indiana and Illinois until the Mississippi is reached.

    Why cannot a road from Springfield to Terre Haute be made a link in this great chain? But, in addition to uniting with two roads, at this point, the saving, in cost of construction, would be one-third less than in a road from Alton to Terre Haute—less in the number of miles and less per mile, from the greater adaptation of the country to rail roads. We would suggest to your consideration, the plan of county subscriptions under the law of the last session, together with private [subscriptions] to the full extent they can be had. These, by the united action of all the counties and inhabitants along the contemplated route, might be made sufficiently large to induce Eastern capitalists to furnish the balance necessary to the construction of the road.

To carry out this plan, it would be advisable to call a convention of the friends of the project, and fix the amount each county should subscribe in its corporate capacity, and also the amount it should raise by individual subscription.

Very Resp'y Yours,
VIRGIL HICKOX
JOHN WILLIAMS
J. BUNN
PASCAL P. ENOS[120]

The Springfield-Terre Haute correspondences demonstrate these citizens' understanding of the importance of joining together railroad systems into ever larger networks. As railroad companies joined together their routes, entire commercial zones were also connected. The Mississippi River was considered to be an invaluable thoroughfare of commerce, and can be said to be a matriarch of rail enterprise. As its waters gave life to riparian flora and fauna, its importance to trade gave life to commercial organizations. The joining together of the rail routes of two railroad companies could effect what might usefully be described as a conjugal union of American commercial territories. Individuals such as Bunn, Williams, Hickox, and Enos, and the lawyers who facilitated all of the germane legal processes, were the "clergy" who arranged and administered these conjugal commercial ceremonies.

Jacob Bunn proceeded to promote regional railroad networks and was listed in the local newspapers as an incorporator in 1857 and a subscription agent for the Springfield & Pana Railroad, in the summer of 1858.[121] The Springfield and Pana Railroad Company helped satisfy the growing demand at that time for the development of railroad networks, particularly in areas where passenger transportation was limited. The articles of incorporation for the company were enacted by statute on 16 February 1857 by the State of Illinois, and read in part as follows:

> Section 1. *Be it enacted by the people of the state of Illinois, represented in the General Assembly,* That James A. Barret, Jacob Bunn, Charles H. Lanphier, Wm. B. Fondey, Virgil Hickox, William Butler, of Springfield, and Preston Breckinridge, of Sangamon County; and Horatio M. Vandever, D. D. Shumway, William A. Goodrich, Wm. S. Frink, Calvin Goudy and William B. Hall, of Taylorville; and Milan S. Beckwith, Mason French and Thomas Finley, of Pana, Christian county, Illinois, and their associates, successors and assigns, are hereby created a body corporate and politic, under the name and style of 'The Springfield and Pana Railroad Company,' with perpetual succession; and under this name and style shall be capable of suing and being sued, impleading and being impleaded, defending and being defended against, in law and equity, in all courts and places whatsoever, in like manner and as fully as natural persons; may make and use a common seal, and alter or renew the same at pleasure; and by their said corporate name and style shall be capable in law of contracting and being contracted with; shall be and are hereby invested with all the powers, privileges, immunities and franchises of conveying real and personal estate which may be needful to carry into effect fully the purposes and objects of this act; and said company are hereby authorized

and empowered to locate, construct and complete a railroad, commencing at Springfield, Sangamon county, and from thence on the most direct and eligible route to Taylorville; and from thence to Pana, in Christian county, with one or more tracks or lines of rails: *Provided*, said company shall commence the construction of said road within four years and complete the same within ten years.

[Section] 2. The capital stock of said company shall consist of six hundred thousand dollars, and may be increased to one million of dollars, to be divided into shares of one hundred dollars each.[122]

Jacob Bunn further perpetuated the assemblage of an Illinois rail system by serving as an incorporator of the Pana, Springfield and Northwestern Railroad Company in the winter of 1865. Bunn served as a founder of the company along with John A. McClernand, John Williams, Shelby M. Cullom, Alexander Starne, Charles W. Matheny, Asa Eastman, Charles Ridgely, James Wilson, Munson Carter, Preston Breckinridge, Joseph G. McCoy, John Bone, Peyton Harrison, and Andrew B. McConnel, all of Sangamon County, along with Horatio M. Vandever, D. D. Shumway, William A. Goodrich, William S. Frink, Calvin Goudy, Lewis E. Thompson, William B. Hall, and Charles A. Manners, all of Christian County, Illinois.[123] Many of the founders listed above were also associated with the establishment of the earlier Springfield and Pana Railroad Company.

Major General John A. McClernand had previously been a law partner of Elliott Herndon, and had served as a member of Congress, in 1859. He fought in the battles of Arkansas and Vicksburg, and returned to Springfield to recommence the practice of law, this time with Norman Broadwell and William Springer.[124]

Shelby Moore Cullom served as a governor of Illinois, as well as a congressman and as a senator from Illinois, and was an unsuccessful candidate for the 1888 and 1892 nomnations for the presidential race, having been unsuccessful in procuring the support of the Illinois delegation.[125] Shelby Cullom had also been a close friend and associate of both Jacob and John W. Bunn. Cullom's greatest importance in the history of United States legislative initiative and administrative history emerged when he was serving as a senator from Illinois. Cullom was associated with the drafting and promulgation of the federal legislative measure which was enacted on 4 February 1887, officially establishing the Interstate Commerce Commission, often known by its abbreviated title, "ICC." The organic statute for the Interstate Commerce Commission is still referred to in numerous tables of popular names for federal statutes as the "Cullom Act," in honor of Shelby Cullom himself. Senator Cullom has left a great legacy as a statesman and as an administrative visionary who discerned the need for imposing greater order upon the rapidly expanding commercial power of the United States. He is to be counted among the great set of leaders that Illinois has provided for the United States. Cullom's railroad experiences in Illinois would have afforded him a comprehensive cognizance of inter-state commerce as a quickly emerging and growing economic phenomenon in the United States.

The Pana, Springfield and Northwestern Railroad Company was intended to form a route from Pana, Christian County, Illinois, to the Illinois River, via Taylorville and Springfield. The route was strategic in that it created a convenient and direct artery of commerce connecting Pana,

Taylorville, and Springfield, to the Illinois River, a major watercourse.

> ... and said Company are hereby authorized and empowered to locate, construct and complete a Railroad, commencing at or near Pana, in Christian County, thence to Taylorville in Christian County, thence to City of Springfield, in Sangamon County, and thence to some eligible point on the Illinois River to be determined by said Company with one or more tracks or lines of rails. Said Company shall commence the construction of said road in good faith within one year and shall complete the same within ten years.[126]

The essence of the railroad ideology current at the time of the enactment of these articles of incorporation is expressed clearly by Section Five of the Act. Companies were encouraged in their corporate charters to form railway networks.

> Said Company shall have power to unite, connect or consolidate its railroads with any other railroad constructed or which may hereafter be constructed in this State... and for that purpose full power is hereby given to said Company to make and execute such contracts with any other Company[127]

The organic statute for the Pana, Springfield and Northwestern Railroad Company authorized an initial capitalization of $1,000,000. The charter also granted authority to the members of the corporation to increase the capitalization to any sum up to $5,000,000.[128] This provision would have served as a mechanism for enabling the directors of the corporation to accommodate financially any additional expenses that might have arisen in connection with the completion or administration of the new railroad company.

Jacob Bunn's prolific involvement with regional railroad companies contributed to the strengthening of Springfield's economy. His interest in railroad promotion and development was also indicative of the contemporary belief that the commercial strength of an urban center was largely dependent upon its proximity to the railroads. While actively engaged as a promoter of smaller railroad companies, Jacob Bunn also participated in the organization of a much larger corporation, in the winter of 1861.

On 18 February 1861, the State of Illinois enacted a statute that incorporated a new railroad company known as the Chicago and Alton Railroad Company. Jacob Bunn served as one of the founders and initial commissioners of the Chicago and Alton Railroad Company, and therefore contributed to what became one of the most notable railroads of the Midwest. The Chicago and Alton was moreover a reorganization and consolidation of the corporate assets of previously existing railroad companies that served and connected the important commercial centers of St. Louis, Alton, Springfield and Chicago.

> Section I   Be it enacted by the People of the State of Illinois represented in the General Assembly, That James Robb, Charles Moran, Adrian Iselin, Nathan Peck, Louis Von Hoffman, Lewis H. Meyer, Septimus Crookes, William B. Ogden, Jacob Bunn, J. J. Mitchell, Joseph B. White and E. M. Gilbert be and are hereby constituted commissioners with power to organize a corporation to be styled 'The Chicago and Alton Railroad Company' subject to all the

conditions franchises rights and privileges conferred by this act.

Section II   That the commissioners named in this act or a majority of them, shall have power to acquire for themselves, and their associates by purchase, transfer or conveyance all and singular the Rail Road and all its property real and personal, with the corporate rights, franchises rights privileges and effects, now or heretofore belonging to or owned, or vested in the Alton and Sangamon Railroad Company, afterwards called the Chicago and Mississippi Railroad Company, and also the Chicago Alton and St. Louis Railroad Company.[129]

The Chicago and Alton Railroad served the city of Springfield, and it is likely that Jacob Bunn, who was residing primarily in Springfield, had been considered to be an ideal individual to include in the formation of the company. Moreover, Bunn would have desired to be associated with the Chicago and Alton Railroad Company because it served Springfield, thereby enhancing the already strong connection that Springfield enjoyed in the system of Midwestern railroads. Bunn's involvement with the road also showed that he was perceived by many of his peers to have already accumulated considerable experience in regional railroad development, and was a well-recognized entrepreneur and financier interested in promoting the industrial expansion of central Illinois.

The Chicago and Alton Railroad Company endured for many decades as an important railway system throughout the Midwest. In 1931, seventy years after the organization of the company, the corporate administration of the Chicago and Alton Railroad effected the sale of all corporate assets to the Alton Railroad Company. At the time of the sale, the capital stock of the Chicago and Alton Railroad amounted to slightly less than $40,000,000.[130] The railroad company eventually accumulated over 1,000 miles of track, through a combination of owned and leased rail lines. With a stock listing on the New York Stock Exchange, the Chicago and Alton Railroad was highly regarded by investors for many years. The volume of the operating revenue of the Chicago and Alton Railroad Company had attained nearly $31,000,000 by 1924, and by 1925 the corporation represented a total investment of more than $150,000,000. By 1930, the Interstate Commerce Commission, pursuant to an officially announced intention to consolidate the vast number of railroad systems in the United States, assigned the Chicago and Alton Railroad to be integrated into the Baltimore and Ohio Railroad Company, System Number 5.[131] Enduring changes in both the economy and in corporate administrations, the Chicago and Alton Railroad Company ultimately traced its origin to 1861, serving the transportation sectors of Midwestern economies for seventy years. The Chicago and Alton Railroad Company was a monument of commercial achievement, and Jacob Bunn had been among the founders who had brought it forth.

John Whitfield Bunn was also an active promoter of the railroad industry of Illinois. He assumed a leading role with the Toledo, Peoria and Western Railway Company, which had been incorporated under Illinois legislative authority on 22 March 1887, as a successor to a corporate precursor of the same name. John W. Bunn served as a director of the concern during the early years of the corporation and, like his brother Jacob, both devoted time and delivered a visionary's touch to the building of the business. The company grew extensively, and in the year 1920 had experienced gross annual revenues of more than $2,000,000. By 1920 the company had a total capital stock of $4,500,000. Also by 1920, the total assets of the railroad company amounted to more than $13,000,000.[132]

The extent of Jacob Bunn's regional entrepreneurial vision was not, however, limited to business concerns of transportation. He had an enormous impact on the construction of the banking sector of Springfield. The ramifications of his achievements in the banking sector spread throughout the entire state of Illinois. And while attempting to build a regional economy that could thrive on the commercial arteries of the railways, Bunn would also serve as a vanguard of the construction of the State Capitol building of 1874. Although the capitol construction project was a local undertaking, its significance pervaded the state, as it represented the growth and vitality of the capital city.

"[Bunn was appointed] as chairman of the commission organized to oversee construction of the new state capitol. This gigantic, neo-classical building with its over-300-foot dome, would eventually become the visual symbol of Springfield."[133] Among the contractors who completed the construction of the new State Capitol was William Douglas Richardson, whose daughter Ada Willard Richardson would marry Bunn's third son, George Wallace Bunn, in 1886.[134]

A brief account of the career of William Douglas Richardson is helpful, as he would be a close associate of both Jacob and John W. Bunn. Richardson himself had contributed handsomely to the industrial growth and business development of Springfield. He served early on in his career as a clerk for the Great Western Railroad

Company.¹³⁵ Later on, he was a partner in the joint venture of Richardson & Latham, an insurance and real estate partnership whose office was situated opposite the J. Bunn Bank,¹³⁶ an institution which will be discussed in the chapter of this paper entitled *Twilight of the Springfield Banker*. Richardson ultimately entered the construction business, as a contractor, and it was within this sector of industry that he gained a national reputation.

Among the construction projects which William D. Richardson assumed were the building of the new Illinois State Capitol, the Lincoln Monument in Springfield, and the First Methodist Episcopal Church of Springfield. He also served as the superintendent of grounds and buildings for the 1893 World's Columbian Exposition in Chicago.¹³⁷ Interestingly, both John W. Bunn and William D. Richardson were associated with the 1893 World's Fair in Chicago. John W. Bunn served as the treasurer of the Board of World's Fair Commissioners,¹³⁸ at the same time when he was also an important leader in Chicago business sectors. John W. Bunn also was present at the dedication ceremonies for the World's Columbian Exposition on 11, 12 and 13 October 1892, and received a complimentary entrance ticket to the ceremonies.¹³⁹

William D. Richardson, like Jacob Bunn and John W. Bunn, was dedicated to the development of the Illinois railroad industry. He also labored to develop national railroad infrastructure when he entered into an association with the rail manufacturing sector of the economy, which would have been a sector of highly dynamic capital and vast wealth at the time. William D. Richardson, John W. Bunn, Dr. George Pasfield, Charles Ridgely, George M.

Brinkerhoff, and Orlin H. Miner, along with John Williams, La Fayette Smith and others, together incorporated the Springfield Iron Company in August of 1871. Furthermore, Richardson and John W. Bunn, in addition to the other men named above, served as members of the first board of directors of the corporation.[140]

> The undersigned being desirous of becoming incorporated under the provision of an act of the General Assembly of the State of Illinois, entitled an act to authorize the formation of corporations for manufacturing, mining, mechanical or chemical purposes approved February 18th 1857- do hereby certify
>
> *First*   The corporate name assumed to distinguish said company, and to be used in conducting its business, is <u>The Springfield Iron Company</u>.
>
> *Second* The objects for which said company is formed are for mining coal and iron, and for the manufacturing and general working of iron and steel.
>
> *Third*   The amount of the capital stock is to be Three Hundred Thousand Dollars.
>
> *Fourth* The term of existence of the company is to be fifty years.
>
> *Fifth*   The capital stock of said company shall consist of Three thousand shares of One Hundred dollars each.
>
> *Sixth*   The number of Directors shall be five, and the following persons are to be Directors for the first year: Charles Ridgely, Geo. M. Brinkerhoff, Orlin H. Miner, William D. Richardson and John W. Bunn.
>
> *Seventh* The operations of said company shall be carried on at or near the City of Springfield, Sangamon County Illinois.
>
> In evidence whereof we have hereunto set our hands and

affixed our seals at Springfield Illinois this Eighteenth day of August AD 1871—

Done in duplicate—

    Charles Ridgely
    John W. Bunn
    Geo. M. Brinkerhoff
    W. D. Richardson
    La Fayette Smith
    Chas. E. Hay
    John Williams
    Alexander Starne
    H. B. Hayes
    Orlin H. Miner
    Geo. Pasfield[141]

The business grew to large proportions, manufacturing 4,500 tons of rails per month, in 1881.[142] In an advertisement from the 1890 issue of the Poor's Railroad Manual, the Springfield Iron Company factory boasted the largest capacity for the manufacture of angle splice bars in the United States.[143] The history of the company mirrored the history of Springfield in that it also was characterized by fast growth.

> In the beginning the works only manufactured railroad iron. The puddle mill belonging to the rail mill was started in June, 1872, and the first rail was made in September of that year, since which time it has continually been in operation. The claim is made by the company that they have made more rails than any similar works in the United States. They now turn out four thousand five hundred tons of rails per month. Other branches of manufacture have been introduced from time to time, so that at present the company is making rails of both iron and steel, bar iron, fish plates, and track bolts. The steel rails are made by the Siemens-Martin, or open hearth process. Some forty clerks

are employed in the different departments of this office, while the entire works give employment to ten hundred and eighty employees. The goods manufactured by the Springfield Iron Company are used by all the principal railroads in the west, and among them we will name the Wabash, Illinois Central, Chicago & Alton, Northwestern, etc., etc.[144]

The factory in 1881 was said to have been consuming 300 tons of coal per day. It procured the coal from the Beard-Hickox Coal Company, whose plant was situated about 200 yards from the Springfield Iron Company factory complex. Virgil Hickox, prominently associated with the Beard-Hickox Coal Company also served as a founder of the Springfield and Pana Railroad Company, with Jacob Bunn. The iron works employed 15 Siemens gas furnaces. The factory also utilized a duplex Worthington pump which comprised two steam cylinders, each 25.5 inches in diameter, a 24 inch stroke, and a 9 inch diameter hydraulic piston that generated a hydraulic pressure of 350 pounds per square inch. The Springfield Iron Company complex consisted of numerous divisions. Included were a rail mill, a Merchant mill, a Blooming mill, a puddle works, a steel conversion factory, and blacksmith shops, carpenter shops, pattern shops, bolt and nut works, and various machine shops.[145]

The factory also was the locus of numerous innovations in the iron and steel industry in the United States. The company introduced a steel-making process in 1880 that was novel in the United States, and undertook an expansion of the factory works so as to provide for the manufacture of rolling bars, merchant steel and plates. Having turned out approximately 26,000 tons of rails and fastenings during the year 1878, the company was among the important concerns of its type in the United States.[146]

The Springfield Iron Company also developed a national reputation for the capacity of its bar iron production. Bar iron was an elementary component in the manufacture of railroad rolling stock, and was therefore an essential specialized product during the great age of railroad accessory manufacturing. The Springfield Iron Company in 1892 manufactured 60,000 tons of merchant iron and steel products, and its factory possessed the largest capacity in the United States for the manufacturing of angle splice bars, and rolling stock bar iron. The iron works were situated near the Chicago and Alton Railroad station, which would have enabled the factory to load its products easily onto Chicago and Alton Railroad freight cars and ship them to Chicago and to St. Louis and to many other areas.

It was the first iron and steel company in the United States to introduce the Siemens gas furnace as a mechanism for heating iron. Another innovation that occurred at the Springfield Iron Company was the ammonia-tar salvaging method that was invented by the corporation's chemist, Dr. Alphonse Hennin. Dr. Hennin discovered a chemical conservation method whereby the residual tar and ammonia left by the gas-manufacturing processes of the company could be retained and reused. By salvaging the resultant tar and ammonia byproducts, the company could reuse the chemical waste products in a chemical combination which could itself be utilized in fueling other sections of the factory. The Hennin Method was, therefore, invented in Illinois, at the Springfield Iron Company. Promptly after Dr. Hennin's discovery, the company hastened to erect all of the machinery requisite for implementing Dr. Hennin's fuel conservation and production method.[147]

The support that Hennin received from the corporate administration was illustrative of the management's wisdom. Charles Ridgely, William Barret Ridgely, John W. Bunn and others, by supporting Dr. Alphonse Hennin in his chemical research, exhibited the finest ideals of visionary executive leadership.

> It is expected that this process will not only prove a great advantage and economy to the Springfield Iron Company and its works, but its general introduction into all the large manufactories of the kind will be a great step in advance in the science of metallurgy, and a great triumph for the application of scientific methods and skillful management in industrial processes so characteristic of the spirit of the age. This process is not only applicable to iron making but to any other industry such as brick making, glass making, and in fact all other cases where a large and continuous supply of fuel is required, and it is attracting very great attention from metallurgists, chemists, gas makers and others.[148]

The company gained a national reputation both for the quality of its output and for the scale of its manufacture. Enduring from 1871 until 1900, when it was sold to the Republic Steel and Iron Company of Chicago,[149] the Springfield Iron Company assumed a prominent seat within the echelon of Springfield's most significant contributions to the industrial expansion of the United States. The Republic Steel and Iron Company was another pacesetter in the iron and steel industry, and had expended more than $6,000,000 to maintain the manufacturing centers that it owned and operated around the United States, between the years 1899 and 1902. The production capacity of the Youngstown, Ohio factory alone amounted to 1,000 tons per day.[150] The Republic Steel and Iron Company was operating at a time when the United States Steel Corporation was in its infancy. Having been chartered in February of 1901, U.S. Steel was the largest corporation in the United States, in terms of capitalization.

As the Springfield Iron Company came to an end, the largest steel corporations ever to exist in world history were taking form, as mergers were being effected on grand scales. Evolving from Chicago, Pittsburgh and Bethlehem, Pennsylvania, among other places, companies such as Republic Steel and Iron, U.S. Steel, and Bethlehem Steel were destined to dominate the industry, at a time when the United States was the leading industrial power in the world.

William Douglas Richardson and John Whitfield Bunn had been two of the founders and original directors of the Springfield Iron Company, and had thereby made their own contribution to the Illinois steel industry, and to the American steel industry as a whole. Richardson, in ways similar to his in-laws Jacob and John W. Bunn, illustrated the visionary entrepreneurship of the time that both facilitated and enabled the economic growth of the region and the industrial success of the country.

Coal companies in central Illinois such as the Beard-Hickox Coal Company owed their existence to the abundance of bituminous coal deposits in the Springfield vicinity. Awaiting its industrial grand awakening, the Illinois coal industry was to experience a rapid development that would be virtually coextensive with the Illinois iron and steel industry. Moreover, the coal industry of Sangamon County would mature with astounding speed. During the period of time when the Springfield Iron Company was in its infant years, coal companies began to flourish, thereby further complementing the economic vitality of central Illinois.

As the diversity of natural resources of Sangamon County was becoming increasingly apparent, Jacob Bunn's entrepreneurial visions were continuing to blossom, and his brother John W. Bunn was also becoming increasingly active in statewide commercial and civic affairs. Coal deposits in Springfield had been discovered inadvertently by the drilling efforts of the Springfield Waterworks Company in 1857. Approximately one decade later, however, coal mines had become plentiful in Sangamon, as the industry had matured rapidly.

Although coal mining had been undertaken in Washington Park in Springfield about a decade before, the coal industry did not gain momentum as a major economic force in Sangamon County until after the cessation of the Civil War, until which time wood served as the primary fuel source for most Springfield manufacturers. The birth of the Sangamon County coal industry is owed predominantly to Parley L. Howlett, a brewer in Riverton, a small town situated to the east of Springfield, and Jacob Loose, a former dry-goods clerk. While drilling into the banks of the Sangamon River, Howlett struck at 210 feet what appeared to be a coal seam that was eight feet thick.[151]

The verity of Howlett's discovery was questioned, however, and it was not until Jacob Loose struck a sizeable coal seam at 237 feet, at Iles Junction, located two miles to the south of Springfield, that coal mining became a salient fixture on the tableau of the Sangamon County economy.

Loose established at Iles Junction the first deep-shaft coal mine in April of 1867. Other entrepreneurs soon followed suit. Howlett soon opened a mine-shaft on his own property. William Beard and William Saunderson commenced the sale of coal from the "North Mine," at the Henry Converse farm, located on land one-and-one-half miles to the north of Springfield. Sangamon County coal productivity blossomed, and within four years, the county was producing approximately 120,000 tons of coal per year.[152]

It was a fortuitous occurrence that Jacob Bunn had been a director of the Springfield Waterworks Company when, in 1857, the company's drilling projects failed to tap water, and instead struck coal. Bunn elected to partake of what many would have considered to be the brilliant future of coal in the vicinity of Springfield. Parley Howlett had borrowed much of the capital he utilized for establishing himself in business in Riverton from Jacob Bunn. The lack of success of his business ventures, however, was sufficient to force Howlett into bankruptcy, in 1868. "... Jacob Bunn, probably the largest creditor of Howlett, purchased everything in 1869."[153] While clearly the event of bankruptcy was unfortunate for Howlett, the timing of his financial tragedy was perhaps even more devastating.

> The first mines at Riverton gave promise of the great wealth to come. Jacob acquired the Riverton coal mine and machinery, the hotel, nearly 400 houselots, a dozen miners' cottages and over 1,500 acres of land with coal rights.[154]

The Riverton mining enterprise of which Bunn was the proprietor was known as the Western Coal & Mining Company. He also owned a Riverton distillery that was known as the Sangamon Company. Bunn would experience success as the proprietor of the Riverton properties until the time when he would have to sell them in order to pay the debts incurred by the failure of the J. Bunn Bank.

"The distillery, coalmine, and town property were dispersed to a variety of purchasers."[155] It is interesting to note the cyclical pattern of speculation, ownership, and financial failure that characterized Riverton business enterprise throughout its 19th century history. Howlett and Bunn, in succession, had both embarked on speculative ventures in Riverton, had become proprietors of significant properties therein, and had both, although for different reasons, become victims of bankruptcy.

Involvement with the numerous enterprises in the various developing sectors of business and industry would not, however, constitute the extent of Bunn's entrepreneurship and vision for the success of Illinois industry. While he was assuming proprietorship of the Riverton properties enumerated above, "...his bank provided the money for a risky venture in northern Illinois—the raising of sugar beets."[156]

A brief treatment of the evolution of the beet sugar industry in Illinois illustrates an entrepreneurial life, that of Charles Henry Rosenstiel, parallel to the business career of Jacob Bunn. Jacob Bunn entered into the beet sugar industry when he commenced a partnership in Chatsworth, Livingston County, Illinois, with Gottlieb and Ernst T. Gennert, who, like Rosenstiel, were German immigrants. The concern was styled The Germania Sugar Company. It constructed a factory for sugar refining in 1865. The company was organized to produce sugar from beets.

Although the Germania factory operated for approximately five years, the sugar production process grew less successful, due to a severe lack of water.[157] The Germania Sugar Company had a capital stock of $165,000, with $55,000 being owned by the Gennert brothers. The company also owned 2,400 acres of land, with a value of $250,000, and a stock of machinery possessing a value of no less than $100,000. Jacob Bunn had not only been a financier of the enterprise, but had eventually attained the executive positions of treasurer and superintendent in the firm. The initial civility that characterized the partnership of Bunn and the Gennert brothers eventually deteriorated entirely, and culminated in an expensive litigation process in the United States Court, in Chicago. For reasons which remain almost entirely obscure even to this day, the Gennerts brought suit against Jacob Bunn. The Gennert brothers petitioned the Court for the following:

> An accounting and division is asked, as well as an injunction to restrain Bunn from disposing of the company or interfering with its affairs.[158]

The *Jacob Bunn vs The Germania Sugar Company* lawsuit resulted in a verdict in favor of Bunn. Bunn was awarded $202,571.54. This was the largest verdict that had ever been rendered in Livingston County.[159] These events undoubtedly left a fog of disdain for Bunn in the Chatsworth region for years. Although the Germania Sugar Company was ultimately a financial failure, it provided Bunn with sufficient experience to organize another beet sugar company elsewhere, in Freeport, Illinois. Furthermore, despite the unfortunate destruction of the friendship which most likely had existed among Jacob Bunn, Gottlieb Gennert, and Ernst T. Gennert, all three of the men should be viewed as having been visionary partners who once contributed to the development of Livingston County business and industry.

Another positive aspect of the Germania Sugar Company experiment was that the business had successfully demonstrated that the cultivation of beet sugar in this region of Illinois was capable of generating a profit. Nonetheless, industrialists and agronomical specialists suspected that greater profits could be made elsewhere in the state. Bunn believed the land in the vicinity of Freeport to be generally more conducive to success in this particular agricultural venture than the land in Livingston County. Consequently, Bunn petitioned Charles Henry Rosenstiel of Freeport for the removal of the factory to Freeport, and for the organization of a new sugar company in Freeport.

After several years of delay, the factory and its $70,000 dollars worth of machinery were relocated to Freeport. On 8 April 1871 a general consensus was attained at a citizens' meeting held at the Freeport Opera House, to relocate the Chatsworth sugar factory to Freeport. Technical expertise was to be found in the opinions of Professor William Kullberg of Germany and of Professor Clark of Massachusetts, in addition to several other scholarly judgements. All were unanimous that the land around Freeport was more aptly suited for the cultivation of beet sugar than the terrain surrounding the township of Chatsworth. Moreover, the region surrounding Freeport possessed superior labor resources, more desirable industrial facilities, and a more abundant availability of water, an essential to the industrial processes of sugar manufacturing.

As a result of the Freeport consensus, the summer of 1872 witnessed the completion of the construction of the new buildings. In August of that year all of the necessary machinery, including the vacuum pans, filters, centrifugals, and ovens had been installed. The factory contained twenty-two miles of pipe, in addition to many copper kettles, and beet grinders, all of which were fundamental components of the sugar manufacturing processes of the time. The cost of construction was *in toto* $167,000. This sum did not include the later construction expenditures that were incurred by the enterprise. The project was carried out to completion by Charles Henry Rosenstiel of Freeport, Jacob Bunn of Springfield, and Jerome Increase Case of Racine, Wisconsin. In September of 1872, the process of manufacturing sugar from beets was underway. The three men owned and operated the establishment during the seasons from 1872 to 1875.[160]

The meeting at the Freeport Opera House was the beginning of what would become the powerful industrial body which the author has termed "The Freeport Triumvirate," because of the rapid and expansive growth of the Freeport Sugar Company and of the American beet sugar industry, as fueled by the industrial vision of Jacob Bunn, Charles Henry Rosenstiel and Jerome Increase Case. Although it survived only for about five years, the Freeport Triumvirate was among the most important, yet remains among the most obscure, chapters in the history of the sugar industry in the United States.

Heinrich Christian Carl Rosenstiel was born in Saxony

18 April 1821 and upon arrival in America changed his given name to "Charles Henry," which name he retained for the remainder of his life.[161] He emigrated to Baltimore in 1840. Rosenstiel traveled west, as Bunn had done four years previously, and settled in Stephenson County, Illinois, arriving there in the summer of 1842. Settling near Eleroy, he initially engaged in the building trade. Thereafter he entered into the manufacture of bricks. The first brick manufactured in Stephenson County has been attributed to the industry of C. H. Rosenstiel. Having removed to Freeport, he erected the first steam-mill in the county, and constructed the woolen mill, as well. Rosenstiel also served on the State Agricultural Board of Illinois for nineteen years, was the founder of the Stephenson County Agricultural Society, and was an extensive landowner and stock dealer. During the period from 1871 to 1872, Charles Henry Rosenstiel erected a sugar factory for the manufacture of beet sugar, thereby entering the sugar industry.[162]

Jerome Increase Case was among the most important and influential industrialists of the Midwest, and remains today not only a pioneer in the sugar industry, but also a leader in the agricultural machinery industry. Jerome I. Case was the founder, in 1842, of the J. I. Case Threshing Machine Company of Racine, Wisconsin. The company was the largest manufacturer of agricultural machinery in the United States in 1920. The company manufactured and sold oil tractors, steam road rollers, rock crushers, horse powers, road graders, tractor plows, harrows, automobiles, farm steam engines, and other types of machinery. In 1920 the factory consisted of a 137 acre manufacturing area, with 60 acres of factory floor space. The factory had an annual production capacity of 5,000 automobiles, 15,000 oil and steam tractors, and 6,000 threshers, in 1920. By that same year the J. I. Case Company operated 65 branch offices in the United States, in Europe and in South America, and possessed more than 9,000 local sales agencies. The company owned a singular subsidiary corporation, the *Compagnie Case de France*, which catered to the agricultural equipment industries of Europe and Africa. With a capital stock of $20,000,000, in 1920, gross sales revenues of more than $32,000,000 in 1919, and total assets of nearly $39,000,000, also in 1919, the company which Jerome I. Case had founded was a global leader in agricultural technology, innovation, and sales.[163]

The Freeport Sugar Company existed at a time when first-mover advantage, the term that refers to the supposed advantages of pioneering companies in new areas of commerce and industry, was a status which ought devoutly to have been desired. For several years, the Freeport Sugar Company exerted its first-mover advantage in the United States, as one of the largest, if not the single largest, beet-sugar operation between the Ohio River and the Pacific Ocean. One historical description of the factory stated:

> In 1872, he [Rosenstiel] erected an immense sugar refinery, with a capacity of fifty tons per day, the largest factory in the West. In this enterprise were associated with him Jacob Bunn, of Springfield, and J. I. Case, of Racine, Wis.[164]

The Freeport enterprise would not, however, be able to build upon its advantages of size and reputation for very long, as it began to suffer a fate which would result in litigation strikingly similar to that which resulted from the disputes surrounding ownership of property titles relating to the Germania Sugar Company.

Jacob Bunn probably owned 50 percent of the firm. The Freeport Sugar Company was producing 200 barrels of sugar per day. Jacob Bunn's bank failure in 1873 forced him to relinquish his interest in the Freeport enterprise, a business that was generating a revenue of $500,000 annually, and was furnishing a monthly compensation of $7,000 to an employment force of two hundred men.[165] Unfortunately, a failure to employ the proper wherewithal for the carbonation of the sugar led to "indifferent results," and the enterprise was further plagued when in the autumn of 1875 there arose "difficulties as to the titles of the several owners."[166]

The factory was eventually leased, in November of 1876, to G. A. Colby & Co. for a six-year term, and was converted by the lessee into a glucose factory. During a period of approximately a year, G. A. Colby & Co. placed 7,500 barrels of syrup on the market, generating what was said to have been a profit of $26,000. Ultimately the lessee relinquished its claim to the sugar works, and the factory came into the possession of the Freeport banking establishment of A. Collman & Co. This company in turn disposed of the concern for $12,000 to Veiller, Jayne & Co, a prominent New York company which was among the vanguards of the American glucose industry. Veiller, Jayne & Co. organized a concern which by 1880 had been consuming 2,000 bushels of corn every 24 hours, and was generating sales revenues of $1,000,000 annually.[167]

The Freeport Sugar Company was riddled with a

multitude of severe dilemmas, not only in processes of manufacturing the sugar, but also in attempts to establish the business on a firm foundation. "The agreement was that Mr. Bunn should draw up the contract, but unfortunately for the other partners, who held quarter shares, this important part of the business was neglected."[168] The reasons for Bunn's alleged "negligence" are not known, but the Freeport Sugar Company began to fail at the same time that the Panic of 1873 was causing nation-wide economic havoc. Jacob Bunn was suffering from the effects of the Panic in Springfield, and would have been preoccupied with trying to salvage the businesses with which he was associated there. Consequently, a more balanced and judicial assessment of his participation in the business is in order. He had played a crucial and vital role in the establishment of the enterprise, having been its primary financier, and was simultaneously engaged in banking and other business concerns. The financial losses suffered by Charles Henry Rosenstiel, Jacob Bunn, and Jerome Increase Case, however, must not be allowed to cast a shadow over the initiative and achievement of these individuals in the beet sugar industry.

> [An agricultural historian referred to] J. Bunn as a pioneer in America's beet sugar industry. He reminded his audience that 'Jacob Bunn, the confiding banker, whose dollars were dissipated looking for beet sugar in the prairies of Illinois, should not be forgotten.'[169]

Equally charitable business eulogies are both appropriate and necessary for Charles Henry Rosenstiel and for Jerome Increase Case, for they, too, were pioneers and engineers of the birth of the American beet sugar industry. The Freeport Triumvirate was an early monument and an important milestone in the American sugar industry.

Allotted wholly to conjecture is whether the Triumvirate, had it lasted another two decades, might have expanded into the cane sugar production sector of the American sugar industry. Perhaps it would have collaborated with the renowned sugar trusts which were built by men such as Claus Spreckels, Rudolph Spreckels, and Henry Osborne Havemeyer. These men built, respectively, the Spreckels Sugar Refining Company and the American Sugar Refining Company, the latter of which controlled at one point approximately 90 percent of the sugar refining capacity of the United States. Could the Freeport Triumvirate have joined the Sugar Trust? If so, would it have done so? Only creative historical speculation can begin to address these inquiries, which, nonetheless, shall forever remain exclusively in the domain of the historical consciousness, where possibilities remain frozen in time.

Jacob Bunn's investments in other species of business enterprise significantly mollified the financial losses which he suffered as a result of the failure of the Chatsworth and Freeport sugar ventures. In addition to involvement with the variety of companies discussed thus far, Bunn was a newspaperman. "Jacob balanced his losses [suffered from the beet sugar venture] with other, more conventional investments at the time such as principal ownership of the major Chicago paper [the *Chicago Republican*] which came to be known as the *Inter-Ocean*."[170]

The *Chicago Republican* was a daily newspaper that existed from May 30, 1865 to March of 1872. The dissatisfaction of numerous businessmen with the *Tribune* was among the primary motivations fueling the inception of the *Republican*. This dissatisfaction hailed from diverse regions, and it culminated in the organization of the *Republican*. Chicago businessmen Ira Y. Munn, John V. Farwell, J. K. C. Forrest, and J. Y. Scammon collaborated with Jacob Bunn and Jesse K. Dubois of Springfield, along with John Wood of Quincy, J. Wilson Shaffer of Freeport, A. C. Babcock of Canton, A. W. Mack of Kankakee, and Henry Childs of Du Page County.[171]

Alonzo W. Mack was an attorney who had served in the Illinois legislature in both chambers. As a Senator he represented Will, Grundy, and Kankakee counties. On 16 January 1865 Senator Mack sponsored a bill in the legislature for the establishment of a newspaper concern to be called the Chicago Republican Company. The bill was enacted into law on 13 February 1865, chartering the Chicago Republican Company with a capitalization of $500,000.

Charles Anderson Dana, the editor-in-chief of the *Chicago Republican*, had had a distinguished career in news media prior to his involvement with the *Republican*. He had served as Assistant Secretary of War under Edwin Stanton, in 1863, 1864 and 1865. He also had gained significant experience with Horace Greeley, while working with the *New York Tribune*. In addition, Dana had served as an editor of The New American Encyclopedia, which was published by the Appleton family.[172] Dana came with other editors who would later enjoy great distinction in New York and in Chicago. J. G. Hazard, who accompanied Dana to Chicago, would later hold the staff position of musical editor of the *New York Tribune*. Dana also came with Frederick H. Hall, who later served as a member of the editorial staff of the *Chicago Tribune*.[173]

The interest that this illustrious group of media figures had in the *Chicago Republican* was indicative of their initial confidence in it as a new newspaper. Furthermore, with such a distinguished editorial staff, the *Chicago Republican* enjoyed a promising initiation. The successes experienced by the management of the newspaper in recruiting Dana, Hazard and the other editors would not, however, characterize the affairs of the company for very long.

Among the dilemmas which confronted the management of the Chicago Republican Company was a disagreement between the business and the editorial sections of the paper, which generated dysfunction within the company. Dana grew intolerant of the conditions which he perceived to be the errors of the management. He soon resigned from the company and returned to New York City, where he resumed his career with newspapers there.[174]

It is interesting that the editorial staff of the *Chicago Republican* would become far more renowned, though, through their involvement with other newspaper companies, such as the *Chicago Tribune*, and the *New York Tribune*, than the entrepreneurs who had put together the Chicago Republican Company. While Charles Anderson Dana and J. G. Hazard proceeded from the *Chicago Republican* to other publishing companies, they became increasingly famous as editors and as fathers of newspaper media. While Dana's image grew more vivid on the pages of history, those of Jacob Bunn and John Villiers Farwell faded.

John Villiers Farwell, a founder of the Chicago

Republican Company, was born in New York in 1825. He came to Illinois with his family during his youth. During the Civil War, Farwell served as an organizer of the Chicago Board of Trade regiment. An active Republican, Farwell was a presidential elector in 1864, and during the presidency of Ulysses S. Grant, served as Indian Commissioner, "traveling some 10,000 miles in the discharge of his duties."[175]

After undergoing a business education at Mt. Morris Seminary, Farwell joined, over a period of time, several dry goods companies. He first worked for the firm of Hamilton & White, a dry goods company in Chicago. After gaining subsequent experience as a merchant and business assistant with the Chicago firms of Hamlin & Day, and Wadsworth & Phelps, Farwell became a partner in the latter, whose name was changed to "Cooley, Wadsworth & Company." Marshall Field and Levi Leiter joined the firm, which was later known as Farwell, Field & Company. Eventually incorporating in 1891, the Farwell business became the J. V. Farwell Company, and was one of the largest dry goods enterprises in the United States.[176] (Marshall Field, who later founded Marshall Field & Company, a globally renowned retail department store, would have received some of his earliest business training while working for elders such as John V. Farwell and Mr. Cooley, at the firm of Cooley, Farwell, Wadsworth and Company, the largest wholesale dry goods company in Chicago.)[177]

John Farwell had collaborated with his brother, Senator Charles Benjamin Farwell, in the construction of the Texas State House. They completed the construction of the Texas state capitol in 1888. John V. Farwell collaborated with Dwight Lyman Moody in the establishment of the North

Market Mission, which provided a home for poor children. Farwell also served as superintendent of the Mission. In addition to having built the Texas State House, through the construction company which he owned, Farwell built the Chicago tabernacle for Dwight Moody.[178] Their affiliation with the State House project would have to constitute one of the most important contributions of Illinois business leaders to the development of another state. "Mr. Farwell's name has become proverbial for his generosity and liberality, and he has been known to give half of his salary to charitable objects.... He was also a prime mover in the establishment of the Young Men's Christian Association of Chicago in 1857."[179] The Farwell brothers, like the Bunn brothers, were visionaries in both business and in national development. Like the Bunns, they were industrial pioneers.

The newspaper was organized prior to the end of the Civil War, and only two months before President Lincoln's assassination. The *Chicago Republican* represented an attempt to bolster the Republican Party in Illinois. It is not surprising that Jacob Bunn, one of Lincoln's most important promoters, was not only a founder of the new company, but an investor who stayed with the company until, by default, he eventually gained complete ownership of it.

Among the initial activities of the newly formed company were the purchases of the plant and the Associated Press Franchise of the *Morning Post*. Charles A. Dana was selected to be the editor of the *Chicago Republican* and Alonzo W. Mack was the publisher of the paper. Dana experienced a dislike for the job that was sufficient for him to withdraw from the *Republican*. Mack and several other founding stockholders relinquished their interests in the company, leaving Jacob Bunn and Jesse Dubois as co-owners, who reorganized the company. Under their administration, V. B. Denslow was assigned the post of editor and George D. Williston was appointed manager.

Turnover continued. Denslow resigned and James F. Ballantyne became editor. James Ballantyne was born in Scotland. He entered journalism in New York City, then came to Chicago, where he served the *Democratic Press*, as their commercial editor.[180] He, in turn, was succeeded by Henry M. Smith who was succeeded by John G. Nicolay, in 1869. By 1870, Jacob Bunn had become the sole owner of the newspaper. He sold it in 1870 to Joseph B. McCullagh, John R. Walsh, H. N. Hibbard, and William H. Schuyler. The *Chicago Republican* printing works were destroyed during the Great Fire of 1871, and the company finally completed a full circle of ownership when it was reacquired by J. Y. Scammon, one of its original co-founders and initial stockholders. It then survived until March, 1872, when it was succeeded by the *Inter Ocean*.[181]

The difficulties faced by the *Republican* were manifold. Many of the alleged dilemmas afflicting the business were briefly delineated in a personal correspondence of Charles A. Dana, who served as the paper's first editor. In a letter dated 30 April 1866, Dana expressed without any noticeable inhibition his views towards the management of the *Republican*.

> 'I have been worked to death since you were here [writing to James Harrison Wilson, his biographer], and much disturbed by the difficulties in the *Republican*. These difficulties are serious, and how they will end I don't know.
> 'I shall get out of the concern if I can, unless it is put on

a different basis, and means are raised by the capitalists who have invested in it to carry it through in a satisfactory manner. The publisher [A.W. Mack] is a bad man, and not as judicious as he is smart. That is the essence of the trouble. I am holding on to see what will turn up, and also to save too great a sacrifice in the process of extricating myself....'[182]

Jacob Bunn would have been included among the "the capitalists who have invested in [the newspaper]" to whom Dana referred in his letter to James Wilson. Consequently, Dana would in all probability have considered Bunn to be one of the people who had failed to establish the newspaper on a sounder financial "basis." Dana and Bunn would have interacted to some degree and knew each other to some degree, as Bunn would almost certainly have assisted with the recruitment of the newspaper's editorial staff. Dana would have been referring to A. W. Mack, the original publisher of the *Republican,* as "a bad man, and not as judicious as he is smart." Clearly there was communication failure amongst the promoters of the paper as well as the paper's staff, and one can discern this dysfunction by reading the account, provided above, of the tempestuous turnover of the company's investors and staff. Nonetheless, the *Chicago Republican* would have been a source, if only a short-lived one, of considerable revenue for Bunn and the other investors.

Bunn's affiliation with the newspaper illustrated several characteristics of his outlook and attitude toward business enterprise. As stated above, he was among those who had been disappointed with some aspect of the *Tribune*. He must have viewed co-founding a new and "improved" newspaper as an opportunity both to act upon his dislike for the

Tribune, and to invest in a business venture that could both yield a profit and serve to promulgate his Republican political positions.

Jacob Bunn was also concerned with the development of regional agriculture, and was a stockholder and member of the Sangamon County Agricultural Board, along with his wife Elizabeth, brother John, sons William Ferguson Bunn, Henry Bunn, George Wallace Bunn, Jacob Bunn, Jr., and in-laws Benjamin Hamilton Ferguson and William D. Richardson.[183]

In addition to serving on the Agricultural Board, Jacob Bunn was an extensive landowner, who discerned the opportunities of investing in Illinois farmland. "Much of [Bunn's] real estate was in the form of Illinois farmland which he recognized as a lucrative investment. He bought over 2,500 acres in Livingston County alone."[184] This was close to the year 1860.

In 1874, his real estate holdings in Clear Lake Township alone, a village in Sangamon County, amounted to 448 acres. Also during 1874, in Chatham, another Sangamon County township, Bunn held two plots, one of 640 acres, and the other of 373 and 9/10 acres.[185] In Riverton Township, he held title to approximately 350 town lots, in at least 37 different town blocks.[186] He owned land in Nebraska as well.[187] In Randolph County, Illinois, Bunn owned plots of 358 acres, 100 acres, 160 acres, and 105 acres.[188] At some point prior to 1890 Jacob Bunn acquired a large quantity of municipal real estate outside of Riverton. The extant liquidation document states that a large quantity of the J. Bunn real estate holdings that were held in other states and in counties other than Sangamon had already been liquidated and reported by the date of the final insolvency statements that were filed in July of 1890.[189] John Whitfield Bunn, who endured the Panic of 1873 without sustaining severe financial damages, also owned immense real estate holdings in Illinois. He, like his brother Jacob who had trained him in the art of investment, also held extensive properties outside of Illinois.

John W. Bunn spent much of his time in Chicago, as he was actively involved in promoting industry in Chicago, as well as industry in Springfield. John W. Bunn was a founder, with Morris Selz, a German immigrant, of "M. Selz and Company," which was a Chicago shoe and boot manufacturer and distributor. John W. Bunn, Morris Selz, Max A. Meyer, and Joseph O. Rutter were the founders of the firm, in 1871. Their place of business was on Wabash Avenue. In the year 1878, Joseph O. Rutter retired, and Charles H. Schwab entered the business. The location of the business was moved from Madison and Franklin Streets in Chicago, to Monroe and Franklin Streets in that city. Selz and Schwab themselves had both emigrated from Germany. Morris Selz was born in 1826 in Württemberg. Charles Schwab was born in 1835 in Alsace.[190]

Eventually incorporating as "Selz, Schwab and Company" in 1878,[191] the firm continued to grow steadily. The firm grew in scale. By the early 20th century, the company was distributing shoes and boots on an international scale, and operated twelve factories, with thousands of employees.

> From a small factory, at first employing not more than 100 men, the enterprise grew until it now has a dozen large

plants employing thousands of workers, sending its product all over this country and the world.[192]

The Selz, Schwab Shoe Company quickly assumed, at the institutional level, the policy orientation of an antitrust advocate when Manuel F. Selz, the general manager of the firm, and a son of Morris Selz, exhibited the concern of the company, and represented the growing concern of the entire industry when he described the rapidly developing monopolistic control of the United Shoe Machinery Company over the shoe machinery industry. United Shoe Machinery had been formed in 1899. Selz claimed that United Shoe Machinery had effectively obliterated the healthy competition that had once characterized the shoe machinery industry. Litigation was initiated against the United, and during the antitrust dissolution proceedings against the United, Manuel Selz testified as to the negative effects of the control that the United had established over the sector. Selz referred to a particularly salient instance of the monopolistic tendency of the United when he described the time when the Selz, Schwab Shoe Company had attempted to raise $1,600,000 for the purpose of acquiring a one half interest in the Thomas G. Plant Shoe Machinery Company. Before Selz had completed raising the necessary capital, the United Shoe Machinery Trust approached the Thomas G. Plant Company and acquired the concern, thus rapidly promoting its monopolistic presence in the shoe machinery sector. Interestingly, there appeared on the same day, and on the same newspaper page, as the article concerning the United Shoe Machinery Trust, and the protest of the Selz, Schwab Shoe Company against it, an obituary for Morris Selz himself, the visionary founder of Selz, Schwab and Company.[193]

Interestingly, John W. Bunn co-organized M. Selz and Company in the same year that he helped found the Springfield Iron Company. John W. Bunn remained an active participant in Chicago commercial and social life. He attended the Board of Trade of Chicago, with a complimentary entrance ticket, in 1889. At that time, John W. Bunn was the treasurer of the Illinois State Board of Agricultural Exhibitions.[194] John W. Bunn also attended in 1894 the New York Produce Exchange, with a visitor's ticket.[195]

The activities of John W. Bunn, Morris Selz and Charles H. Schwab in Illinois were not, however, restricted to commercial associations. John was also a member of the Union League Club and the Chicago Club, both of Chicago. He also was appointed by Governor Dunne to the Illinois Centennial Commission. Serving the Republican State Committee as a loyal member for approximately six years, from 1872 until 1876, and from 1900 until 1902, John W. Bunn also was chosen to serve as the first treasurer of the University of Illinois, occupying that position from 1868 until 1893.[196] Morris Selz and Charles H. Schwab were both members of the Union League Club, like Bunn, and the three partners undoubtedly spent many hours together formulating innovative business strategies in conference, in the rooms of the Club. Charles H. Schwab, like John W. Bunn, was closely connected with the World's Columbian Exposition, in 1893. Schwab was a director of the World's Fair, and John W. Bunn was treasurer of the Illinois Board of World's Fair Commissioners.[197] John W. Bunn, Charles H. Schwab and Morris Selz were close friends, as well as being close business partners. Bunn's respect and admiration for Morris Selz was demonstrated vividly when Bunn served as an honorary pallbearer at the funeral for Morris Selz, in 1913, in Chicago.[198] The three men shared beliefs in the Republican Party, commercial development, and in philanthropy. A committed visionary philanthropist, Selz bequeathed much of his personal estate to the employees whom he affirmed were such an important part of the success of Selz, Schwab and Company. "When he died in 1913 he left $150,000 to the workers who had helped him achieve success."[199] Beginning his career in the United States with seventy-five cents, as a new German immigrant, Morris Selz eventually accumulated approximately $20,000 while undertaking business enterprises in California.[200] Coming to Chicago signified the beginning of his greatest contribution to American industry, when he formed M. Selz and Company, with John W. Bunn and the other partners. His legacy to his employees, to Chicago and its institutions, and to Illinois were extraordinary, and could have emanated from nobody less than a genuine civic and commercial visionary and social capitalist with the highest sense of integrity and philanthropy.

Charles H. Schwab sought to assist with institutions that could offer orphaned and impoverished children shelter, food, care and opportunities for employment. He provided very generous support for the Chicago Home for Jewish Orphans. Schwab also gained experience in public office, when he assumed the responsibilities of Comptroller of the city of Chicago, from 1886 until 1887. Schwab belonged to the Standard Club, in addition to belonging to the Union League Club.[201]

Jacob Bunn was to the Chicago Republican Company what John W. Bunn was to Selz, Schwab and Company: visionary businessmen who desired to build Illinois, in all regions commercially, civically, and socially. While living primarily in Springfield, John W. Bunn was very much a Chicagoan. Jacob Bunn, as well, was a Chicago business leader, when one considers his involvement with the *Chicago Republican*, and his interests in promoting the Republican Party in Chicago.

In addition to a multifaceted involvement with the foregoing enterprises in various geographical and corporate areas, Jacob Bunn was one of the founders of the banking sector of Springfield. Two important institutions in the history of Springfield, in the history of the State of Illinois, and in the history of Jacob Bunn's career were the Springfield Marine and Fire Insurance Company and the J. Bunn Bank. One can neither understand Springfield nor know Jacob Bunn without understanding both of these organizations and the historical contexts from which they emerged.

33. Orlin H. Miner. A founder and original director of the Springfield Iron Company, and business partner in that concern with John Whitfield Bunn and William Douglas Richardson. (Photo courtesy of *Men of Illinois,* Chicago: Halliday Witherspoon, 1902.)

34. Shelby Moore Cullom. Cullom was a Senator from Illinois, and was prominently involved with the drafting of the legislation which would, on 4 February 1887, be enacted as the organic statute for the Interstate Commerce Commission. Cullom was also a close friend of Jacob and John W. Bunn. (Photo courtesy of *Men of Illinois,* Chicago: Halliday Witherspoon, 1902.)

35. Charles Henry Rosenstiel as an older man. Rosenstiel was one of the most important agricultural and industrial visionaries of northern Illinois. He was a business partner with Jacob Bunn and Jerome Increase Case, in the Freeport Sugar Company, among the foremost beet sugar production companies in the United States. (Author's personal collection.)

The Freeport Triumvirate

36. *Jacob Bunn.* (Photo courtesy of the Sangamon Valley Collection at the Lincoln Library, Springfield, Illinois.)

37. *Charles Henry Rosenstiel.* (Author's personal collection.)

38. *Jerome Increase Case.* (Photo courtesy of Gerald Karwowski and the Oak Clearing Museum, Union Grove, Wisconsin.)

39. *Jerome Increase Case and the "Big Four" of the Agricultural Machinery Industry. Clockwise from far left: Stephen Bull, Jerome Increase Case, Massena B. Erskine, and Robert Baker. These partners formed the firm of J. I. Case & Company, which they managed until the death of Jerome I. Case in 1891.* (Photo and historical information courtesy of Gerald Karwowski and the Oak Clearing Museum, Union Grove, Wisconsin.)

40. Charles Richardson. Charles was a brother of William Douglas Richardson. Like his brother William, Charles was a Springfield businessman. He served as the general manager of the Leland Hotel in Springfield, Illinois. (Author's personal collection.)

LELAND HOTEL, SPRINGFIELD

41. The Leland Hotel of Springfield, Illinois. The Leland was known throughout the Midwest as one of the finest hotels of central Illinois. Many visiting politicians, artistic performers, businessman, and other notables stayed at this hotel. (Photo courtesy of *Historical Encyclopedia of Illinois and History of Sangamon County,* Vol. II. Newton Bateman and Paul Selby, Eds. Chicago: Munsell Publishing Company, 1912.)

42. The Chicago and Alton Railroad Company train depot in Springfield. Jacob Bunn had been one of the founders of the Chicago and Alton Railroad Company, a railroad firm that served the transportation sectors of the Midwest for seventy years, before being absorbed into the Baltimore & Ohio Railroad Company. (Photo courtesy of *Souvenir of Springfield*, Portland: L. H. Nelson Company [year of publication unkown].)

MORRIS SELZ, Chicago.
Born Wurtemberg, Germany, Oct. 2, 1826. Located in America in 1845, and in Chgo. in 1854; in 1871 formed the company of Selz, Schwab & Co., wholesale boot and shoe manufacturers, of which he is the President.

J. HARRY SELZ, Chicago.
Born in Chgo., April 22, 1864, 2d Vice-Pres. Selz, Schwab & Co., mfrs. and wholesalers of boots and shoes.

43. *Morris Selz and his son J. Harry Selz of Chicago. John Whitfield Bunn had collaborated with Morris Selz in the organization of the firm of M. Selz and Company, which later became Selz, Schwab and Company. The firm was one of the largest Chicago-based manufacturers and distributors of shoes and boots, distributing globally. John Whitfield Bunn served as the vice president of the company in his later years. Morris Selz was Third District Republican Congressional Committeeman. Morris and his son Harry were members of the Standard Club. J. Harry Selz was second vice president of Selz, Schwab and Company, and a member of the Union League Club of Chicago along with his father, Schwab and John W. Bunn, and of the Illinois Athletic Club. J. Harry Selz was also a director of the Corn Exchange National Bank of Chicago.* (Photo courtesy of *Men of Illinois,* Chicago: Halliday Witherspoon, 1902.)

44. *Charles H. Schwab. Schwab was a partner in the firm of Selz, Schwab and Company, and with Morris Selz, was a close friend of John Whitfield Bunn. Schwab was a member of the Standard Club and the Union League Club of Chicago. He was Comptroller of Chicago and a director of the World's Columbian Exposition [1893]. He was actively affiliated with the Chicago Home for Jewish Orphans.* (Photo courtesy of *Notable Men of Chicago and Their City* [Anon.], Chicago: *Chicago Daily Journal,* 1910.)

45. *John Villiers Farwell. Farwell was a business partner with Jacob Bunn and others in the establishment of the Chicago Republican Company, in January of 1865, which published the important Chicago newspaper, "The Chicago Republican." He was associated at various times with the dry goods businesses of Hamilton & White; Hamlin & Day; and Wadsworth & Phelps. John Farwell and his business associate Cooley had served as mentors of a young merchant-apprentice named Marshall Field. Field would eventually be the founder of Marshall Field & Co., which became one of the foremost department stores of the world.* (Photo courtesy of *Men of Illinois,* Chicago: Halliday Witherspoon, 1902.)

46. *Charles Benjamin Farwell. Brother of John Villiers Farwell, and a Republican Senator from Illinois. He was a partner in the John V. Farwell Co.* (Photo courtesy of *Men of Illinois,* Chicago: Halliday Witherspoon, 1902.)

47. *A portrait of John Whitfield Bunn painted by Cecilia Beaux, who accepted the commission to paint the portrait in 1913. Bunn was 82 years old when this portrait was painted. Beaux had been particularly interested in learning of John W. Bunn's recollections of Abraham Lincoln. Bunn relayed many of his reminiscences to Beaux during the portrait sessions. Bunn is holding a copy of Richard Watson Gilder's book about Lincoln. After her meeting with Bunn, Beaux characterized him as having been "fine, big and full of life." Bunn would live another seven years, outliving his brother Jacob by nearly 23 years. This portrait was on display at the Smithsonian for a period of time in the 1990's as part of a Beaux retrospective.*[202] (Photo courtesy of Bank One, Springfield, Illinois.)

48. The Springfield Marine Bank, originally known as the Springfield Marine and Fire Insurance Company. Jacob Bunn had been a founder of the bank in 1851. The Marine Bank at the time of its acquisition in the 1990s by Bank One Corporation, was the oldest bank in the state of Illinois. See picture at upper center left. (Photo courtesy of the Sangamon Valley Collection at the Lincoln Library, Springfield, Illinois.)

49. The Lincoln Library in Springfield, Illinois. John Whitfield Bunn had actively promoted the organization and development of a public library in Springfield, and served as a member of the Lincoln Library board. (Photo courtesy of *Historical Encyclopedia of Illinois and History of Sangamon County,* Vol. II, Newton Bateman and Paul Selby, Eds., Chicago: Munsell Publishing Company, 1912.)

50. Benjamin Hamilton Ferguson. Ferguson was the first president of the Springfield Marine Bank (after the bank changed its corporate name from Springfield Marine and Fire Insurance Company), a noted crockery and china merchant, and served as the vice-chairman of the board of the Illinois Watch Company in his later years, under the Jacob Bunn administration during the 1890s. (Photo courtesy of Bank One, Springfield, Illinois.)

51. A portrait of Antrim Campbell, a leading Springfield attorney, who was the first president of the Springfield Marine and Fire Insurance Company. (Photo courtesy of Bank One, Springfield, Illinois.)

52. Portrait of Robert Irwin who became the secretary of the Springfield Marine and Fire Insurance Company, and was the banker who opened an account for Abraham Lincoln at the bank. (Photo courtesy of Bank One, Springfield, Illinois.)

53. *The facade and entrance to the Springfield Marine Bank. The man standing on the far right is Henry Bunn, the second son of Jacob and Elizabeth (Ferguson) Bunn. Henry Bunn was a founder of the Sangamo Electric Company, the last president of the Illinois Watch Company, and held various other business positions prior to his retirement.* (Photo courtesy of the Sangamon Valley Collection at the Lincoln Library, Springfield, Illinois.)

SPRINGFIELD MARINE BANK.

54. An artist's rendition of the Springfield Marine Bank. (Photo courtesy of the Sangamon Valley Collection at the Lincoln Library, Springfield, Illinois.)

55. *F. K. Whittemore. Whittemore received much of his training in business and finance from Jacob Bunn, as an employee of the J. Bunn Bank in Springfield. Whittemore became a noted Chicago official.* (Photo courtesy of *Men of Illinois,* Chicago: Halliday Witherspoon, 1902.)

56. The Springfield Marine Bank in the late 20th century during some renovation. (Photo courtesy of the Sangamon Valley Collection at the Lincoln Library, Springfield, Illinois.)

57. Judge Christopher C. Brown, Esq. Judge Brown was an associate in business with Jacob Bunn. Brown also was the judge who helped administer the liquidation of the Jacob Bunn real estate holdings and other assets, after Bunn's bank had failed. (Photo courtesy of *Men of Illinois*, Chicago: Halliday Witherspoon, 1902.)

58. *An original check written on an account at the J. Bunn Bank.* (Photo courtesy of the Sangamon Valley Collection at the Lincoln Library, Springfield, Illinois.)

59. *An unused notebook bearing the corporate seal of the Springfield Marine Bank.* (Author's personal collection.)

VIII

Twilight of the Springfield Banker

The history of the banking industry in Springfield is a turbulent one. The first banking institution to have been organized in Springfield was the State Bank of Illinois, which was chartered by the state legislature in 1835. Banks were then established at Vandalia, Alton, Galena, Jacksonville, and Chicago. The Panic of 1837, however, signified the beginning of the crises that would eventually precipitate the liquidation of the bank. "During the panic of 1837, the bank was compelled to suspend specie payment along with other banks of the United States, and from that time on until the bank was finally liquidated it had trouble."[203]

Liquidation, which had been initially provided for by statute on 26 January 1843, was completed in 1848.[204] The liquidation of the State Bank created an institutional vacuum that would endure until 1851, when on 28 January 1851, the Illinois Legislature passed a bill which stated *"there shall be established in the city of Springfield an insurance company, to be called the Springfield Marine and Fire Insurance Company."*[205] In the absence of an official banking system, "merchants such as John Williams and Jacob Bunn had taken customers' money for safekeeping, but only as a courtesy."[206]

The absence of a banking system was apparent not only in Springfield, but also throughout the rest of the state of Illinois. Moreover, the poor condition of banking in Illinois handicapped the progress of other types of nascent business enterprise. Among the difficulties in the money markets of this time, in Springfield, were high levels of uncertainty in the value of paper money, and the importation of paper money from banks outside of the state of Illinois. As a result of these outside banks' geographical distance from the areas in Illinois from which people were making use of their services, the people who were dependent upon the banks rarely became closely familiar with the banks' practices and reliability.[207]

There were additional difficulties. Banking service functions such as deposits, exchange, and discounts were occasionally performed by private merchants, who could charge exorbitant rates of interest. Yet another difficulty was an absence of abundant money borrowing. These were among the parameters of the period of time that lasted from the failure of the State Bank, in 1848, until 1851. Furthermore, there was not even a private bank in Springfield.[208]

Without sufficient mechanisms for money circulation, loans, deposits, exchange, and discounts, Springfield's businessmen were mired in a state of financial stagnation. A statement made in 1850 by the editor of the *Illinois Journal* contained a theory of the potential growth and stability that institutions of resident capital would engender.

> To... those doing prudent and profitable business, small loans, occasionally, would be of great advantage. There are many of them—young men of good habits, known industry and business tact—who, with a small loan and the means

they have on hand, would erect for themselves dwellings, and thus make themselves more comfortable—stimulate them to greater industry, and render them permanent and valuable citizens. What we want is capital here that can be borrowed, at all times, on good security, and which may tend to encourage and stimulate industry, and to enable those to get along and make money and render themselves useful to society....[209]

A combination of strategic incorporation principles and strategic business planning enabled the birth of the company that would come to fill the institutional vacancy left by the failure of the State Bank, in Springfield.

The climate of constitutional jurisprudence at that time presented difficulties for the establishment of banks. The editor of the *Illinois Journal*, however, proposed a solution.

[Insurance companies] secure those citizens against losses by fire who apply for their benefits, and they furnish money for loans on moderate terms, and by these combined operations are able to pay handsome dividends upon their stock. It is well known that the insurance companies of St. Louis have furnished more facilities for carrying on the immense business of that place than the bank located there. Why not an insurance company for Springfield?[210]

The theory inherent in this proposal materialized soon after it was presented, and the banking industry of Springfield was recommenced. On 28 January 1851, the State of Illinois granted a charter mandating "that there shall be established in the city of Springfield an insurance company, to be called the 'Springfield Marine and Fire Insurance Company'."[211]

The company was organized with a capital stock of

$100,000, which was divided into individual shares of $50. The corporation was legally endowed with a wide range of powers. It possessed the authority to underwrite the loss of buildings and houses by fire, write marine insurance on goods and vessels, and purchase real estate not to exceed $30,000 in value, as might be requisite for its business transactions. The new "insurance company" was also empowered to receive deposits, to make loans at the established rate of interest, to purchase and to sell bills of exchange. The Springfield Marine and Fire Insurance Company was endowed not only with the powers of an insurance company, but also with the power to undertake every function of a bank, except that of issuing currency, a function which was withheld from the bank.[212]

A public notice appeared in the *Springfield Journal* in 1851, providing information on the new insurance company.

> PUBLIC NOTICE is hereby given that by virtue of an Act of the General Assembly of the State of Illinois, passed on the 28th day of January, A. D. 1851, entitled, 'an Act to incorporate the Springfield Marine and Fire Insurance Company.' Books will be opened by the undersigned Commissioners named in said act, at the Counting room of Jacob Bunn, in Springfield, Ills., on the FIRST MONDAY IN APRIL NEXT, (A. D. 1851) for subscriptions to the Capital Stock of said company.
>
> ROBERT IRWIN,
> JOHN WILLIAMS,
> JACOB BUNN,
> WILLIAM B. FONDEY,
> JOHN C. LAMB,
> *Commissioners*[213]

In accordance with the provisions of the charter of the corporation, books for the subscription of stock were opened on the first Monday in April, which was 10 April 1851. All of the stock had been taken in six weeks. "On the list [of subscribers] were to be found such names as Jacob Bunn, Robert Irwin and John Williams, merchants of proved integrity..."[214] Action was soon taken to procure a location for the new business. The old State Bank building was offered at auction, and was purchased by J. G. Loose, "for a company of our citizens."[215] Upon having secured the new business location, steps were taken to establish the new management. On 11 June 1851 the stockholders convened for the purpose of electing directors. The men elected to serve as the first board of directors were Jacob Bunn, John Williams, James L. Lamb, Robert Irwin, Antrim Campbell, Stephen T. Logan, and Mason Brayman. The directors elected on 12 June 1851 were the executive officers of the firm: Antrim Campbell was elected president, Robert Irwin vice president, and John C. Sprigg secretary.[216]

The Springfield Marine and Fire Insurance Company opened its doors in July of 1851, and experienced rapid establishment of clientele. The first insurance policies were granted within five days of the company's opening date. One cargo policy was granted to J. A. Hough and one fire policy was granted to S. M. Tinsley, both of Springfield. At the close of the year 1851 the new company's loans totaled in excess of $9,000, while bills of exchange approximated $20,000, and the bank's assets had grown to $140,000. By 1861, the bank books indicated loans totaling $195,000, bills of exchange of $80,000, and a banking house with a value of $25,000. Deposits amounted to $35,000, and a contingent fund of $125,000 had been established. Moreover, total assets attained $383,000 in that year.[217]

Utilization of the company's insurance function was sparse. Only twelve policies were issued, and the last of these was issued within one year of the company's organization. "For some reason, fire insurance had never got beyond a mere beginning."[218] After all, the insurance company had been founded under the legal title of an insurance company, but was essentially a bank, even from its inception.

The following historical fact regarding the clientele of the Springfield Marine and Fire Insurance Company is worth noting, for the tall client mentioned in this anecdote would become far more than a mere patron.

> On March 1, 1853, a tall, awkward individual, well known throughout central Illinois as an honest, competent attorney, walked into the Springfield Marine and Fire Insurance Company. Mr. Robert Irwin proceeded to open a new account with the $310 his acquaintance handed him... And it must have been the least of Mr. Irwin's suspicions that he was in a sense immortalizing himself when, across the top of a blank page in Depositor's Ledger B, he wrote, 'A. Lincoln.'[219]

The Springfield Marine and Fire Insurance Company is where Abraham Lincoln deposited his money. The historic ledger is on display in a glass case in the bank lobby of the building, which in 1992 was acquired by Bank One Corporation, which was itself acquired by J. P. Morgan and Company in 2004.

Jacob Bunn served as a guiding force behind the Springfield Marine and Fire Insurance Company. As a director, he would have assisted in carrying the company through its infancy, and through difficult economic periods, such as the Panic of 1854, if he were still on the board at that time. The 1854 panic was due largely to an over-extension of resources in railroad construction projects, and was followed by a more severe economic crisis, the Panic of 1857, which caused 117, out of the 1,350 businesses in Chicago, to fail.[220]

The 1857 Panic was a cyclical depression that followed the boom decade after the Mexican War. Land speculation coupled with excessive railroad construction during the period from 1849 until 1856, in addition to the expansion of poorly regulated banks, contributed to the Panic of 1857.[221] The sudden withdrawal of bankers' balances held in New York City, which had increased from $17,000,000 in 1850 to more than $30,000,000 by 1857, and the collapse of the New York branch of the Ohio Life Insurance Company on 24 August 1857, were among the most prominent precipitants of the Panic of 1857.[222]

The cotton economy of the South had survived the Panic without severe damage, and this inspired Senator James H. Hammond of South Carolina to conclude that "Cotton is King." The fact that cotton successfully weathered the Panic added to the existing sectional tensions that led to the Civil War,[223] as the South with its flourishing cotton economy would not have been desirous of "sharing" in the economic tribulations of the North. Slavery, of course, was another issue, and a major component of the Southern economy. Issues raised by individuals such as Senator James Hammond of South Carolina were just the issues which formed the foundation for the sentiments that would motivate actual secession only a few years later.

As a promoter and as a director of the Springfield Marine and Fire Insurance Company, Jacob Bunn was also an instrumental force in the rebirth of the banking system both in Springfield and in Illinois. As one of the most active figures affiliated with the formation and success of the company, which itself was an agent of the inception of new businesses and industrial expansion, Bunn was one of the visionaries who successfully revitalized the regional economy. He assisted with the rejuvenation of Springfield business sectors. The company provided for an alteration in its name on 5 May 1884 to "Springfield Marine Bank," effective 1 July 1884.[224] The change in corporate name was an appropriate one, as the newly adopted title reflected the true nature of the concern with far greater aptitude. The Springfield Marine Bank retained its corporate name until its acquisition in 1992.

Desirable economic circumstances were conducive to business venture, and Jacob Bunn always managed to capitalize on the opportunities of such an environment. "Financially and politically, the 1850s and 60s were exciting years for Springfield. As the economy expanded Jacob decided that, rather than remaining just one of several bank directors at the Marine, he would start his own bank."[225]

The J. Bunn Bank was housed in the building that was owned jointly by Jacob Bunn and George Woods, a tailor and clothing merchant. George Woods was a partner in the firm of Woods & Henkle, an important clothing enterprise in the capital. The Bunn-Woods building also housed Van Ness & Company, a dealer in china and home furnishings. A dentist by the name of Dr. French had his office in the building, and the law firm of Stuart and Edwards occupied an office there as well. The International Order of Odd Fellows, and a music store owner named Pearson also occupied spaces in the building. Among the contractors who completed the painting and glazing of the Bunn-Woods building was the firm of Willard & Zimmerman. Alexander Perry Willard was a partner in Willard & Zimmerman, and he was the grandfather of Ada Willard Richardson, the daughter-in-law of Jacob Bunn. At about the same time of their contract with the Bunn-Woods building, Willard & Zimmerman had contracted for the construction of a new building for their own business. The paint company also contracted to complete the paint work for the Nicholas H. Ridgely store building, on the east side of the old capitol square.[226]

 Little extant historical data concerning the J. Bunn Bank seems to have surfaced, but the legacy of the bank extends beyond the documents concerning its inception and business organization. More data concerning the J. Bunn Bank building seems to exist than information surrounding the J. Bunn Bank itself. The bank did serve to help begin the successful career a young man named F. K. Whittemore, a native of New York who had come to Springfield as a boy. At some juncture, Whittemore became acquainted with Jacob Bunn, and almost certainly John W. Bunn, as well. Jacob Bunn employed Whittemore as a cashier in the J. Bunn Bank. Whittemore also worked as a cashier at the State National Bank, also in Springfield. After his experience in banking with the J. Bunn Bank and with the State National Bank, Whittemore relocated to Chicago, and there commenced a successful career as a public official. In Chicago he served the administration of President Benjamin

Harrison, by serving as the Acting Assistant Treasurer of the United States in Chicago. In 1898 Whittemore served as the State Treasurer of Illinois, and in 1900 he filled the position of Assistant State Treasurer of Illinois.[227]

Whittemore undoubtedly received training in money management from Jacob Bunn, who would have provided Whittemore with many of the valuable components of a business education. Moreover, Whittemore would likely have encountered John W. Bunn, who would have given similarly of his own experience in commerce. Like John W. Bunn and Benjamin H. Ferguson, F. K. Whittemore was another beneficiary of the generosity that Jacob Bunn always exhibited when helping others to build a career vision for themselves. Again, Jacob Bunn provided an aspiring civic leader with experience and support.

While the Bunn banking house provided a career beginning for F. K. Whittemore, who experienced success as a noted member of Chicago officialdom, the Bunn bank also provided a general introduction to the financial world to a young New Englander who would become an important figure in the New York financial sector. The J. Bunn Bank served as a beginning point for a young man named Watson Bradley Dickerman. Dickerman, a native of Connecticut, was first employed by the J. Bunn Bank, shortly after graduating from the Williston Seminary in Easthampton. After gaining work experience in finance in Springfield, Dickerman relocated to New York City, where he entered business as a stock broker. In 1868, Dickerman joined the Open Board of Brokers, which was later absorbed by the New York Stock Exchange. During that time Dickerman devoted two years to learning the nature of the securities market, and in 1870, he formed a brokerage firm with W. G. Dominick, known as "Dominick and Dickerman." Dickerman experienced great success as a stock broker, and in the years 1890 and 1891, he was elected to the presidency of the New York Stock Exchange. Additionally, Dickerman served as the president of the Norfolk & Southern Railroad Company and served as a director of the Long Island Loan & Trust Company.[228]

The J. Bunn Bank opened in 1858. Its reputation can be stated fully in an assertion that was made by the youngest child of Jacob Bunn, Alice Edwards Bunn, who lived well into the 20th century. She recalled, of her father's business reputation, that "a phrase current in this part of the state for many years [was that]… Not only was a sure investment 'as good as wheat in the mill,' it was also 'as safe as J. Bunn's Bank.'"[229] The J. Bunn Bank would survive, however, for only twenty years, and it would be the failure of this bank, due to the violent economic dynamics of the Panic of 1873, that would constitute the most crucial milestone in the life of its founder, Jacob Bunn.

An understanding of the last quarter century of Jacob Bunn's life, vision, and sense of honor in business can be gained only by comprehending the social and economic circumstances of the period of time from 1873 until 1897. These years constituted a period of panic and cyclical depression that contained the Panic of 1873 and its aftermath. To provide a fundamental outline of the nature of the Panic of 1873, a brief summary follows.

The Panic of 1873 was among the most violent economic disasters in the history of the United States. Numerous factors contributed to the culmination of crisis. Unrestricted railroad speculation, especially in the railroad construction sector, in addition to over-expansion of commerce, agriculture, and industry, as well as a shrinkage in the European markets for United States farm products after 1871, all contributed to the weakening of the economic stability and strength of the United States. Due largely to its association as financial agent for the Northern Pacfic Railroad, the failure of the Philadelphia banking house of Jay Cooke & Company, on 18 September 1873, precipitated the Panic.[230]

The Panic, which has often been referred to as the point of inception of a "long wave" depression which endured arguably until approximately 1896, initiated a period of a mercurial economic climate. Numerous recessions and upturns occurred. Recovery from 1873 began in 1878, continued until 1882, was then followed by a recession lasting from 1883 until 1885, which in turn was followed by a period of recovery, lasting from 1885 until 1890. Yet another recession took place, enduring from 1890 to 1891, and it was followed by economic and industrial recovery in 1892. The failure of the Philadelphia and Reading Railroad and the National Cordage Company, in 1893, signified the termination of the "boom." "Before 1893 had ended, 491 banks and over 15,000 commercial institutions were reported to have failed. Before the turning point was reached by 1897, almost one third of the total railroad mileage was in the hands of receivers."[231]

In 1890, the United States contained 163,597 miles of railroad track. In 1900 the United States contained 193,346 miles of track. During the period from 1890 to 1900 approximately 30,000 miles of track had been built.[232] Consequently, one third of this total, in 1897, might have amounted to a number in the vicinity of 64,000 miles of railroad track. As stated above, some amount close to this total of railroad mileage was estimated to have fallen into receivership by the year 1897.

Also as stated previously, the banking institutions of the United States suffered immense damage as a result of the Panic of 1873, and the virtually cyclical economic turbulence ensuing from the financial troubles of that year. The J. Bunn Bank was among the casualties of this devastation. Evidence of his superlative abilities as a banker and as a business administrator and leader was apparent when his depositors retained their faith in his bank.

At first it seemed as if Springfield and Jacob Bunn might weather the worst effects of the storm. "Not even when the country was plunged into financial distress in 1873 did confidence waver in the J. Bunn Bank," reported one *Saint Louis Post-Dispatch* article, which continued,

> Bunn did not escape the blow. It staggered him, but he thought he could pull through. For five years he tried to save himself and the stricken farmers and tradesmen who depended upon him to save them. Himself he might have saved if he had been less intent upon saving others.[233]

The Panic of 1873 generated a pervasive devastation that plagued the entire country, and people engaged in many different types of business and trade were affected by its destructive force. The people of Springfield were not exempt from this devastation, and Jacob Bunn, in particular, sustained the full force of the damages that a nationwide panic can deliver unto a city.

But even Jacob Bunn had not reckoned with the devastating financial collapse resulting from this nationwide panic. His bank was ultimately unable to pay out its creditors due to the drastic drop in the price of farmland which it held as collateral. It was in this terrible hour, when his bank and fortune were already lost to him, that the true merit of Jacob Bunn's character shone at its brightest.[234]

The closing of the J. Bunn Bank generated widespread publicity in Illinois. Detailed coverage of the closure and bankruptcy proceedings appeared on numerous occasions in numerous newspapers. On New Year's Eve, 1877, Jacob Bunn realized the necessity of suspending the bank. He was able to solicit the assistance of Christopher C. Brown, an old friend and associate who answered Bunn's plea for help with compassion and loyalty.

> BUNN'S BANK SUSPENDS
>
> The Old Establishment Forced to Suspend—C. C. Brown, Esq., Appointed Assignee.
>
> The Banker Transfers All His Property for the Benefit of His Creditors—Approximate Assets and Liabilities of the Bank.
>
> The suspension of the old established banking house of Jacob Bunn, was announced to the public yesterday morning, by a notice to that effect on the door of the bank, together with announcement of the appointment of C. C. Brown, Esq., as assignee. The intelligence created a very considerable degree of interest, and crowds gathered around the bank doors, to read and speculate upon the probable causes which brought about a result unlooked for by the public generally.
>
> These causes may be briefly stated: At the time of the recent suspension of the Savings Bank, that of Mr. Bunn

had about $170,000 in savings deposits. There has since been quiet [sic] a drain on these deposits, which might perhaps have been even more extensive but for a desire to await the accumulation of interest which, according to custom, is credited up on January 1st. It was expected that the drafts would be most numerous at that time; but on Monday there was a large amount, nearly $45,000 withdrawn. Meanwhile, Mr. Bunn had gone to Chicago to provide further means to anticipate heavy drafts expected January 1, but upon his return he found that the additional funds were scarcely more in amount than to cover the withdrawals on Monday, so the money was not used but promptly returned. In his embarrassment Mr. Bunn consulted friends and it was seen that there was no alternative but suspension. Mr. Bunn asserted an intention to assign all his property for the benefit of his creditors, in which purpose he was joined by Mrs. Bunn, C. C. Brown, Esq., was chosen as assignee, and advised of his selection upon his return, New Year's night, from a brief absence in the country, where singularly enough he had, in response to expressed doubts, by some one, asserted his belief in the bank's entire solvency, which he had further attested by depositing a large amount in it a day or two before. He was greatly surprised. Mr. Bunn upon his return to his residence New Year's night, executed the following deed, in which he was joined by Mrs. Bunn, and which was filed in the Recorder's office shortly after nine o'clock yesterday morning....[235]

The deed was made on 1 January 1878, and showed the strength of character that Elizabeth Bunn possessed. Her primary concern was the honorable repayment of the debts, for the benefit of the J. Bunn Bank depositors who were suffering. Jacob Bunn was heavily invested in real estate in numerous states, and also owned considerable investments in various corporations.

This indenture made and entered into this 1st day of January, A. D. 1878, between Jacob Bunn and Elizabeth J. Bunn, his wife, of the county of Sangamon and State of Illinois, parties of the first part, and Christopher C. Brown, of the same county and State, party of the second part, witnesseth.

That the said parties of the first part for and in consideration of the trusts hereinafter mentioned and of the sum of one dollar to them in hand paid, by the said party of the second part, the receipt whereof is hereby acknowledged, do hereby grant, bargain, sell and convey and assign, transfer and set over to the said party of the second part, his heirs, executors, administrators and assigns, all the real estate of the said parties of the first part situated in the States of Illinois, Indiana, Iowa and Nebraska, and also all the goods, chattels, rights, credits, bills, notes, accounts, choses [sic] in action and other property personal of the said Jacob Bunn, wherever situated.

To have and to hold... in trust, however, for the following purposes, to wit: To sell and dispose of all said property for cash, and out of the proceeds to pay all of the creditors of the said Jacob Bunn the amounts due them in full; and if there should not be sufficient [funds]to pay all such debts in full, then to pay the same *pro rata* and to administer said trust in compliance with the laws of the State of Illinois.

[Here follows the obligation of the assignee to execute the trust]

Signed,   JACOB BUNN
           ELIZABETH J. BUNN
           CHRISTOPHER C. BROWN
Acknowledged before N. Divelbiss, Notary Public.[236]

The failure of the J. Bunn Bank was not viewed to be a result of any failure of Bunn himself. The sympathy that he received from the Springfield community gained state-wide attention.

JACOB BUNN

GENEROUS ENCOMIUMS   FROM THE PRESS
TO THE SPRINGFIELD BANKER

Astonishment of Chicago Papers that a Man's Creditors Should Not be His Enemies

From the Lincoln Ill. Times.

When Jacob Bunn, the Springfield banker, closed his doors, so great was his reputation as an able financier, an honest, hard-working man, that everybody regarded the event as not only a great public calamity, but as one entirely beyond the power of Mr. Bunn to prevent. No one but himself will ever know the mental agony he has suffered during, perhaps, the entire year just closed, and it may be for a much longer period,—how he has studied, planned and calculated; how often he has retired at night and never closed his eyes in sleep; how often he would go back in imagination forty years when he came to Springfield a poor boy, became a grocer's clerk, afterwards a partner, and how the people, reposing confidence in him, brought their money to him for safe keeping; how he subsequently became a banker, gained the almost unlimited confidence of all who knew him, built elegant and commodious business houses, encouraged and built up manufactures, and always in the lead with any enterprise calculated to improve and build up his adopted city, the friend and constant helper of the poor, surrounded and blessed with all that beautifies and comforts civilized life—now to think that after forty years of hard work, all must go and he to start in the world again without a dollar—yes, without a place in which to shelter himself and family. There are few—very few—men who have the moral courage to face such an issue, but Jacob

Bunn was equal to the task. He realized the perilous condition of his banking institution; he advised with his most confidential friends and attorneys; laid the facts before them; after concluding that suspension was the inevitable and only course to pursue, the papers were made out, and at 10 o'clock that evening (the evening previous to closing) they were taken to Mrs. Bunn for her signature. This was the first intimation that she had of the matter. On being told by the attorney that her dower interest in the property was worth at least $50,000, and that she could reserve that if she desired, she replied, 'No,' 'It will help to pay the creditors,' she continued, 'and I do not want it.' She signed her name to the document and by it she conveyed not only valuable lands and property, which she could have reserved, but even her own home and jewels. Afterwards she sent out for her two sons who were attending a New Year's party and told them of the matter, adding that it would be impossible for them to return to school as they had no home much less money to pay for their schooling; and that night saw Jacob Bunn and the members of his family bound together by stronger chords of sympathy and love than they have been for five years. The magnitude of his business had hitherto occupied his attention constantly; he could think of nothing else, and had really become a stranger in his own family, and it is no wonder that Mr. Bunn told a friend the following morning that that night was the happiest he had spent in five years. Such an example of honesty and fidelity of principle is as rare as it is commendable, and is abundant proof of the fact that Jacob Bunn never deceived the confidence of the people in his integrity.[237]

Before the Panic of 1873 had caused the J. Bunn Bank to close its doors permanently, a check written upon the J. Bunn Bank had been among the most reliable and solid of all negotiable instruments in Springfield, and indeed, in central Illinois, from 1858 until the early 1870s.

The failure of the J. Bunn Bank caused Bunn himself to rethink the blessings in his life. Although without a home and without fortune, he still had his family. The setting was dramatic. On a winter's evening in a very cold city, Jacob Bunn lost everything he had labored to build up in business, since the summer of 1840. It was as if a frigid windstorm had swept across the land and removed the house and provisions of a family, leaving in its wake a barren landscape, incapable of being recognized by the people who had once made it their home. The Panic of 1873 was the storm, and the world of business that Jacob Bunn and so many others had worked to construct, was the house. The one thing the winds could not remove was the family's sense of dedication to each other, and the candle of honor whose flame now burned brighter than ever.

Retrospectively, the failure of the J. Bunn Bank, the loss of personal fortune, and perhaps most importantly the financial devastation of the many people who had been dependent on the bank and its founder, were the ultimate precipitants of the final chapter of the Springfield legacy of Jacob Bunn. Through vision and determination he brought about, from the damaged economic landscape created by the economic storms of the Panic of 1873, a business enterprise that would generate technological reverberations throughout the world. For, once again, this industrious visionary would be a vital part of Illinois' contribution to technology and business by becoming involved in a company that would impact the world. He lost the J. Bunn Bank because of economic and financial forces that were entirely beyond his control. After such devastation, Bunn would have had a peculiar relationship with the times, because they had changed so drastically. But, unlike his previous ventures, which took him into the businesses of groceries, railroads, farming, real estate, publishing, coal production, and civic infrastructure, this final venture would take him into the business of "time" itself: watch making.

IX

The Timepiece Savior

In order to understand the last twenty years of Bunn's career and life one must first understand several crucial circumstances of this period in his life and this era in Springfield's corporate history. The late 19th century in Springfield witnessed the growth and prosperity of numerous businesses, many of which contributed to the growth of industry at the national level. Among this industrial progress was the birth of the watch manufacturing industry in Springfield, and what would become a global industry.

The gestation of the Springfield watch-making industry began in 1869, with the arrival of John C. Adams. Adams originated the concept of organizing a watch manufacturing company in Springfield, and upon his arrival promptly promulgated his causes. Adams discussed the profits that could be enjoyed by investors, and the advantages to Springfield that a timepiece company could bring. As the initiator of the formal cause of the enterprise, Adams should be considered the true founder of the Springfield Watch Company. The Springfield Watch Company was organized in 1870, with a capitalization of $100,000. The first administration consisted of John Todd Stuart as president, and William B. Miller as secretary. The first board of directors consisted of John W. Bunn, Dr. George Pasfield, a close friend of John W. Bunn and a leading industrialist of Illinois, John Williams and George N. Black.[238] All of these individuals had known each other for many years in business, social, or civic associations, and a friendship seemed to exist among all of them.

After having successfully procured the signatures of numerous Springfield businessmen, Adams and these collaborators established the Springfield Watch Company in January of 1870. Jacob Bunn was not directly affiliated with the founding of the Springfield Watch Company, but he held a large quantity of the outstanding stock. Now that the corporate structure and capitalization had been successfully established, the time had come to procure the technicians and employees who could manage the production divisions of the company, and begin the actual manufacture of the timepieces.

John C. Adams returned briefly to Elgin, Illinois, for the purpose of securing expert personnel for the fledgling enterprise. Adams was able to recruit Charles E. Mason as the foreman of the escape department; Otis Hoyt, as the foreman of the train room; John Nickerson to assume responsibility over the jeweling department; D. G. Currier as the foreman of the finishing room, and chief model maker. W. Dean was given the position of die-maker; John K. Bigelow was recruited as the factory superintendent; and George White was appointed pattern maker.[239]

Moreover, the location of the business was temporarily settled by a rental agreement of $100 per month, which was signed with Barryman & Rippon whereby the Springfield

Watch Company was entitled to use of the upper level of their machine shop. This arrangement was temporary, as plans were being completed for the construction of a factory on 14 acres of land situated on North Grand Avenue, between Ninth and Eleventh Streets. The contract for the factory's construction was signed with John T. Rhodes, and the cost was $18,025. The anticipated completion date was 1 November 1870. By December of 1870, necessary machinery and fixtures were being installed in the new factory, and by May of 1871, watch parts were being manufactured.[240] In January of 1872 the first set of completed watch movements was completed.[241]

The sales strategies of the Springfield Watch Company included an attempt to pitch the product to the retail market. As accomplishing a firm standing in the market became a more demanding enterprise, the company adapted to the challenges of the task by expanding the scope of its sales representation.

> Like so many others have tried to do since, the company attempted to sell direct to the retail trade, and the marketing of the product was placed in the hands of the Secretary, Mr. Miller, who took the road for that purpose and visited all the large cities. This soon proved to be too great a task, and in 1873 a New York office was established at 11 Maiden Lane, in charge of J. M. Morrow, who placed the product with the jobbers and continued with the company until 1884.[242]

Establishing a sales branch office in New York would have been advantageous to the Springfield Watch Company. The mere presence of the sales office in a city of that magnitude not only would generate sales, ideally, but also would create for the company a reputation which by word-of-mouth promotion and possible publicity in local newspapers, would help establish the reputation of the company in a large city. A New York presence would be of value.

As the reputation of the company in the retail market was developing, the workforce and production methods were growing and evolving. As the company matured, it gradually began manufacturing and processing a greater number of the components necessary for watch movement manufacturing. Prior to that time, watch movement components including jewels, hairsprings and dials had all been imported.[243]

The watch movement production rate of the factory in the early 1870s was indicative of a prospering factory. "The first watch movement, a 'Stuart' Grade [named after the company president John Todd Stuart] with 15 jewels, was finished on December 23, 1871, and by March, 1872, a production rate of over 100 movements per month had been achieved." The company employed 125 people in 1873.[244]

The new company would, however, suffer a devastating financial setback in the Panic of 1873, which would affect business enterprises throughout the United States. The specific nature of the economic damage sustained by the Springfield Watch Company during the Panic, and during the aftermath of the crisis, involved an almost complete failure of the firm. Having been in existence for only three years, the company had not sufficient capital strength to weather the Panic.

> The panic of 1873, which paralyzed the business of the country, placed the company in an embarrassing position, as they had not been in business long enough to have a

surplus of capital to sink during the depression which followed, and they soon found themselves with a large stock of watches on hand, with little or no demand for them, and no money with which to keep the factory running. To meet the emergency, fifty thousand dollars ($50,000.00) of preferred stock was issued, but it was not enough to do more than postpone the inevitable.[245]

The Springfield Watch Company sold in excess of 10,000 watches by the close of 1872. Despite apparent growth, the company's capital was dwindling, and competition from the Elgin and Waltham watch companies was difficult to overcome. "The reluctance of jewelers to turn away from the well-established Waltham and Elgin products was difficult to overcome and was not helped by the generally poor economic conditions which prevailed during 1873 and 1874."[246] The years from 1874 until 1877 signified a period of crisis for the Springfield Watch Company, and it was this period of financial tumult that provided the opportunity for what would become the final business venture that Jacob Bunn would undertake.

The company was failing to raise additional capital, failing to generate revenues in excess of its expenses, and its creditors began turning to the courts for remedial action. On 3 January 1877, John W. Bunn, Otis Hoyt, and W. J. Konkling were appointed a committee to "devise some means of relief from the embarrassed condition of the affairs of the company."[247] The plan that resulted from the deliberations of this committee stated that:

> ...the company should be sold to 'any new company which would assume and pay all debts of said company and relieve its stockholders of all liability.' (In return, the stockholders

would release the company of any claims and forego their personal investments; in other words, their stock would be worthless.)[248]

The motion was approved on 21 February 1877, and a suggestion was floated that called for the presenting of a quantity of watches equal to the value to the stock held by each investor, in order to "ease the pain of their losses." It is not known whether this suggestion was ever executed.[249]

On 22 March 1877, Secretary of State George N. Harlew gave official approval to a petition to form "A new corporation for the manufacture of watch movements, cases, materials and parts with capitalization of $100,000 consisting of 1,000 shares, $100 par, duration 99 years, to be known as the Illinois Springfield Watch Company at Springfield, Illinois."[250] The reason for the official alteration in the corporate name stems primarily from a desire to distinguish the company from the New York Watch Company, which was located in Springfield, Massachusetts, and whose watches were labeled "Springfield." Apparently, some confusion had arisen in the watch trade as to the respective identities of the New York Watch Company and Springfield Watch Company products, and as a result, in 1874, the Springfield Watch Company labeled its watches "(Illinois) Springfield Watch Company." Not all watch dials that were labeled "Illinois" bore the parentheses, and there appeared as early as January of 1873 watches of this make. The Springfield Watch Company officially became the Illinois Springfield Watch Company in July of 1877.[251]

In no manner could the newly formed company have been considered to have been in a secure financial condition, at the end of 1877.

Despite the new products and the efficiencies in manufacturing which accrued as the company gained experience, nevertheless, the books showed a net loss of $44,000 at the end of 1877. In fact, the reorganization which cancelled a significant portion of the company's debt in July of that year was the only reason the company was still solvent.[252]

The year 1878 witnessed several employees abandon the Illinois Springfield Watch Company, several of them leaving to return to their previous jobs at the works of their former employer. Mason now was the only one of the original five people whom Adams had brought to Springfield in 1870. The first open-face stem-winding watch in America was produced under Mason's superintendence, at the Illinois Watch Company.[253]

By this time, the company was losing its staff and its capital. Furthermore, its credibility, which was already tarnished due to its near failure in 1877, was dwindling rapidly. E. N. Bates, the company's second president, resigned in July of 1878, only eighteen months after his entering into that office. It was during the autumn and winter of 1878 that the Illinois Springfield Watch Company was reborn, and it would be the company's third president who would transform it into one of the most dynamic and influential driving forces in the industrial development of the United States. The man who served as the third president was Jacob Bunn.

The company was to experience one more alteration in its name before it would embark on the most successful and influential period of its corporate existence. A notice, dated 18 November 1878, appeared in the Springfield newspapers stating that the board of directors of the Illinois Springfield Watch Company had summoned a meeting of the stockholders of the same for the purpose of voting on the change in corporate names from the current one to *Illinois Watch Company*. A second newspaper notice appeared that signified the rebirth of the company. "On December 31st a second notice was published announcing that the name change had been approved. This was signed 'Jacob Bunn, President'. Thus, entered Jacob Bunn and so began the Bunn dynasty which was to last for the next 48 years."[254] It is worth noting also that he had served as a commissioner and as a member of the board of directors of the Illinois Springfield Watch Company.[255]

The minutes of the meeting of the board of directors of 31 December 1878 do not explain the reasons behind the change in the corporate name. It is reasonable to suppose that the motivation was simply a desire for a simpler name. It has been thought, however, that the name change signified the culmination of "several months of behind-the-scenes maneuvering to bring Jacob Bunn in as president. A new company name would serve to identify the point in time where the new management assumed command."[256]

Conjectural though it is, this theory remains compelling, especially when one considers that there was no financial crisis to remedy, such as the case of the company only eighteen months before, and that an alteration in the corporate name would not likely have taken place as a result of trivial events. "In any event, December of 1878, was an important turning point in the company's history and it marked the beginning of the 'Bunn years.'"[257]

Jacob Bunn had a manifold motivation to ensure

personally the success of the Illinois Watch Company. Not only had he lost something in the vicinity of $1,000,000 in the company up to the point when he was made its president,[258] but he had an undying moral determination to repay the bank debts, that he owed to the many creditors of the collapsed J. Bunn Bank. The Illinois Watch Company would serve as one of the primary sources of the money that he would use to repay the bank debts.[259]

As part of his vision for the expansion of the business, Bunn extended the potential consumer base of the company. Among his first acts as president of the Illinois Watch Company was the establishment of an office in Chicago in 1879.[260] The Jacob Bunn administration fueled the growth of the Illinois Watch Company.

> In 1877, the company was re-organized with Jacob Bunn President, and Charles Smorowski Secretary, since which time the business has constantly increased, so that up to this time (1881) they have been unable to keep up with their orders.[261]

Product demand was by no means the only rapidly increasing parameter of the enterprise. The employment level increased with astounding speed. The table below charts the various growth patterns of the financial, labor, and productive capacities of the Illinois Watch Company, during the period from 1872, when the concern was a fledgling enterprise, to 1880, when Jacob Bunn had presided over the company for nearly two years.

Year	Average Number Employed	Watch Movement Production	Annual Pay
1872	-----	3,845	$63,000
1873	-----	9,095	$104,000
1874	-----	14,241	$121,000
1875	-----	8,550	$72,000
1876	-----	10,076	$50,000
1877	160	18,040	$84,000
1878	180	19,035	$96,000
1879	260	33,285	$125,000
1880	400	47,065	$207,000[262]

Jacob Bunn carried out a vision for the company that strengthened its financial condition, increased the size of its labor force, the scale of its manufacture, and the volume of the wages it paid the people in its employ. "Six hundred persons are now employed, and this number will be increased to eight hundred during the coming year [1882]."[263] As can be ascertained from the table shown above, the initial years [1877–] of the Bunn administration were years of solid growth and burgeoning prosperity for the Illinois Watch Company.

The effects of Bunn's belief in the future of the Illinois Watch Company were astounding. He helped bring about a 500 percent increase in watch production over the period of his time as company president. "Jacob threw all of his vast energies and expertise into making improvements. Before his death, output would increase to 600 watches daily [from 100 watches daily in about 1877-1878]."[264]

Under his administration the factory also manufactured

the first nickel watch movement in the United States, in 1879, and by 1886 the company was said to have been turning out the smallest watches in America.[265]

The Illinois Watch Company catered to numerous and diverse watch markets. In 1886, the company sought to strengthen its hold in the ladies' watch market, and introduced the 6 and 4-size Grades; the latter type was the smallest watch type manufactured in the United States at that time. In 1889, the company entered into competition with the Elgin Watch Company and other similar concerns for the men's watch market, by introducing the size-16 watch. Illinois Watch campaigned to extend its market to encompass the children's timepiece market, and in one advertisement it said, "Every schoolboy needs and desires a watch," and introduced the 14-size Grade "120" for the purpose of securing a position in this particular market.[266] [Please see the 2004 book *The Illinois Watch: The Life and Times of A Great American Watch Company* by Fred Friedberg for all the details about watches.]

In 1918, the Illinois Watch Company possessed total corporate assets of more than $2,500,000, and had watch movement sales that year of nearly $2,000,000.[267] The manufacturing departments represented a high concentration of mechanical expertise. The various manufacturing specialties and personnel were:

> Timing and Adjusting, L. F. Acker; Finishing, T. A. Sondal; Train, Wm. H. Hibbs; Jeweling, G. J. Haendle; Screw, Jacob Nennett; Machine, G. W. Meredith; Escape, Chas. Glassler; Plate, Cyrus Shinkle; Dial, Chas. Nichols; Damaskeening, Jos. Silva; Punch, Louis Scharf; Engraving,

J. S. Clarke; Balance Staff, Wm. Clarke; Gilding, Ilert Wieties; Mech. Superintendent, Geo. F. Johnson.[268]

Although the Illinois Watch Company sought to capture business in several watch markets, its greatest success would occur in the railroad timepiece market. The company's greatest renown derived predominantly from its recognizing the growing demand in the railroad industry for reliable timepieces. The true historical impact of the watch-making industry on the railroad industry was articulated eloquently in the following statement made by Lewis Mumford, in his 1934 *Technics and Civilization*, "The clock, not the steam-engine, is the key-machine of the modern industrial age."[269] Although the Illinois Watch Company manufactured watches, and not clocks, it made *timepieces* for the railroads, and was one of the vanguards of the timepiece industry in the United States.

The year 1884 was notable for Illinois because it marked a change in marketing philosophy for the company. The American railroads had agreed to adopt standard time that year and the railroad industry was beginning to have significant impact on the daily lives of people all over the country. This, in turn, was affecting the watch industry as watches began to be viewed as more than just ornamentation. The qualities of reliability and accuracy were beginning to assume importance to those who had to catch trains as well as those who operated them.[270] The Illinois Watch Company took into account this transmogrification of the watch markets and timepiece industry. Furthermore, it is almost certain that the company's issuance of the Grade "104" and Grade "105" watches transpired in response to a careful consideration of these changing market conditions,[271] as they started to produce watches specifically for the railroads' need for accurate timepieces. During the beginning of the final decade of the 19th century Illinois Watch advertisements targeted railroad men with increasing tenacity.[272] By 1890 the Illinois Watch Company had office locations in New York City, in Chicago, and in San Francisco, in addition, of course, to their central office location in Springfield.[273] In 1891, a railroad accident involving the collision of two trains that had been traveling in opposite directions incited railroads to establish a national standard for timepiece accuracy. Illinois Watch became the foremost standard-setter.

> To qualify, a watch had to remain accurate within 30 seconds a week at temperatures ranging from 34 to 100 degrees. To ensure that accuracy, Illinois watches were tested in a variety of positions in both a refrigerator and a heat box. It was 'six positions hot and cold,' one former factory worker remembered.[274]

The company's timepieces ultimately pervaded the United States. "[The] Illinois Watch Company [made] the accurate timepieces that were relied upon by railroad men from the Maine Central to the Southern Pacific."[275] Furthermore, in 1937 the company was referred to as the "leading watch manufacturing concern in America," by the *Illinois State Register*.[276] The Illinois Watch Company was renowned not only in the United States, but also throughout the world.

> With branch offices in San Francisco, Chicago, and New York City, the company was known across the nation and around the world.

At a time when the American watch industry was so highly regarded that the Swiss were copying American watch designs, the Illinois Watch Company ranked third in the United States in production of high-quality watches.

In its lifetime, the company made nearly 6 million jeweled watch movements, putting it behind only the Elgin and Waltham watch companies...the U. S. government ordered 15,000 high-grade military watches in 1918. In the early 1900s, the National Observatory in Washington, D.C. held a sort of competition for watches. Of the 11 that were finally accepted, 10 were made by the Illinois Watch Co.[277]

Additional indication of the global reputation of the company became evident when the watches were used on a key voyage of the 20th century. "In 1911, Norwegian explorer Roald Amundsen selected Bunn Specials as the official watches for his successful effort to reach the South Pole."[278] The commercial successes of the Illinois Watch Company after 1897, when Jacob Bunn died, traced ultimately to his success in administering the company from 1878 to 1897. The company was far more than a manufacturing concern. In addition to being an industrial force that put the names Illinois and Bunn on millions of watches and made Springfield a familiar name around the world, Illinois Watch possessed cultural force. The company contributed to its local and regional cultures through activities that entertained the employees and other members of the Springfield community, and the people of communities from all over Illinois.

The watch company had its own athletic teams, including a Bloomer Girls baseball team in the 1920s. It also had the Illinois Watch Co. Band, which was known throughout the Midwest, and played as far away as

Colorado... Formed in 1881, the 26-member band was led for 42 years by Prof. Louis Lehmann, who had been imported from Poughkeepsie, N. Y., expressly for that purpose...the band later merged with the Capitol City Band to form the Springfield Municipal Band.[279]

The company also boasted an "ideal" labor environment. Labor conditions at the company were highly regarded. "If the company's product was held in high repute, the factory's working conditions had an equal reputation among its employees."[280] One recollection by a former Illinois watch employee summarized the benefits of the company's working conditions.

> I was told by a former worker at the plant that, if you were going to work in Springfield, the place to work was at the Watch Factory,' said Jo Anna Lynn Harner... 'How can you be happy working in a factory?' Harner asked [an interviewee]. 'When you think of a factory, you think of dirt, grime and grease. This wasn't that type of factory.' Because it's nearly impossible to make fine watches in dark, grimy surroundings, the Watch Factory was a clean, well lit plant. Its wide, tree-lined lawns gave it a pleasant appearance from the outside, as well.[281]

Illinois Watch was an agent of sociological change, particularly as its policies pertained to female laborers. The company permitted women who had gotten married to remain on the work force, although few who did marry elected to remain on the workforce. Several of the female employees worked in the "timing room," where they were charged with the responsibility of "[keeping] hundreds of watches wound while they were being tested for accuracy."²⁸²

Yet another of the broad array of innovations that the Illinois Watch Company was entitled to enumerate on its institutional resume was the Illinois Watch Company wireless station. This station, known as 9ZS, made use of a 55,000 volt transmission generator, for the purpose of broadcasting time and weather checks for the Central Time Zone. The generator could transmit the messages over distances of 1,000 miles or greater in all directions from Springfield. The generator was controlled by a master clock, which, at precisely 11:55 would cause the generator to transmit the time signals, over a five-minute period, culminating in a final signal indicating that it was 12:00 noon. Shortly after the time signal process had been completed, the transmission master would send out a weather report, which would in turn be received by other operators who had receiving devices. A Mr. Johnson served for a great length of time as the wireless operator for the Illinois Watch Company, and had gained such a solid reputation for his knowledge and skill in this particular area of technical expertise that many wireless operators would come to apprentice under Johnson's tutelage. "This station was a great school for amateur wireless operators during the war and Mr. Johnson is known far and wide for his work in connection with it."²⁸³

The Illinois Watch Company wireless station became the object of national attention when it was the central subject of a magazine article that appeared in *Radio News*. The article read in part as follows:

> This concern is probably the first one in this country, if

not in the world, to actually transmit time signals and weather reports each day. The transmission of time signals is, of course, not a new thing, but it is new for a watch making organization to do it. We need not rack our brains in this case for the prime motive. A concern making a watch is naturally anxious that the watch will keep good time. If that concern is reasonably certain the finished watch is accurate they naturally enough want them to have a likewise accurate means of comparison. The sending of daily time signals, so that nearby owners of watches may have a dependable source of 'checking up' is therefore a step in the right direction and in keeping with the gospel of service.[284]

The success of the Illinois Watch Company throughout the last twenty years of the 19th century was due primarily to the leadership of Jacob Bunn. He had truly been the savior of the company, which in turn, through the revenues that it generated, greatly enabled him to salvage the financial conditions of his bank customer creditors.

Consequently, the historical impacts of the Illinois Watch Company were varied. Whereas on the one hand the company was the most important corporate force behind the standardization of American railroad time, setting new standards for timepiece quality, on the other hand, the enterprise was one of the leading contributors to Springfield industry, and was a major source of revenue for Jacob Bunn who used much of the money that he gained from it to repay the bank debts. "Typically, when someone remonstrated that that there was no need to work so hard, he would reply, 'For myself no, I need but little. But I must pay those bank debts before I die.'"[285] The autumn of 1897 would mark the end of Bunn's final business venture, the end of his life, and the end of an epoch in Illinois business.

While returning home from dinner at Benjamin and Alice Ferguson's home, Jacob Bunn became ill. He was accompanied by his seven-year-old grandson, George Wallace Bunn, Jr., who recalled his grandfather having to stop and rest along the way home.

> George remembered that, 'Two or three days later, still feeling a bit under the weather, he went into a little room adjoining his office [at the Illinois Watch Company], where there was a couch, and lay down for a short nap. He never woke up.'[286]

On 16 October 1897, Jacob Bunn died, at the age of eighty-three. His death came as a shock to Springfield. A local paper stated that, "[his death] was wholly unexpected, and was a great shock to the people of this community."[287] He was a man who had been greatly admired and respected by a President, by his employees, co-workers, friends, family, and other associates.

But amid the flowery tributes, his humanity was most eloquently recalled by an employee who said,

> If I live 50 years and forget everything else in the world, I believe that I will remember Jake Bunn was the first man that I found that would hear what I had to say.[288]

Among the most prominent features of his legacy was a combination of social altruism and a determination to help others. He believed so strongly in honor that he paid back everything that he could to those whom he considered to be the ones he had failed. His financial condition at the time of his death was evidence of his sincerity.

> But the most startling thing about his death was the fact that he died without any money of his own—it was all in account for his creditors. So small was his estate that there is no file of it in the county probate offices. Jacob Bunn had been a man of his word.[289]

He died leaving a multitude of legacies in the realms of business and civic endeavor. Each achievement, irrespective of its size or scale, was important to the development of Springfield. Jacob Bunn can be remembered for having been a founding force in the Springfield Marine Bank, and in the railroad industry of central Illinois. While trying to pay back the bank debts, and while trying to salvage the financial conditions of over one thousand creditors, Bunn saved the watch company, and therefore saved the watch-making industry of Springfield, and managed to build up what was perhaps the leading business enterprise responsible for the standardization of American railroad time.

After the death of Jacob Bunn, his sons Henry and Jacob Bunn, Jr., perpetuated the civic spirit of the Illinois Watch Company. They ensured that the corporation that they were now managing remained true to its commitment to improve its community and its dedication to aid people in all areas of the United States and abroad. The company continued to exhibit commercially-oriented civic spirit, continued to promote civic improvement through constructive social organizations, and perpetually retained the respect that it had earned from its employees.

In a brief corporate history that dates from approximately 1920, the Illinois Watch Company was said to have paid, throughout the course of its entire existence, $20,000,000 in wages to its workers. Additionally, the factory at the same time was manufacturing 600 jeweled watch movements per day, and employed 1,200 people.[290]

The extraordinary growth that the Illinois Watch Company experienced occurred primarily because of the abilities of its executive leadership. Jacob Bunn, John W. Bunn, Benjamin H. Ferguson and others all contributed to the complete transmogrification of the company, from a small, exceedingly unstable, notably unsuccessful, and steadily declining concern, to a massive industrial complex whose products had become globally renowned. Jacob Bunn, as president of the corporation, and as one who had been present with the company, as a stockholder, director, and eventually as president and board chairman, oversaw, from 1878 until 1897, the most critical stage in the life of the Illinois Watch Company. After Jacob Bunn's death in 1897, his son, Jacob Bunn, Jr., assumed the presidency of the company, and served in that office until his untimely death in 1926. Jacob Bunn, Jr., not only successfully managed the affairs of Illinois Watch, constantly seeking opportunities for the company's growth, but also organized, through the watch company, an educational program which ultimately was established at high schools around the world: the Abraham Lincoln Essay Contest. In Bunn's announcement of the contest, "... he assured high-school officials that the company's sponsorship was 'without selfish motives.'"[291]

The Abraham Lincoln Essay Contest was initiated in 1924. Jacob Bunn, Jr., "invited twenty-three thousand American high schools to organize a Lincoln essay contest."[292] Programs such as the Lincoln essay contest were ultimately possible because Jacob Bunn, Sr., had envisioned the success of the Lincoln presidency and, later, of the Illinois Watch Company. The watch company had experienced severe financial setbacks in its early years. Jacob Bunn salvaged the enterprise. The elder Bunn was the "timepiece savior." He transformed a failing enterprise into a global leader in timepiece technology and standard railroad timekeeping, with a factory genuinely concerned with the welfare and comfort of its more than 1,000 employees. He salvaged the company, and through his own efforts and through the efforts of his children, salvaged the financial conditions of his depositors, to whom he felt an undying moral obligation. All of these activities strengthened Illinois and the nation as a whole.

He was committed to building what would become one of the most significant industrial legacies that Illinois would leave to American industry, and while salvaging the watch company, he saved a large sector of the Springfield economy, and earned for Springfield a permanent seat in the hall of United States technological and industrial achievement.

60. *John C. Adams. Adams originated the concept for the establishment of a watch company in Springfield. He had also been a founder of the Elgin Watch Company, of Elgin, Illinois, the largest manufacturer of jeweled watch movements in the United States, and a major rival of the Illinois Watch Company.* (Photo courtesy of the Sangamon Valley Collection at the Lincoln Library, Springfield, Illinois.)

61. *John Todd Stuart, Esq. Stuart was a law partner of Abraham Lincoln's. Stuart served also as the president of the Springfield Watch Company, the ultimate seed company which would nearly eight years later evolve into the Illinois Watch Company, under the leadership of Jacob Bunn.* (Photo courtesy of the Sangamon Valley Collection at the Lincoln Library, Springfield, Illinois.)

62. *John Williams. Williams was another leading merchant and industrialist of Springfield, and had served with Jacob Bunn in promoting the railroad industry of central Illinois.* (Photo courtesy of the Sangamon Valley Collection at the Lincoln Library, Springfield, Illinois.)

63. Jacob Bunn (seated at left) and his son, Jacob Bunn, Jr., (seated at right) sitting in the principal administrative office of the Illinois Watch Company. Jacob Bunn was the president of the Illinois Watch Company at the time when this photograph was taken, and served on many occasions as the chairman of the board of directors. The large poster that is situated to the immediate upper right of the door is a poster advertisement for the Chicago and Alton Railroad Company, a company which Jacob Bunn had served both as a founder and commissioner. (Photo courtesy of the Sangamon Valley Collection at the Lincoln Library, Springfield, Illinois.)

64. *The factory and principal offices of the Illinois Watch Company.* (Photo courtesy of the Sangamon Valley Collection at the Lincoln Library, Springfield, Illinois.)

65. *A detailed illustration of the Illinois Watch Company campus.* (Photo courtesy of the Sangamon Valley Collection at the Lincoln Library, Springfield, Illinois.)

66. *The interior label of an Abraham Lincoln essay contest award medal case. The essay contest was sponsored by the Illinois Watch Company, and became an international academic phenomenon at high schools.* (Author's personal collection.)

67. *A Lincoln Essay Medal.* (Author's personal collection.)

68. *The reverse side of the Lincoln Essay Medal.* (Author's personal collection.)

69. *Postcard of Illinois Watch Company.* (Author's personal collection.)

70. *Reverse of color postcard of Illinois Watch Company. The postcard reads on the left hand side, "Our Mr. George W. Chatterton, Jr. will call upon you in a few days. Very Respectfully, Illinois Watch Company." George W. Chatterton was a highly regarded and very successful sales and product agent for the Illinois Watch Company, and also represented another one of the leading commercial families of Springfield.* (Author's personal collection.)

71. Color collage postcard promoting Illinois Watch Company. (Author's personal collection.)

72. Reverse of color collage postcard of Illinois Watch Company. (Author's personal collection.)

73. Stock Certificate of Springfield Watch Company. (Author's personal collection.)

74. A wooden box bearing the corporate name and corporate emblem of the Illinois Springfield Watch Company, an interim corporation which existed for about one and a half years before being reorganized as the Illinois Watch Company. The corporate name has been carved intricately into the face of the wood. (Author's personal collection.)

75. Landscaped entrance to Illinois Watch Company. (Photo courtesy of the Sangamon Valley Collection at the Lincoln Library, Springfield, Illinois.)

76. Photograph taken of primary building of the Illinois Watch Company. (Photo courtesy of the Sangamon Valley Collection at the Lincoln Library, Springfield, Illinois.)

77. Advertisement in Saturday Evening Post *for Illinois Watch Company wristwatches.* (Author's personal collection.)
The three watches advertised here are:
    The Claudette $32.50 (today's ribbon watch)
                                        (14k gold filled, natural or white)
    The Glenna $42.50 (Lady's bracelet watch)
                                        (14k filled white gold)
    Beau Royale $35.00 (Men's strap watch)
                                        (14k gold filled, natural or white)

The Illinois Watch • A Great American Watch • Made to Time America

78. *Illinois Watch Company advertisement in* Saturday Evening Post. *(Author's personal collection.)*

The Dean (Men's pocket watch, 17 jewels, 14k solid white gold — $85.00)
The Vanity Fair (Lady's ribbon watch, 17 jewels, 14k gold filled, natural or white — $45.00)
The New Yorker (Men's strap watch, 17 jewels, 14k gold filled, natural or white — $50.00)

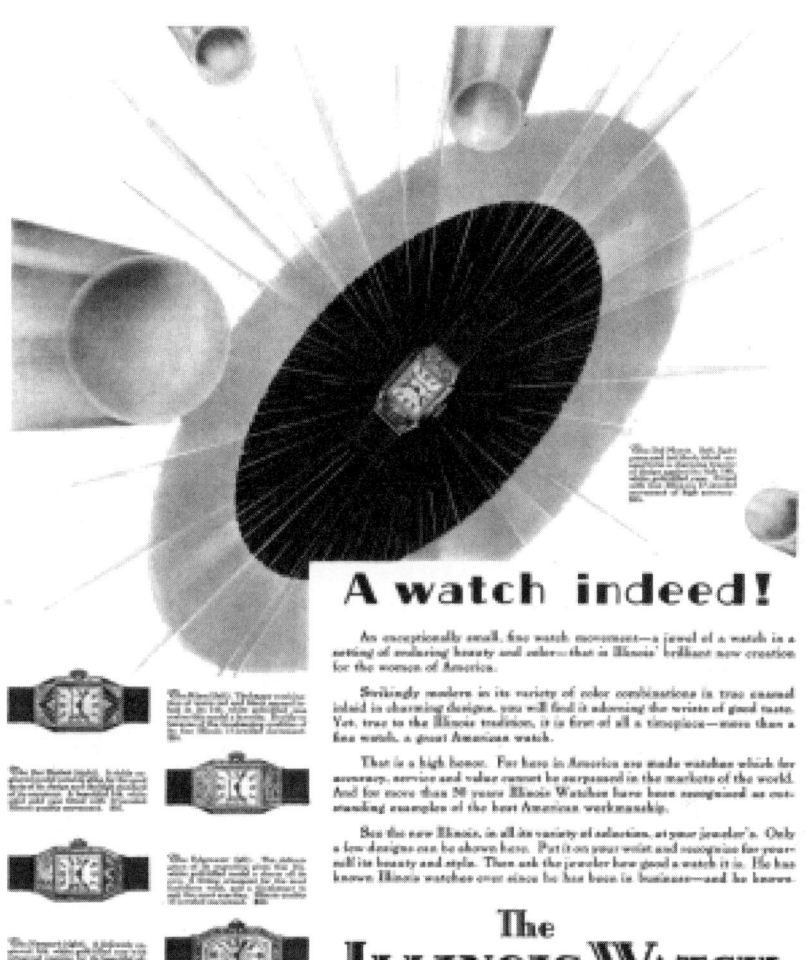

79. Another wristwatch advertisement in Saturday Evening Post *from the Illinois Watch Company.* (Author's personal collection.)
At top: The Del Monte Watch. Clockwise: The Miami, The Bar Harbor, The Newport, The Edgewater.

80. Another wristwatch advertisement in The American Magazine *(Feb. 1929), from The Illinois Watch Company.* (Author's personal collection.)
Above: The Ensign, The Beau Brummel, and The Marquis-Autocrat.

81. Photograph of Illinois Watch Company employee and executive party. (Photo courtesy of the Sangamon Valley Collection at the Lincoln Library, Springfield, Illinois.)

82. Photograph of one of the Women's Clubs that was organized by female employees of the Illinois Watch Company. (Photo courtesy of the Sangamon Valley Collection at the Lincoln Library, Springfield, Illinois.)

83. Large group photograph of employees of the Illinois Watch Company. (Photo courtesy of the Sangamon Valley Collection at the Lincoln Library, Springfield, Illinois.)

84. Another employee gathering at the Illinois Watch Company. (Photo courtesy of the Sangamon Valley Collection at the Lincoln Library, Springfield, Illinois.)

85. Illinois Watch Company employees working in one of the production halls of the factory. (Photo courtesy of the Sangamon Valley Collection at the Lincoln Library, Springfield, Illinois.)

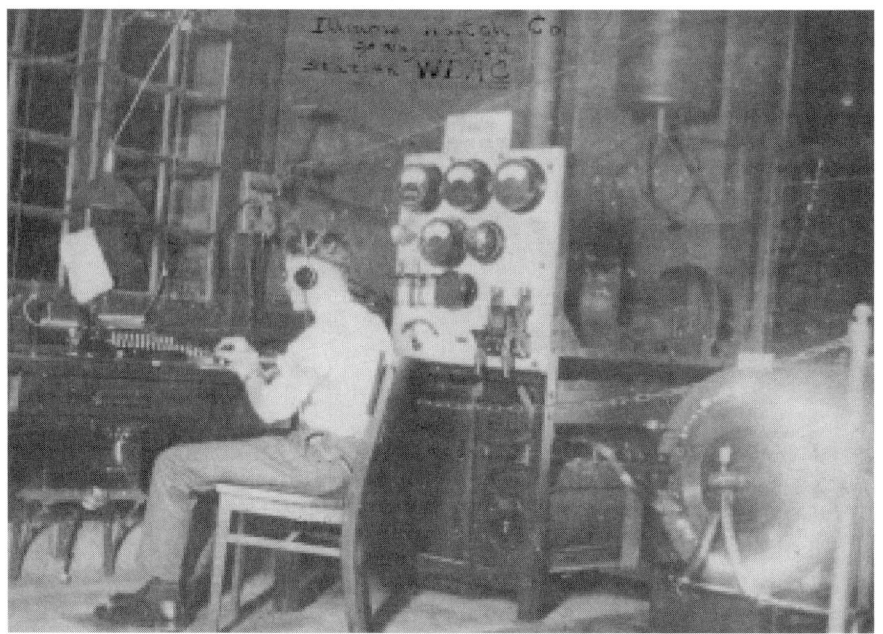

86. Interior of the Illinois Watch Company Wireless Station. The young man shown here is in charge of administering transmissions from the 55,000 volt generator that the Illinois Watch Company used for time and weather broadcasts. (Photo courtesy of the Sangamon Valley Collection at the Lincoln Library, Springfield, Illinois.)

87. Another photograph of the production process at the Illinois Watch factory. (Photo courtesy of the Sangamon Valley Collection at the Lincoln Library, Springfield, Illinois.)

88. The Illinois Watch Company factory and campus after a severe ice storm. (Photo courtesy of the Sangamon Valley Collection at the Lincoln Library, Springfield, Illinois.)

89. John Whitfield Bunn in one of his corporate offices, as an elderly gentleman.(Photo courtesy of the Sangamon Valley Collection at the Lincoln Library, Springfield, Illinois.)

90. Pocket watch that belonged to a great-grandson of Jacob Bunn. (Author's personal collection.)

91. Wristwatch that belonged to Ruth (Regan) Bunn, the wife of the last vice-president of the Illinois Watch Company, Willard Bunn, a grandson of Jacob Bunn, and great-nephew of John Whitfield Bunn. (Author's personal collection.)

92. An Elgin Watch Company pocket watch. The Elgin Watch Company of Elgin, Illinois, organized by John C. Adams, was once the largest manufacturer of jeweled timepiece movements in the world, and along with the Waltham Watch Company of Massachusetts, and the Hamilton Watch Company of Pennsylvania, was a primary competitor with the Illinois Watch Company in the jeweled timepiece movement industry. Interestingly, it would be Adams who would also help organize the Springfield Watch Company, the corporate precursor of the Illinois Watch Company. (Author's personal collection.)

93. Illinois Watch Company pocket watch. (Author's personal collection.)

94. Illinois Watch Company pocket watch. (Author's personal collection.)

95. Illinois Watch Company, "Bunn Special" railroad pocket watch. The "Bunn Special" was one of the leading types of railroad timepieces in the industry and was viewed both as a standard in the railroad industry, and as an essential instrument for railroad timekeeping and scheduling logistics. (Author's personal collection.)

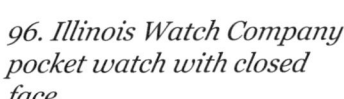

96. Illinois Watch Company pocket watch with closed face.

97. Open-faced Illinois pocket watch. (Author's personal collection.)

ROBERT CARR LANPHIER
1878-1939

98. Robert Carr Lanphier. A graduate of the school of engineering at Yale, Lanphier brought both technological ingenuity and business vision and expertise to the Sangamo Electric Company, eventually becoming the chairman of the board of directors. Lanphier was also a director of the General Time Instruments Corporation, a company with which he had been associated through the Sangamo Electric Company. (Photo courtesy of Sangamo: A History of Fifty Years, *by Robert Carr Lanphier and Benjamin P. Thomas; Chicago: Privately printed, 1949.)*

JACOB BUNN
1864-1926

99. *Jacob Bunn, Jr. He was the youngest son and second to youngest child of Jacob and Elizabeth (Ferguson) Bunn. He served as president of the Illinois Watch Company, as president of the Sangamo Electric Company, and as an executive with several other noted commercial enterprises.* (Photo courtesy of *Sangamo: A History of Fifty Years,* by Robert Carr Lanphier and Benjamin P. Thomas; Chicago: Privately printed, 1949.)

100. A section of a poster depicting the principal Illinois factory of the Sangamo Electric Company. Please note the distinctive corporate logo in the lower center of the image. (Author's personal collection.)

101. Photograph of the Springfield factory and campus of the Sangamo Electric Company. (Photo courtesy of the Sangamon Valley Collection at the Lincoln Library, Springfield, Illinois.)

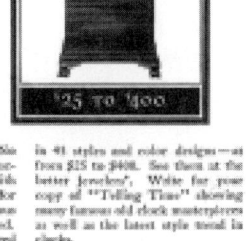

102. Advertisement for the Sangamo Electric Clock. Sangamo manufactured electric clocks for several years before finally selling the clock business to the General Time Instruments Corporation, at that time headed by Ralph Matthiessen. (Author's personal collection.)

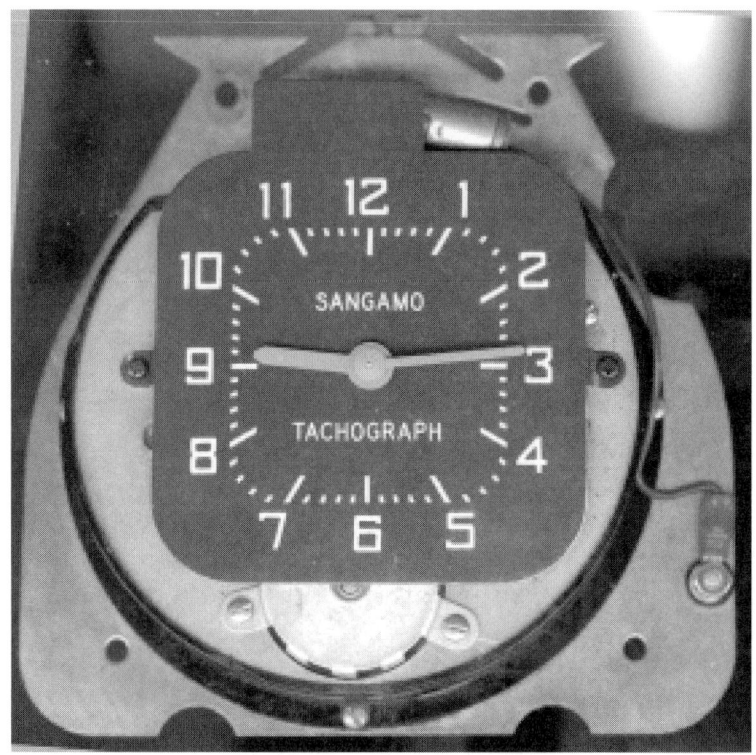

103. A Sangamo Electric Company tachograph. The tachograph was an instrument that was utilized in the engines of motor vehicles, to monitor and record the speeds of the vehicles. (Author's personal collection.)

X

Echoes of Industry and Reflections of Integrity

The commercial and civic development of Springfield, Sangamon County, Illinois, can be viewed as a series of ever-complex kaleidoscopes, in which each pioneer merchant, doctor, educator, politician, lawyer, intellectual, and laborer was a gemlike shard. Each of the people encountered in this work played an important role in Illinois history, and can be understood as being a part of the kaleidoscopic array of achievement that occurred from approximately 1818 until 1897.

One cannot examine the history of Springfield, or for that matter the history of Illinois, without taking inventory of the ramifications of the career of Jacob Bunn and those of his contemporaries who sought to build up their region in every way possible. To understand the railroads, the banks, the grocery companies, the land speculation, the politics, the law, the industries, and the economy of central Illinois, one must look to Jacob Bunn as perhaps the most dynamic *individual* force in the business development of Illinois from 1836 until 1897.

Two banks, a newspaper, one city railway and at least four regional railroad companies, several public utilities, a grocery company, a watch company, the Springfield telegraph industry, a coal company, an iron company, a liquor company, land development, the beet-sugar industry, the new state capitol building, the Lincoln presidential campaign, the Lincoln Monument, and many other civic, benevolent, social, and business enterprises owe their existence at least in part to the vision and to the spirit of societal commitment of Jacob Bunn. One cannot gain a full understanding of any of these developments in Illinois without knowing Bunn and his contributions to their success.

The Springfield legacy of Jacob Bunn was not restricted to the business enterprises and civic projects that he oversaw during his own lifetime. In order to understand fully the legacy of this American one must take inventory of all that came into existence as a result of his accomplishments, both directly and indirectly.

The primary historical phenomena that owe their existence to his lifetime of work in business and to his infrangible sense of honor, but which took place after his death, were varied and significant: fulfillment of his objective of paying back in full the amount of money lost to those whom he considered bound to restore financially, the successful organization of an electric company that would play numerous important roles in 20th century American and international technological development, and the formation of a company that would set many standards in the beverage equipment industry and become a hugely-successful corporation with products all over the world. The family's legacy is honor and industrial achievement. But the successes and failures present an intriguing history.

The Panic of 1873 presented after five years an unendurable pressure upon the J. Bunn Bank, and the bank's assets, which were predominantly in the form of real estate, were not sufficient to enable the continued business of the bank. When his bank closed its doors on 1 January 1878, his debts amounted to $800,000. His assets exceeded this amount considerably, but their value plummeted, due to forced sales, much to the detriment of his endeavor to salvage the financial condition of the bank, its depositors, and his own condition. Jacob Bunn was excused from any legal liability for the balance of 28.5 per cent, after the liquidation of his assets had generated the reimbursement of 71.5 per cent of the total debt. His sense of duty and honor, however, would not be abated by the fact of a legal decision, namely, discharge from liability.

> Nevertheless, he fully recognized that morally he was still obligated for this balance and his one hope was that eventually he would be able to pay it. The remaining years of his life were dedicated to that purpose, but he was doomed to disappointment and passed away in 1897 without accomplishing it.[293]

Although Jacob Bunn died in 1897, his spirit and sense of duty and honor continued to be felt in Springfield and in his family. He bequeathed to his children that very spirit, and with that inspiration and sense of dedication to honor and civic duty they carried out what death had prevented their father from completing in his own time. "Mr. Bunn's children knew and were in complete sympathy with his wishes in this matter.... In order to facilitate the handling of these payments, Mr. Bunn's children have formed the

Bunn Memorial Trust, through which checks are being issued."[294] The payments were completed on the day after Christmas, 1925. A 1925 newspaper story explains:

> Approximately one million dollars—$800,000 to be exact was the Christmas and New Years gift of Miss Alice Bunn, George W. Bunn, Henry Bunn and Jacob Bunn, Jr., heirs of the late Jacob Bunn, Sr., in voluntary payment to nearly 5,000 persons of all moral obligations left through suspension of the old J. Bunn Bank which closed its doors at the southwest corner of Fifth and Adams streets, Springfield, Illinois, January 1, 1878.
>
> Without legal obligation, with no element of compulsion whatever and actuated only by the highest idealism the heirs of Jacob Bunn named above through their attorney, B. L. Catron, in collaboration with the 'Bunn Memorial Trust,' of which J. F. Bunn and J. H. Holbrook are trustees, sent out in December, 1925, the following statement:
>
> 'In the year 1840, Mr. Jacob Bunn, who was the father of Alice Bunn, George Bunn, Henry Bunn and Jacob Bunn, Jr., engaged in the private banking business in this city. His business progressed rapidly and assumed large proportions. However, in the general depression which settled on this country in 1873 and the succeeding years, it was necessary for him to take a large amount of real estate in settlement of loans to customers who found themselves financially embarrassed during that period. After five years of that depression Mr. Bunn found his bank overloaded with slow assets, chiefly real estate, with insufficient cash means to continue his business. Consequently, on January 1, 1878, he placed his bank in voluntary liquidation. His debts amounted then to $800,000, and his assets largely exceeded that amount in actual value. Forced sales, however, reduced them to such an extent that the total payments made to his depositors amounted to only 71-1/2%, or $572,000.

'After liquidation and settlement, Mr. Bunn was discharged from legal liability for the balance of 28-1/2% remaining unpaid. Nevertheless, he fully recognized that morally he was still obligated for this balance and his one hope was that eventually he would be able to pay it. The remaining years of his life were dedicated to that purpose, but he was doomed to disappointment and passed away in 1897 without accomplishing it.

'Mr. Bunn's children knew and were in complete sympathy with his wishes in this matter. Now, after 48 years, they are prepared to carry out his purpose and propose to pay in full the balance remaining unpaid, as above stated, together with interest thereon at the rate of 5% per annum, or approximately 240% interest. This balance, with interest, will nearly equal the amount of the original claims. For example, on an original claim January 1, 1878, of $1,000.00, 71-1/2% was paid amounting to $715.00. On the balance of $285.00, interest is computed for 48 years at 5% per annum for 50 years.

'In order to facilitate the handling of these payments, Mr. Bunn's children have formed the Bunn Memorial Trust, through which checks are being issued. Many of the original claimants have died, and in such cases payment is being made to such persons as are determined to be the proper beneficiaries of their respective estates. The attached memorandum will show the original amount of your claim, if you were a claimant, or if you have been found to be the beneficiary of a deceased claimant, it will show his or her name and the amount of the claim, with your relationship and share in the amount paid.

'A check payable to your order for the amount of your shares enclosed herewith. If for any reason you find this incorrect kindly return the check, with a full statement of the facts.'

The action of Mr. Bunn's children at this time is indeed remarkable. It appeals not to the mind alone but to the heart. Justice, kindness, honor, benevolence lend the genuine Christmas spirit to this magnificent gift.

Unpretentious, modest, seeking to avoid publicity, but yielding to requests to permit publication of basic facts because in that way aid would be rendered in efforts to find heirs of some of the deceased depositors who have not been located there is indeed the Christian spirit back of this gift.

Miss Alice Bunn, George W. Bunn, Henry Bunn and Jacob Bunn, Jr., the four living children of Jacob Bunn, Sr., who conducted the J. Bunn bank from 1840 [sic]—1878, have honored not only themselves and their father, but have brought honor to Springfield, Illinois, their home. Of course bankruptcy wiped out every legal claim. But to Jacob Bunn and his descendants a debt was a matter of honor. Who will say that this was not a finer achievement than the accumulation of any fortune, however large. They have written a chapter into the history of Springfield and Illinois as inspirational as it is remarkable—a chapter illuminated by the light of honor which reflects it beautifully against the back ground of selfishness and greed of this money-mad age of material progress.[295]

The family's persistence in this endeavor was manifest also in the manner whereby they reimbursed families whose original J. Bunn Bank depositors had passed away. The Bunn Memorial Trust was an extension of the life, ethics, and achievements of Jacob Bunn, Sr. Although he had been bankrupt, and therefore legally absolved from financial liability, Jacob Bunn and his descendants fulfilled what they recognized as their moral obligation.

The Jacob Bunn legacy was the foundation for many subsequent family-run achievements in business and in philanthropy. While Jacob Bunn had no money to bequeath to his children, he instead passed on to them a vast "fortune" of morality and integrity. While this "moral estate" of honor, motivation, and vision would lead to the establishment of the Bunn Memorial Trust, as a civic action, it would also give rise to other business enterprises.

One of the first to note is the Sangamo Electric Company, the entrepreneurial offspring of the Illinois Watch Company. Tom Sheridan, the Master Mechanic for Illinois Watch and a highly respected Chicago patent lawyer, had become acquainted with German engineer Ludwig Gutmann, who had studied under Dr. von Siemens in Berlin, Blathy in Budapest, and Gaulard and Gibbs in France. Gutmann was developing a type of electrical meter, but required sufficient technological apparatus, in addition to ample financial patronage. Sheridan realized that both could be provided abundantly by Illinois Watch. Sheridan informed Jacob Bunn, Jr., who was the Vice President of Illinois Watch, and he in turn told his father and company President, Jacob Bunn, Sr., who declined the proposal in 1896.[296]

Jacob Bunn, Sr., determined to pay back the bank debts, and to perpetuate the success of Illinois Watch, would have shunned entrepreneurial ventures that could pose the threat of financial loss. If the possibility of such a venture had occurred before 1873, Bunn, Sr., would probably have partaken of the venture. He must have calculated the potential advantages and disadvantages of the proposal, and then decided that his first priority was to discharge the bank debts that were incurred by the bank failure in 1878. To repay the bank debts he would have to minimize the chances of further financial losses; to minimize the possibilities of further financial losses he would have to forego investment in the future of Gutmann's invention.

Although Jacob Bunn, Sr., was not himself a direct promoter of the electric meter industry, he was the pioneer of standard railroad time in America. As a result of his visions for the success of the Illinois Watch Company and the railroad industry, he built Illinois Watch into a successful concern, and therefore created the environment in which the Sangamo Electric Company could be born. Consequently, when Jacob Bunn, Jr., an officer of the watch company, chose to finance Gutmann's invention, he laid the foundation of the Sangamo Electric Company.

The existence and success of the Sangamo Electric Company would be incomprehensible without the mechanical ingenuity and the brilliant business acumen of Robert Carr Lanphier, Sr. He was born in 1878, in Springfield, to another family of great civic importance in the history of both Springfield and Illinois. Upon returning to Springfield from Connecticut, after completing his engineering studies at Yale University, the young Lanphier encountered Jacob Bunn, Jr., who approached him at a Springfield social event, with the prospect of organizing a corporation for the manufacture of the Gutmann electric meter. After Lanphier and Bunn discussed the notion of undertaking the venture, Lanphier accepted an offer from Bunn to devote two months to investigating the technological potential of the Gutmann electric meter. The success with which Lanphier demonstrated the technological potential of the meter was indisputable, and was one of the most important factors leading to the incorporation of the Sangamo Electric Company.

Lanphier served as the third president of the Sangamo Electric Company, and served for many years as a member of the board of directors, guiding the affairs of the growing concern with sincerest dedication and expertise. Trained as an engineer at Yale, and trained in the art of corporate enterprise by Jacob, Jr., and Henry Bunn, Lanphier represented the ideal combination of the expert technician and the forward looking business visionary and corporate diplomat.

The Sangamo Electric Company was incorporated 11 January 1899, with headquarters and principal manufacturing facilities located in Springfield. "Like most other successful American business enterprises, the Sangamo Electric Company had humble beginnings...."[297] Within five decades, however, the company had become a world leader in the electrical equipment sector, and its contributions to domestic and global industry were vast. The company's array of products was as diverse as the spectrum of industries that it served. Within five decades the company was a globally renowned manufacturer of electrical equipment that served the automotive industry, the United States and the British military, the railroad industry and many other sectors that required electrical devices. Sangamo manufactured meters used widely in automobile engines, flash devices made for use in road signs, sonar devices used abundantly by the United States Navy, motors for electric clocks, various refrigeration apparatus, and many other items.[298] (For an extensive chronological account of the company's innovations, see the appendix that follows this chapter.)

The Sangamo Electric Company became a global corporation, and by 1931 had offices or manufacturing facilities in Springfield; New York City; Chicago; San Francisco; Los Angeles; Toronto; Montreal; Paris, France; London, England; Osaka, Japan; Buenos Aires,

Argentina;[299] Boston; Philadelphia; Birmingham, Alabama; and Jackson, Mississippi, in addition to sales offices in 25 other cities throughout the United States and Canada.[300]

The company had either parent corporation or subsidiary corporation stock listings on the Chicago Stock Exchange,[301] the Midwest Stock Exchange, the New York Stock Exchange,[302] the London Stock Exchange,[303] the Canadian Stock Exchange, the Montreal Curb Market, and the Toronto Stock Exchange. By 1949 the company's logo was a registered trademark in nearly thirty countries of the world.[304] Sangamo Electric was an international leader in the manufacture of electrical devices. By 1950, nearly every country on earth had received electrical equipment from the Sangamo Electric Company.[305]

The Sangamo Electric Company organized subsidiary companies in various locations throughout the world, during the first half of the 20th century. By doing so, the Sangamo administration was able to cater to the increasing demands of the meter and electric apparatus industries. Several events in the history of Sangamo Electric Company are of particularly salient importance. Although the history of this corporation contains many more data of interest than the ones relayed below, the ones which follow are especially illustrative of the principles of vision, integrity and legacy that course through these chapters.

As stated earlier, the administration of the Illinois Watch Company, the concern which would serve effectively as the ultimate corporate parent of the Sangamo Electric Company, decided to sell the firm to the Hamilton Watch Company of Lancaster, Pennsylvania, in 1927. Interestingly, the Sangamo Electric Company would return ownership of what had become the Springfield division of the Hamilton Watch Company to Springfield industrial interests when in June of 1937 Sangamo Electric acquired the grounds and facilities of the Springfield division of Hamilton. The decision behind the acquisition was founded on principles of utility and profit, as the Hamilton factory contained a boiler plant that provided heat, and the factory also contained additional space, which created opportunities to generate revenue through rental of the space.[306]

The positive state of sales revenues and financial growth was accompanied by the highly positive state of relations between the employees and the administration at Sangamo and was evidenced by a general evaluation given by Chairman Robert Carr Lanphier in 1938:

> Relations with our employees continue most cordial. During the year a wage increase of 5% was put into effect and, as in the past, our wage rates compare favorably with any in the electrical industry... We are indeed fortunate in having a group of employees able and willing to present their problems to the management with dignity and intelligence, thus providing the basis for mutually agreeable decisions and actions that cannot be other than beneficial to both employer and employee.[307]

British-Sangamo was prospering during the 1930s, and in October of 1935, its stock was listed on the London Stock Exchange. According to the opinion of Robert Carr Lanphier, the board chairman of the Sangamo Electric Company (the parent corporation in Springfield), "[The stock listing] has had the favorable effect of creating a wide public interest in Sangamo in Great Britain."[308]

In the autumn of 1936, British-Sangamo, the British

subsidiary of the Sangamo Electric Company, acquired a controlling interest in the Weston Electrical Instrument Company Ltd. Of Great Britain. The Weston Electrical Instrument Company Ltd., had until its acquisition existed as a wholly owned subsidiary of the Weston Electrical Instrument Corporation, a New Jersey corporation that was claimed to have been the foremost manufacturer of indicating instruments in the world. The acquisition of the British subsidiary of Weston Electrical Instrument Corporation was completed on December 31, 1936. Soon after that date, British-Sangamo commenced the removal of the Weston operations from its original location to the British-Sangamo plant, which was located in Enfield, England, close to London. British-Sangamo undertook the construction of several new buildings for the purpose of accommodating the recent expansion in business operations. It was stated by Robert Carr Lanphier, in the Annual Report To [the] Stockholders, of 1936, that,

> To provide [the additional space required], plus much needed facilities for the Engineering Department and for other purposes at British-Sangamo, new buildings have recently been started which will round out the British plant very completely and provide a factory second to none in Great Britain for the manufacture of meters, electrical instruments, time switches and related products.[309]

Robert C. Lanphier died in January of 1939. His services as a pioneer in the meter and electrical instrument industries, along with those of Ludwig Gutmann, and those of his mentor, friend and associate, Jacob Bunn, Jr., who had died in May of 1926, constitute a vital chapter in the annals of the American defense industry. As Jacob Bunn, Sr., had been a pioneer in the newly settled geographical regions of Illinois in the 1830s, Lanphier, Gutmann, Henry Bunn and Jacob Bunn, Jr., had been pioneers in the newly emerging economies and industries that were developing around the defense technology industry. In addition to his association with Sangamo, Lanphier had served as a director of the General Time Instruments Company of New York City (the General Time Instruments Corporation held the controlling interest in the Western Clock Company of La Salle, Illinois, and in the Seth Thomas Clock Company of Thomaston, Connecticut[310]), a director of the Springfield Marine Bank, a prominent member of the Springfield Rotary Club, a trustee of Illinois College in Jacksonville, Illinois, and a dedicated supporter of the Red Cross.[311]

Robert Carr Lanphier and his associates in the Sangamo Electric corporate family must always be remembered as having been among the foremost industrial patriarchs of the electric meter industry, developers of the defense sectors of the United States, and students of the commercial art of defense contracting as a field of enterprise. Lanphier was succeeded as president of Sangamo Electric by Donald S. Funk, who had previously served as vice-president and general manager of the parent company in Springfield. Funk was succeeded as vice president by Charles H. Lanphier, the older son of Robert Carr Lanphier.

In Donald Funk's inaugural report to the stockholders of Sangamo, he exhibited his own deep appreciation for Lanphier's contributions to the corporate community of Sangamo, and to the electrical industry generally. In the first paragraph of the 1938 Annual Report to the

Stockholders, Funk gave a corporate eulogy that should serve as a model for all such extolment in business and industry:

> With the deepest regret, I report the death on January 29, 1939 of Mr. Robert Carr Lanphier, president of the company. For more than forty years, his outstanding energy, genius and wisdom have been unselfishly devoted to the interests of the Sangamo Electric Company. Under his wise business guidance and through his deeply human understanding, which inspired respect and loyalty throughout the entire organization, the company has grown to its present magnitude. His passing brings a deep sense of personal loss to every employe [sic] and to his hosts of friends. The directors have passed and spread upon the Minutes of the company, a Resolution testifying to the outstanding contribution which he has made to the industry and to Sangamo.[312]

Donald Funk's tribute to Lanphier, which the author of this book calls the "Lanphier Eulogy," with which Funk inaugurated his tenure as company president, and reporter to stockholders, not only extolled the virtues of respect, loyalty, dedication and vision in business enterprise as being essential to a positive working environment and community, but also itself exhibited these same qualities in its own content, showing that Funk, like Lanphier (and the Bunns) also subscribed to the conviction that these values were essential to the formation, development and continuation of successful and value-bound business communities.

The "Lanphier Eulogy" should serve as a didactic instrument in the management, public relations, employer-employee relations, and business ethics courses offered in the business schools of the present day, because it exhibits the perpetuation of the values of integrity, dedication to excellence, vision, respect, and legacy, from one generation of business administration to the succeeding generations of the subsequent administrations, and could serve as a rubric of positive and honorable individual ambition, achievement, outlook, and commitment to the business institutions with which one is employed. These values must be actively promoted and perpetuated if business enterprises are to be communities of vision, respect, and legacy—quite simply, if they are to be successful at all. Taken as a block, these values form a *sine qua non* for healthy business environments, and must never be sacrificed.

Donald S. Funk continued to lead the company, and under his administration the concern continued to expand in employment, sales, and production, exerting profound technological influence across the globe. Funk also oversaw the successful and profitable participation of the Sangamo corporate family in the defense technology markets that blossomed during World War II.

During World War II, Sangamo Electric advanced the technology of anti-submarine defense technology. The company manufactured specialized electronic products under contract with the Underwater Sound Section of the United States Bureau of Ships. Donald S. Funk stated,

> Apparatus for both combat and training purposes were produced and the design of the various devices was entirely the work of Sangamo engineers. We are informed that this Sangamo apparatus played an important part in the detection and destruction of German and Japanese submarines.[313]

In addition to supporting the United States, British and

Canadian war efforts, Sangamo Electric also sought to promote engineering education among college age students throughout the United States. With the concept of vision in mind, Donald S. Funk and Charles H. Lanphier, as chairman and president, respectively, set forth their rationale for establishing a scholarship program that would support students wishing to pursue an engineering education:

> The continued success of any enterprise is dependent on competent younger personnel to take over the duties of retiring employees and to provide manpower for expansion in the Company's activities. For a number of years, the Company has conducted an employee training program to train men for increased responsibilities. As part of this program in the last ten years, all departments of the Company have been strengthened by the addition of over one hundred college graduates. Special emphasis has been given to recruitment of graduates in the field of Engineering, and, to assist in this program, a scholarship plan was initiated during the year which will ultimately provide for some twelve $1,000 scholarships per year. Summer work programs in our Engineering Department are also conducted in order to stimulate interest in the Company on the part of Engineering undergraduates. It is the opinion of the Company that one of the most critical problems facing industry lies in this area.[314]

Donald S. Funk and Charles H. Lanphier exhibited in their concept for this scholarship plan a vision that benefited many students of engineering. The key operative factor in this scenario is the fact that Funk and Lanphier had a *vision* and acted on their vision for the success of the next generation of employees, who would eventually become the next generation of business and industry leaders.

The three elemental principles that flow through these

pages are vision, integrity, and legacy. One must develop a vision for one's career; one must seek to achieve one's objectives with integrity at every step and stage in one's life; one must bear in mind the entire time the importance of leaving a legacy to family, community, society, at some level, so as to provide a source of inspiration to the next generation of social, civic and commercial leaders.

The author calls this phenomenon of inheriting the fundamental and essential ethics of vision, integrity and legacy from business mentors, and then in turn "bequeathing" these same principles to the next generation of leaders, the "Principle of Visionary Succession." The concepts of legator, the one who bestows, and legatee, the one who receives, are appropriate in this instance, as they accurately describe the nature of the relationship between the parties in the context of Visionary Succession.

From the "Wheelbarrow Dialogue" to the "Lanphier Eulogy," the Principle of Visionary Succession is manifest, representing numerous chains of vision and legacy, characterized invariably by the highest sense of integrity.

Jacob Bunn, Sr., had exhibited a sense of vision for his brother, John Whitfield Bunn, during the "Wheelbarrow Dialogue," in which he changed his brother's life forever, setting before him a new path of livelihood in the frontier regions of Illinois. Both Jacob and John Whitfield Bunn had exhibited vision for the political success of Abraham Lincoln and the Republican Party.

Jacob and John Whitfield Bunn both exhibited vision for Henry Bunn, George Wallace Bunn, and Jacob Bunn, Jr., when they invited them to participate in the grocery company, the bank, the watch company, and other concerns, therefore setting before them careers in business and industry.

Jacob Bunn, Jr., had exhibited a vision for Robert Carr Lanphier, when he invited Lanphier, who had just returned home from his studies at Yale University, to investigate the Gutmann meter in order to make a prediction regarding potential industrial and commercial viability of the invention. Jacob Bunn, Jr., and Henry Bunn had exhibited a vision for the success of Ludwig Gutmann's invention, and thereby helped establish the "career" of an entire industry— the meter industry.

Donald S. Funk and Charles H. Lanphier exhibited vision for potentially hundreds of young students of engineering and electrical science. Clearly, Funk and Charles Lanphier had perpetuated the same ethics of vision, integrity and legacy that they had inherited from Jacob Bunn, Jr., Robert Carr Lanphier, and Ludwig Gutmann, Henry Bunn, and men like them.

Indisputably, Funk and Lanphier were the legatees of vision, integrity and legacy; and because of their inheritance of these ethics from men like Robert Carr Lanphier, Jacob Bunn, Jr., and Henry Bunn, they were able to become the legators of a vision that would help create the careers of so many young and aspiring business people and professionals.

May we hope always that this principle may forever abundantly characterize the relations between the older and the younger generations of business people, so that those who are embarking upon careers in business, industry and commerce may themselves inherit the ethics of vision, integrity, and legacy, from those who have completed their journeys in the realms of commerce. An inheritance of these principles is infinitely superior to any inheritance of money or other materials items.

While the values of precious metals, currency, and grain fluctuate, the values of the principles of vision, integrity, and legacy never fluctuate. Unfortunately, however, people's perceptions do. Consequently, it is vital that the business communities of the present day ambitiously promote these morals, because without the moral "currency" that is comprised of these three fundamental ideals, all commerce will ultimately fail.

The Sangamo Electric Company was not, however, the only business enterprise to spring from one of the original Jacob Bunn companies. As the Illinois Watch Company had been the parent of the Sangamo Electric Company, the Bunn Capitol Company was the company which provided both the opportunity and the business environment in which the Bunn-O-Matic Corporation, a global leader in beverage equipment and accessories, was founded. The company was founded by a great-grandson of Jacob Bunn.

> General wholesale grocery trade was discontinued in 1952 and Bunn Capitol began specializing in institutional grocery supplies. The business name became famous nationwide with George Regan Bunn's invention of the astoundingly successful Bunn-O-Matic coffeebrewer, much as the name Sangamo was immortalized as a meter manufacturer.[315]

Robert H. Bunn, the current president of the Bunn Capitol Company, in an interview characterized Jacob Bunn, Sr., and his civic and business achievements as an "old oak tree," from which have sprung many prominent branches.[316] Robert H. Bunn's insight into, and characterization of, the business ventures of Jacob Bunn and their ramifications, describes them perfectly.

Without Jacob Bunn, Sr., there would have been neither an Illinois Watch Company nor a Bunn Capitol Company, and therefore neither a Sangamo Electric Company nor a Bunn-O-Matic Corporation. Also, Jacob Bunn helped with the founding and nurturing of the careers of individuals such as John Whitfield Bunn, Benjamin H. Ferguson and F. K. Whittemore, seeing in them the potential for great business achievement coupled with integrity. Jacob Bunn was a father of visionaries, and a patriarch of industry.

For a city that "seemed to hold little promise for greatness,"[317] Springfield was the birthplace of many important institutions and organizations. The Bunn-Lincoln Machine—the prototype of corporate sponsorship of a Republican Presidential candidate, The Bunn Capitol Grocery Company, the Illinois Watch Company, the Springfield Iron Company, the Springfield Marine Bank, the Springfield Home For the Friendless, and the Springfield Library Association were only a few of the notable businesses and charities that were brought about by Jacob Bunn and his associates.

He came as a pioneer from the stony farmland of New Jersey and helped build an empire on the rich farmland of the prairie. The "Old Northwest" has now become the Midwest. Chicago has now taken the lead for industry and power in the state. But Jacob Bunn and his peers helped make it all happen. As an industrial pioneer who managed to build the sociopolitical infrastructure of Illinois, Jacob Bunn was an architect of American empire. Jacob Bunn left a legacy of honorable behavior, civic responsibility, and concrete accomplishments that spawned international corporations that have made a difference to lifestyle, economic health, technology, and creative problem-solving around the world.

During a time when corporate and political scandal seem to be increasingly commonplace phenomena, when mergers continually change the corporate landscape, when business history is rarely taught in business schools, when honor is an increasingly alien concept among students and workers, and when our nation's industrial infrastructure is being disassembled and "outsourced" to laborers in other lands, one should be reminded of what individual honor, integrity, and vision can accomplish at all levels. Truly, Jacob Bunn and others like him have set many examples of achievement, integrity, and success that can be models for the civic, political, philanthropic, educational, and business leaders of the communities of the present day. Let us hope that our current active and aspiring leaders will be willing to follow the many examples of excellence that Illinois commercial and civic leaders, both past and present, have to teach.

Appendix I

General Chronology of the Mechanical Innovations of the Sangamo Electric Company

Year	Product Introduced/Manufactured[318]
1904	Type C meter
1905	Mercury motor watt-hour meter
1906	Type E condenser alternating current mercury meter
1907	Permanent magnet (This device was manufactured for the Wheeler and Schebler Carburetor Company)
1909	Type F for A.C. and Type D-5 for D.C. mercury meters
1910-1911	Type H meter
1911	Delco ampere meter (This meter was manufactured for the Cadillac Motor Car Company)
	Distant dial ampere-hour meter
1912	Molded mercury chamber
	Variable resistor for ampere-hour meters
1913-1916	Ampere-hour meter (This type of Ampere-hour meter was attached to the bodies of approximately 6000 Pullman railroad cars)
1914	H-2 meter

	(This meter was an improved version of the Type H meter of 1910)
	MS ampere-hour meter (The MS ampere-hour meter was manufactured for Delco-Light plants)
1915	Refrigeration apparatus (Refrigeration devices were developed under the Springfield Refrigeration Company, a subsidiary of Sangamo Electric Company)
1917	Street railway meter
1919	LC ampere-hour meter
1921	Type N ampere-hour meter
1923	S-2 meter for export trade
1924	Pressley kit
1924-1931	Type E non self-starting synchronous motor
	Type F synchronous motor
	Electric clock
1925	Type A condenser
	Illini condenser
1930	Electric switch
1932	Electric sign flasher
1933	Three-coin prepayment meter (The three-coin prepayment meter was the first mechanism of its type offered in England, and was made available through British Sangamo, a subsidiary of the Sangamo Electric Company)
1937	Tachograph
1940	Type J meter

(The Type J was an improvement upon its predecessor, the Type H meter)

1941 Components for mechanical time fuses
(The time fuse mechanisms were manufactured pursuant to a war contract between the Sangamo Electric Company and the Frankford Arsenal at Philadelphia)

BC-608 contactor

Range recorder or SONAR equipment
(Range recorders were manufactured for the British Admiralty, through Sangamo Limited, the Canadian subsidiary of the Sangamo Electric Company, and for the United States Navy, through Sangamo Electric Company, the parent operating and holding company based in Springfield, Illinois)

Attack Teacher
(The attack teacher was an electronic mechanism that trained submarine crew in the strategies of antisubmarine operations)

1941-1943 Mica capacitor
(The production of mica capacitors in 1943 increased to fifty times what it had been in 1941)

Paper capacitor

1942 Radio compass tuning loop motors

Transmitter and receiver radio compass indicators

Electrical instrumentation for Link trainers
(These three 1942 products were manufactured in collaboration with the Kollsman Instrument Division of the Square D Company)

1943 Portable anemometer

(Portable anemometers were instruments for determining the speed and direction of the wind, and they were manufactured for the Signal Corps)

Timing mechanism
(Timing mechanisms were manufactured for Navy Ordinance)

Relay mechanism
(Relay mechanisms were manufactured for use in mines and in depth charges)

1943-1944   Indicating instrument
(Sangamo Electric Company manufactured approximately 400,000 indicating instruments during the period from June of 1943 until December of 1944)

1947-1948   Type H motor

Type S time switch

Appendix II

Some Key Institutional Components of the Sangamo Electric Company Corporate Family

The following is a list of several of the subsidiary companies that were either organized or acquired by the Sangamo Electric Company, to achieve a stronger position in the developing electric meter and defense industries of the United States and the world. Each subsidiary is accompanied by a brief description of its primary purpose within the Sangamo Electric family of companies.

- British-Sangamo was organized in 1921 to serve the meter industry and other electrical instrument industries in Great Britain. Later known as "Sangamo-Weston Limited," after its acquisition of Weston Electrical Instrument Company Limited of Great Britain (until the point of becoming a component of Sangamo-Weston, Weston Electrical Instrument Company Limited had been a subsidiary of the Weston Electrical Instrument Corporation of New Jersey, USA), the corporation manufactured a complete line of watthour meters, and had experienced particular success in manufacturing prepayment meters.[319]

- Sangamo Company Limited (Toronto) was organized to establish a market presence in Canada. During the 1930s, the subsidiary specialized in the manufacture of numerous types of watthour meters, as well as industrial motors. The meters were modified slightly to satisfy the various regulations of Canadian industry and trade.

Sangamo Limited was an important center for the exporting of meters.[320] Sangamo Limited received considerable orders from countries such as New Zealand, and the Latin American countries during the 1930s. The subsidiary owned and operated two plants in Toronto, one on George Street, and the other on Stafford Street.[321] Under the leadership of Scott Lynn and George Wellesley Lawrence, Sangamo Company Limited achieved an international market for its numerous products, and achieved a comparably grand reputation.

- The Allied Tool and Machine Company of Chicago was acquired in 1942 pursuant to a need for an internalized tool and die facility, which was becoming increasingly necessary as the production of military apparatus, whose manufacture required tool and die functions, was steadily growing.[322]

- The Lincoln Meter Company of Springfield became a part of the Sangamo family in 1928, and served primarily the public utility sectors, manufacturing ampere and watt demand meters.[323]

- Sangamo Generators, Inc. was formed to acquire the machinery, inventory and facility of the Gothard Manufacturing Company of Springfield, which specialized in the production of civilian and military generators and dynamotors.[324]

- Capitol Aviation, Inc. was acquired in 1958, for the purpose of providing service and maintenance for the aircraft that belonged to the Sangamo Electric Company.[325]

- Sangamo International, Inc. was formed in 1958 as a sales corporation, for the purpose of promoting the sale of Sangamo Electric products in the export trade.[326]

- The D. G. C. Hare Company of New Canaan, Connecticut. In February of 1958, the Sangamo Electric Company acquired all outstanding common stock of the D. G. C. Hare Company of New Canaan, Connecticut. D. G. C. Hare was a small company, but had become well-established as a developer of instrumentation magnetic tape recorders, whose applications as data recording and reproduction mechanisms in the defense industry were manifold.[327]

- The Pickens Realty Corporation was established for the purpose of erecting a new Sangamo Electric factory at Pickens, South Carolina.[328]

Appendix III

Table of Executives and Various Positions Occupied

NOTE: Not all executives are listed in chronological order of succession. The roster is meant to allow the reader to search for a particular name and see generally some of the chief positions that these persons occupied within the enterprise scheme of this book. This roster neither is exhaustive nor is assembled in a rigidly chronological sequence.

The J. Bunn Grocery Company

EXECUTIVES/EMPLOYEES	POSITIONS OCCUPIED
Jacob Bunn	President, Proprietor
T. K. Babcock	Bookkeeper
Elisha Drummond	Assistant Bookkeeper
John Whitfield Bunn	Clerk, President, Proprietor
James Canfield	Clerk
Benjamin Hamilton Ferguson	Clerk
John H. Merriweather	Clerk
John Moran	Porter

Springfield Marine and Fire Insurance Company

EXECUTIVES	POSITIONS OCCUPIED
Antrim Campbell	President
Thomas Condell	President
R. F. Ruth	President
Benjamin Hamilton Ferguson	President
Robert Irwin	Vice President, Secretary
John C. Sprigg	Secretary
Noah Divilbiss	Clerk (chief assistant to Secretary)

Springfield Marine Bank*

Corporate Name changed from Springfield Marine Fire Insurance Company in May 1884; effective July 1, 1884.

EXECUTIVES	POSITIONS OCCUPIED
Benjamin Hamilton Ferguson	President, Chairman
John Whitfield Bunn	President, Chairman
Jacob Bunn, Jr.	President, Chairman
George Wallace Bunn	President, Chairman

Springfield Watch Company

EXECUTIVES	POSITIONS OCCUPIED
John C. Adams	Founder
John Todd Stuart	President
W. B. Miller	Secretary
J. M. Morrow	Sales Manager for NY Branch
John K. Bigelow	Superintendent of Factory
Otis Hoyt	Train Department Foreman
Charles E. Mason	Escape Department Foreman
John Nickerson	Jeweling Dept. Foreman

Illinois Springfield Watch Company

EXECUTIVES	POSITIONS OCCUPIED
Erastus Newton Bates	President
John Whitfield Bunn	Vice President
Frank W. Tracy	Secretary
Otis Hoyt	Superintendent of Factory
Charles E. Mason	Superintendent of Factory

Illinois Watch Company

EXECUTIVES	POSITIONS OCCUPIED
Jacob Bunn	President, Chairman
John Whitfield Bunn	Vice President
Charles Smorowski	Secretary
Jacob Bunn, Jr.	Vice President, President, Chairman
Henry Bunn	Vice President, President, Chairman
Benjamin Hamilton Ferguson	Vice Chairman, Chairman
George F. Johnson	Mechanical Superintendent
George A. Bates	Secretary
Frederic W. Morgan	General Cashier, Credit Manager
Julius W. Armbruster	General Salesman
George W. Chatterton, Jr.	Sales Agent
L. F. Acker	Timing and Adjusting Department Foreman
T. A. Sondal	Finishing Dept. Foreman
William H. Hibbs	Train Department Foreman
G. J. Haendle	Jeweling Dept. Foreman
Jacob Monnett	Screw Department Foreman
George W. Meredith	Machine Dept. Foreman
Charles Gassler	Escape Department Foreman
Cyrus Shinkle	Plate Department Foreman
Charles Nichols	Dial Department Foreman
Joseph Silva	Damaskeening Dept. Foreman
Louis Scharf	Punch Department Foreman
J. S. Clarke	Engraving Dept. Foreman
William Clarke	Balance Staff Dept. Foreman
Ilert Wieties	Gilding Department Foreman

Springfield Iron Company

EXECUTIVES	POSITIONS OCCUPIED
Charles Ridgely	President
John Whitfield Bunn	Vice President
George M. Brinkerhoff	Secretary, Treasurer

Dr. Alphonse Hennin   Senior Chemist, Chemical Engineer
W. E. Mack   Sales Manager, Chicago Branch
C. I. Wickersham   Sales Manager, Chicago Branch
B. L. Keen   Sales Manager, Chicago Branch
William Barret Ridgely   Vice President
Franklin Ridgely   Secretary

Selz, Schwab & Company

EXECUTIVES | POSITIONS OCCUPIED
Morris Selz — Founder, President
Charles H. Schwab — Partner
John Whitfield Bunn — Founder, Vice President
J. Harry Selz — Vice President
Manuel F. Selz — General Manager

Freeport Sugar Company

EXECUTIVES | POSITIONS OCCUPIED
Jacob Bunn — Founder, Financier, Partner
Charles Henry Rosenstiel — Founder, Financier, Partner
Jerome Increase Case — Founder, Financier, Partner

Chicago Republican Company

EXECUTIVES | POSITIONS OCCUPIED
Alonzo W. Mack — Publisher
Charles Anderson Dana — Editor-in-Chief
Van Buren Denslow — Editor-in-Chief
James F. Ballantyne — Editor-in-Chief
Henry M. Smith — Editor-in-Chief
John G. Nicolay — Editor-in-Chief
George D. Williston — Manager
I. Newton Higgins — General Manager
Jacob Bunn — Principal Proprietor, Publisher

Sangamo Electric Company

EXECUTIVES AND ASSOCIATED INSTITUTIONS	POSITIONS OCCUPIED
Jacob Bunn, Jr.	Founder, Financier, President
Henry Bunn	Founder, Financier
Ludwig Gutmann	Founder, Electrical Innovative Visionary
Robert Carr Lanphier	Secretary, President and Chairman
Otis White	Vice President
Donald S. Funk	General Manager, Vice President, President
F. C. Holtz	Vice President of Engineering
Charles Lanphier	Vice President of Purchasing
R. C. Bennett	Vice President of Production
J. H. Holbrook	Treasurer
G. W. Good	Treasurer
J. A. Schimenz	Assistant Treasurer
J. Henry "Dutch" Hodde	Secretary
H. E. Greene, Jr.	Assistant Secretary
C. R. Horrell	General Sales Manager
J. A. Muir	General Superintendent
Continental Illinois National Bank & Trust Company of Chicago	Registrar
First National Bank of Chicago	Transfer Agent
Arthur Young & Company	Auditor

Sangamo Company Limited (Canada)

EXECUTIVES	POSITIONS OCCUPIED
Scott Lynn	President
George Wellesley Lawrence	Vice President, President
W. S. Ewens	Vice President of Sales
Herbert Nehls	General Export Sales Manager

Notes

[1] John Bartlett, *Bartlett's Familiar Quotations*, Justin Kaplan, Ed. 16th ed. Boston: Little, Brown, 1992. 296.

[2] Robert D. Putnam, *Bowling Alone: The Collapse and Revival of American Community*, New York: Simon & Schuster, 2000. 288, 289.

[3] Edward J. Russo, *Jacob Bunn And His Descendants*, Springfield: 1986. 12.

[4] *Ibid.* 4.

[5] *Ibid.* 6.

[6] *Ibid.* 7.

[7] Alta Mae Speulda, "Men Who Made Sangamon," *Illinois State Register*, Springfield: January 31, 1937. Note also that the cemetery marker for Jacob Bunn, Sr., located in the Bunn Family plot in Oakridge Cemetery in Springfield, Illinois, also states Bunn's date of birth as March 18, 1814, and his date of death as October 16, 1897.

[8] Edward J. Russo, *Jacob Bunn And His Descendants*, Springfield: 1986. 7.

[9] *Ibid.* 8.

[10] John Bartlett, *Bartlett's Familiar Quotations*, Justin Kaplan, Ed. 16th ed. Boston: Little, Brown, 1992. 475.

[11] Edward J. Russo, *Jacob Bunn And His Descendants*, Springfield: 1986. 8.

[12] *Ibid.* 10.

[13] *Ibid.* 9.

[14] Richard B. Morris, *et al.,* Eds., *Encyclopedia of American History,* 7th Ed. New York: HarperCollins, 1996. 592.

[15] Arthur M. Schlesinger, Ed., *The Almanac of American History*, New York: Barnes & Noble, 1993. 188.

[16] Edward J. Russo, *Jacob Bunn And His Descendants*, Springfield: 1986. 10.

[17] *Ibid.* 11.

[18] *Ibid.* 11

[19] *Ibid.* 11.

[20] Bruce A. Campbell, *The Sangamon Saga,* Springfield: Phillips, 1976. 17, 18.

[21] *Ibid.* 21.
[22] *Ibid.* 25, 26.
[23] *Ibid.* 25, 26, 42, 43, 49.
[24] *Ibid.* 38.
[25] *Ibid.* 39.
[26] *Ibid.* 38, 39.
[27] *Ibid.* 52.
[28] Edward J. Russo, *Jacob Bunn And His Descendants,* Springfield: 1986. 11, 12, 13.
[29] *Ibid.* 13.
[30] *Ibid.* 13.
[31] *Ibid.* Cited from an advertisement on a page between pp. 14, 15.
[32] *Illinois State Journal*, June 22, 1848. 1 : 2.
[33] *Illinois State Journal*, May 10, 1850.
[34] *Illinois State Journal*, August 15, 1849. 3.
[35] Edward J. Russo, *Jacob Bunn And His Descendants*, Springfield: 1986. 16.
[36] *Illinois State Journal*, November 28, 1849. 2.
[37] Edward J. Russo, *Jacob Bunn And His Descendants*, Springfield: 1986. 16.
[38] *Ibid.* 15.
[39] "Springfield, Illinois City Directory, 1855," Online. *Ancestry.com*, 2 April 2003.
[40] "John W. Bunn," *Journal of the Illinois State Historical Society*, Vol. XIII, No. 1, Springfield: Illinois State Historical Society, April, 1920. 273.
[41] Articles of Incorporation of Bunn And Humphreys, Inc. Approved, October 22, 1928.
[42] *Ibid.*
[43] Certificate of Change in Location of Principal Office, Approved, February 20, 1930.
[44] Articles of Amendment to the Articles of Incorporation of Bunn and Humphreys, Inc. Approved, January 18, 1934.
[45] Articles of Merger of Bunn Capitol Grocery Company and Capitol Grocery Company, June 30, 1937.
[46] James Alfred Ellis, *History of the Bunn Family In America*, Chicago: Romanzo Norton Bunn, 1928. 210.
[47] "John W. Bunn," *Journal of the Illinois State Historical Society*, Vol. XIII, No. 1, Springfield: Illinois State Historical Society, April, 1920. 273, 274.
[48] *Ibid.* 274.
[49] Paul Selby, Ed., *History of Sangamon County Illinois*, Part II. Chicago: Munsell Publishing Company, 1912. 1215.

[50] Paul Selby, Ed., *History of Sangamon County Illinois*, Chicago: Munsell Publishing Company, 1912. 1215, 1216.
[51] Edward J. Russo, *Jacob Bunn And His Descendants*, Springfield: 1986. P. between pp. 31 and 32.
[52] *Ibid.* 28.
[53] Bruce A. Campbell, *The Sangamon Saga*, Springfield: Phillips, 1976. 87.
[54] *Ibid.* 87.
[55] *Illinois State Journal*, August 14, 1857. 3:1
[56] *Ibid.*
[57] Bruce A. Campbell, *The Sangamon Saga*, Springfield: Phillips, 1976. 87.
[58] *Illinois State Journal*, August 14, 1857. 3:1
[59] Bruce A. Campbell, *The Sangamon Saga*, Springfield: Phillips, 1976. 87.
[60] Edward J. Russo, *Jacob Bunn And His Descendants*, Springfield: 1986. 15.
[61] Bruce A. Campbell, *The Sangamon Saga,* Springfield: Phillips, 1976. 64, 71, 101, 122.
[62] *Ibid.* 63.
[63] *Ibid.* 63.
[64] *An Act to promote the construction of Horse Railways in the City of Springfield*, February 18, 1861, General Assembly of Illinois. 1.
[65] *Ibid.* 1, 2, 3.
[66] Annual Reports for Springfield City Railway Company, 1902, 1904, 1908.
[67] Bruce A. Campbell, *The Sangamon Saga*, Springfield: Phillips, 1976. 93.
[68] Edward J. Russo, *Jacob Bunn And His Descendants*, Springfield: 1986. 14, 15.
[69] *Illinois State Journal*, August 29, 1849. 2.
[70] Bruce A. Campbell, *The Sangamon Saga*, Springfield: Phillips, 1976. 109.
[71] Edward J. Russo, *Jacob Bunn And His Descendants*, Springfield: 1986. 27.
[72] *Ibid.* 27.
[73] *Ibid.* 27.
[74] Paul Angle, Ed., *Abraham Lincoln By Some Men Who Knew Him: Being Personal Recollections of Judge Owen T. Reeves, Hon. James S. Ewing, Col. Richard P. Morgan, Judge Franklin Blades, John W. Bunn*, 1950. Reprint by Books For Libraries Press, Freeport, New York, 1969. 102.
[75] *Ibid.* 103, 104.

76 *Ibid.* 109, 111, 112.

77 *Ibid.* 111, 112, 113, 114.

78 *Ibid.* 114, 115.

79 *Ibid.* 115, 116, 117.

80 Richard B. Morris, *et al.* Eds., *Encyclopedia of American History*, 7th Ed. New York: HarperCollins, 1996. 1041.

81 Dumas Malone, Ed., *Dictionary of American Biography*, Vol. 8. New York: Charles Scribner's Sons, 1932. 225-226.

82 George W. Bunn, *The Old Chatterton: A Brief History of a Famous Old Opera House*, Cullom Davis, Ed. Springfield: Sangamon County Historical Society, 1974. 12.

83 Franklin William Scott, *Newspapers And Periodicals Of Illinois 1814 – 1879*, Springfield: Illinois State Historical Library, 1910. 85.

84 *Illinois State Journal*, April 8, 1857. 2 : 1.

85 Dumas Malone, Ed., *Dictionary of American Biography*. Vol. 8. New York: Charles Scribner's Sons, 1932. 228.

86 Richard B. Morris, *et al.* Eds., *Encyclopedia of American History*, New York: HarperCollins, 1996. 699.

87 Dumas Malone, Ed., *Dictionary of American Biography*. Vol. 8. New York: Charles Scribner's Sons, 1932. 226.

88 *"10th Annual Meeting of ISHS," Transactions of the Illinois State Historical Society For the Year 1909*, Springfield: Illinois State Historical Library, Publication No. 14, May 13, 14, 1909. 182.

89 *"Necrology," Journal of the Illinois State Historical Society*, Vol. XVII, No. 3. Springfield: Illinois State Historical Society, October, 1924. 540.

90 John Carroll Power, *History of the Early Settlers of Sangamon County, Illinois*, Springfield: Reprinted, Phillips Brothers, Inc. 1970. 769.

91 Bruce A. Campbell, *The Sangamon Saga*, Springfield: Phillips, 1976. 81.

92 Edward J. Russo, *Jacob Bunn And His Descendants*, Springfield: 1986. 30.

93 Bruce A. Campbell, *The Sangamon Saga*, Springfield: Phillips, 1976. 108.

94 *History of Sangamon County Illinois*, Chicago: Inter-State Publishing Company, 1881. 310.

95 Edward J. Russo, *Jacob Bunn And His Descendants*, Springfield: 1986. 28.

96 Bruce A. Campbell, *The Sangamon Saga*, Springfield: Phillips, 1976. 350.

97 *History of Sangamon County Illinois*, Chicago: Inter-State Publishing Company, 1881. 311, 312.

[98] John W. Bunn's letters to Gen. R. K. Swift, *Final Report of the Military Expedition from Chicago to Cairo*, Part I. Online, Illinois In The Civil War, http://www.illinoiscivilwar.org/orders2.html.

[99] *Ibid.*

[100] *Ibid.*

[101] *Ibid.*

[102] Edward J. Russo, *Jacob Bunn And His Descendants*, Springfield: 1986. 28.

[103] Mary E. Humphrey, "Springfield Home For The Friendless," *Journal of the Illinois State Historical Society*, Vol. XX, No. 1, Springfield: Illinois State Historical Society, Apr. 1927. 138.

[104] Edward J. Russo, *Jacob Bunn And His Descendants*, Springfield: 1986. 29.

[105] Mary E. Humphrey, "Springfield Home For The Friendless," *Journal of the Illinois State Historical Society*, Vol. XX, No. 1, Springfield: Illinois State Historical Society, Apr. 1927. 138, 139.

[106] *Ibid.* 139.

[107] *Ibid.* 140.

[108] Edward J. Russo, *Jacob Bunn And His Descendants*, Springfield: 1986. 29.

[109] Mary E. Humphrey, "Springfield Home For The Friendless," *Journal of the Illinois State Historical Society*, Vol. XX, No. 1, Springfield: Illinois State Historical Society, Apr. 1927. 141.

[110] *Ibid.* 142.

[111] *Ibid.* 142, 143.

[112] *Ibid.* 147, 148.

[113] Edward J. Russo, *Jacob Bunn And His Descendants*, Springfield: 1986. 29.

[114] *Ibid.* Page between pp. 12 and 13

[115] *Illinois State Journal*, August 15, 1849. 3.

[116] *Illinois State Journal*, May 16, 1844. 3:3.

[117] Bruce A. Campbell, *The Sangamon Saga*, Springfield: Phillips, 1976. 56, 57.

[118] *Illinois State Journal*, July 6, 1847. 1: 6.

[119] *Illinois State Journal*, July 6, 1847.

[120] *Illinois State Journal*, January 19, 1850.

[121] *Illinois State Journal*, April 15, 1858. 3:1. July 29, 1858. 3:1.

[122] *An Act to incorporate the Springfield and Pana Railroad Company*. Private Laws of the State of Illinois, Passed At The Twentieth General Assembly, Begun and Held At The City Of Springfield, January 5, 1857. Vol. II. 1024, 1025.

[123] *An Act to incorporate the Pana Springfield and Northwestern*

Railroad Company, 24th General Assembly, State of Illinois, A.D. 1865.

[124] Bruce A. Campbell, *The Sangamon Saga*, Springfield: Phillips, 1976. 95.

[125] *Ibid.* 125, 126.

[126] *An Act to incorporate the Pana, Springfield and Northwestern Railroad Company,* 24th General Assembly, State of Illinois, A.D. 1865. 2.

[127] *Ibid.* 4.

[128] *Ibid.* 3.

[129] *An Act to incorporate the Chicago and Alton Railroad Company*, February 18, 1861. 22nd General Assembly, State of Illinois. 1.

[130] Annual Report of the Chicago and Alton Railroad Company, February 27th, 1932.

[131] *Poor's Railroad and Bank Section*, 1930, 70th Anniversary Edition; New York: Poor's Publishing Co., 1930. 427, 428, 429, 431.

[132] John Moody, *Moody's Analyses of Investments and Security Rating Books*, Part I: Railroad Investments; New York: 1921. 1072, 1074, 1075.

[133] Edward J. Russo, *Jacob Bunn And His Descendants*, Springfield: 1986. 33.

[134] *Ibid.* 45.

[135] C. S. Williams, *Williams' Springfield Directory: City Guide and Business Mirror for 1860-61*, Springfield: Johnson, 1860. 123.

[136] *Springfield City Directory and Business Mirror For 1866*, Springfield: Bronson & Nixon, 1865. 210.

[137] Joseph Wallace, *Past And Present of the City of Springfield and Sangamon County Illinois*, Chicago: Clarke, 1904. 200, 203.

[138] John Whitfield Bunn, Business Card; Illinois Board of World's Fair Commissioners, 1893.

[139] John Whitfield Bunn, Complimentary Entrance Ticket to World's Columbian Exposition Dedication Ceremonies. Chicago, October 11th, 12th and 13th, 1892.

[140] *Certificate of Incorporation of Springfield Iron Company*, August 18, 1871.

[141] *Ibid.*

[142] *History of Sangamon County, Illinois*, Chicago: Inter-State Publishing Company, 1881. 573.

[143] *Poor's Manual*. New York: American Bank Note Company, 1890. 1284.

[144] *History of Sangamon County, Illinois*, Chicago: Inter-State Publishing Company, 1881. 573, 574.

[145] *Ibid.* 573-574.

[146] Victor S. Clark, *History of Manufactures in the United States: 1860-1914*, Washington, D.C.: Carnegie Institution of Washington, 1928. 239.

[147] *Illinois State Journal: Springfield in 1892, Souvenir Supplement*, Springfield, 1892. 83, 84.

[148] *Ibid.* 84.

[149] *Springfield News*, August 7, 1902. 2:3.

[150] *Ibid.* 2:3.

[151] Bruce A. Campbell, *The Sangamon Saga*, Springfield: Phillips, 1976. 105, 106.

[152] *Ibid.* 106.

[153] Curtis Mann, *What's In A Name! The Early History of Riverton, Illinois 1837–1880, Historico*, Springfield: Sangamon County Historical Society, Oct., 2000.

[154] Edward J. Russo, *Jacob Bunn And His Descendants*, Springfield: 1986. 32.

[155] Curtis Mann, *What's In A Name! The Early History of Riverton, Illinois 1837–1880, Historico*, Springfield: Sangamon County Historical Society, Oct., 2000.

[156] Edward J. Russo, *Jacob Bunn And His Descendants*, Springfield: 1986. 32.

[157] Newton Bateman, and Paul Selby, Eds., *Historical Encyclopedia of Illinois and History of Livingston County*, Vol. II, Chicago: Munsell Publishing Company, 1909. 763, 764.

[158] *Pontiac Sentinel*, November 5, 1874. 2.

[159] *Pontiac Sentinel*, October 29, 1874. 2.

[160] M. H. Tilden, *The History of Stephenson County, Illinois*, Chicago: Western Historical Company, 1880. 470, 471.

[161] Genealogical document concerning Charles Henry Rosenstiel and his descendants. (Courtesy of Joe Rosenstiel.)

[162] M. H. Tilden, *The History of Stephenson County, Illinois*, Chicago: Western, 1880. 650.

[163] *Moody's Manual of Railroads and Corporation Securities*, New York: Blair & Co., 1920. 2396, 2397.

[164] *Portrait and Biographical Album of Stephenson County, Ill.*, Chicago: Chapman Brothers, 1888. 443.

[165] M. H. Tilden, *The History of Stephenson County, Illinois*, Chicago: Western, 1880. 471.

[166] *Ibid.* 471.

[167] *Ibid.* 471, 472.

[168] *Portrait and Biographical Album of Stephenson County, Ill.*, Chicago: Chapman Brothers, 1888. 443.

[169] Edward J. Russo, *Jacob Bunn And His Descendants*, Springfield: 1986. 33.

[170] *Ibid.* 33.

[171] Franklin William Scott, *Newspapers And Periodicals of Illinois: 1814-1879*, Springfield: Illinois State Historical Library, 1910. 85.

[172] A. T. Andreas, *History of Chicago*, Chicago: A. T. Andreas, 1884-1886. Reprint, New York: Arno Press, 1975. 497.

[173] J. Seymour Currey, *Chicago: Its History and Its Builders: A Century of Marvelous Growth*, Chicago: S. J. Clark Publishing Company, 1912. 201.

[174] *Ibid.* 201.

[175] *The National Cyclopaedia of American Biography*, Vol. XIV, New York: James T. White & Company, 1910. 228.

[176] *Ibid.* 228.

[177] Axel Madsen, *The Marshall Fields: The Evolution of an American Business Dynasty*, Hoboken: John Wiley & Sons, Inc., 2002. 21, 22.

[178] *The National Cyclopaedia of American Biography*, Vol. XIV, New York: James T. White & Company, 1910. 228.

[179] *Ibid.* 228, 229.

[180] A. T. Andreas, *History of Chicago*, Chicago: A. T. Andreas, 1884-1886. Reprint, New York: Arno Press, 1975. 497.

[181] Franklin William Scott, *Newspapers And Periodicals of Illinois: 1814-1879*, Springfield: Illinois State Historical Library, 1910. 85.

[182] James Harrison Wilson, *The Life of Charles A. Dana*, New York: Harper, 1907. 376.

[183] *History of Sangamon County Illinois*, Chicago: Inter-State Publishing Company, 1881. 548, 549.

[184] Edward J. Russo, *Jacob Bunn And His Descendants*, Springfield: 1986. 25.

[185] *Illustrated Atlas Map of Sangamon County, Ill. Carefully Compiled from Personal Examinations and Surveys*, Illinois: Brink, 1874. 27, 35.

[186] Inventory of the Real and Personal Estate of Jacob Bunn. July 14, 1890. The Hon. Christopher C. Brown, Assignee. 2, 4.

[187] Edward J. Russo, *Jacob Bunn And His Descendants*, Springfield: 1986. 32.

[188] *Illustrated Historical Atlas of Randolph Co. Illinois*, Dallas: Taylor 1990. 37.

[189] Inventory of the Real and Personal Estate of Jacob Bunn. July 14, 1890. The Hon. Christopher C. Brown, Assignee. 4.

[190] A. T. Andreas, *History of Chicago*, Chicago: A. T. Andreas, 1884-1886. Reprinted by Arno Press, New York, 1975. 730, 731.

191 Albert Nelson Marquis, Ed., *The Book of Chicagoans: A Biographical Dictionary of Leading Living Men of the City of Chicago*, Chicago: Albert Nelson Marquis, 1911. 607.

192 *Transactions of the Illinois State Historical Society for the Year 1921*, Publication Number 28 of the Illinois State Historical Library; 22nd Annual meeting of the Society, May 10-11, 1921. 69.

193 *Chicago Daily News*, June 3, 1913.

194 Board of Trade of the City of Chicago, Complimentary Entrance Ticket for John W. Bunn, Treasurer of the Illinois State Board of Agricultural Exhibitions. 1889.

195 New York Produce Exchange, Visitor's Ticket for John W. Bunn. 1894.

196 "John W. Bunn," *Journal of the Illinois State Historical Society*, Vol. XIII, No. 1. April, 1920. Springfield: Illinois State Historical Society, 1920. 277.

197 Anonymous, *Notable Men of Chicago and Their City*, Chicago: *Chicago Daily Journal*, 1910. 325.

Business Card for John W. Bunn; Illinois Board of World's Fair Commissioners. 1893.

198 "For Morris Selz Funeral," *Chicago Daily News*, June 4, 1913.

199 *Transactions of the Illinois State Historical Society for the Year 1921*, Publication Number 28 of the Illinois State Historical Library; 22nd Annual meeting of the Society, May 10-11, 1921. 69.

200 *Ibid.* 69.

201 Anonymous, *Notable men of Chicago and their city*, Chicago: *Chicago Daily Journal*, 1910. 325.

202 "John Whitfield Bunn," *Cecilia Beaux and the Art of Portraiture*, Washington: The National Portrait Gallery, Smithsonian Institution. 122,123.

203 Bruce A. Campbell, *The Sangamon Saga*, Springfield: Phillips, 1976. 40.

204 *Ibid.* 40.

205 *Ibid.* 70, 71.

206 *Ibid.* 71.

207 Paul M. Angle, *The Marine Bank: The Story of the Oldest Bank in Illinois*, Springfield: Springfield Marine Bank, 1931. 4.

208 *Ibid.* 4, 5.

209 *Ibid.* 5.

210 *Ibid.* 5, 6.

211 *Ibid.* 6.

212 *Ibid.* 6, 7.

213 *Illinois State Journal*, March 3, 1851. 3:3.

[214] Paul M. Angle, *The Marine Bank: The Story of the Oldest Bank in Illinois*, Springfield: Springfield Marine Bank, 1931. 7.

[215] *Ibid.* 7.

[216] *Ibid.* 7, 8.

[217] *Ibid.* 8.

[218] *Ibid.* 10.

[219] *Ibid.* 12.

[220] *Ibid.* 15.

[221] Thomas H. Johnson, and Harvey Wish, *The Oxford Companion to American History*, New York: Oxford UP, 1966. 612.

[222] Richard B. Morris, et al. *Encyclopedia of American History*, New York: HarperCollins, 1996. 249, 731.

[223] Thomas H. Johnson, and Harvey Wish, *The Oxford Companion to American History*, New York: Oxford UP, 1966. 612, 613.

[224] Paul M. Angle, *The Marine Bank: The Story of the Oldest Bank in Illinois*, Springfield: Springfield Marine Bank, 1931. 17.

[225] Edward J. Russo, *Jacob Bunn And His Descendants*, Springfield: 1986. 25, 26.

[226] *Illinois State Journal*, March 24, 1859, 1:6.

[227] *Men of Illinois*, Chicago: Halliday Witherspoon, 1902. 425.

[228] Henry Hall, Ed., *America's Successful Men of Affairs: An Encyclopedia of Contemporaneous Biography,* Vol. I, New York: *The New York Tribune,* 1895-1896. 192.

[229] Edward J. Russo, *Jacob Bunn And His Descendants*, Springfield: 1986. 19.

[230] Richard B. Morris, *et al., Encyclopedia of American History*, 7th ed. New York: HarperCollins, 1996. 281, 1005.

[231] *Ibid.* 739.

[232] John F. Stover, *The Routledge Atlas Of The American Railroads*, New York: Routledge, 1999. 41, 48, 49.

[233] Edward J. Russo, *Jacob Bunn and His Descendants*, Springfield: 1986. 35.

[234] *Ibid.* 35.

[235] *Illinois State Journal*, January 3, 1878. 4.

[236] *Illinois State Journal*, January 3, 1878. 4.

[237] *Illinois State Journal*, January 14, 1878. 1:3.

[238] Anonymous, *Illinois Watch Company, Springfield, Illinois, U.S.A.*, Circa. 1913. In possession of the Sangamon Valley Collection at the Lincoln Library, Springfield, Illinois. 1, 2.

[239] *Ibid.* 2.

[240] William Meggers and Roy Ehrhardt, *American Pocket Watches*, Vol. 2. 21.

[241] Anonymous, *Illinois Watch Company, Springfield, Illinois, U.*

S. A., Ca. 1913. In possession of the Sangamon Valley Collection at the Lincoln Library, Springfield, Illinois. 3.

[242] *Ibid.* 3, 4.

[243] *Ibid.* 4.

[244] William Meggers and Roy Ehrhardt, *American Pocket Watches*, Vol. 2. 22.

[245] Anonymous, *Illinois Watch Company, Springfield, Illinois, U. S. A.*, Ca. 1913. In possession of the Sangamon Valley Collection at the Lincoln Library, Springfield, Illinois. 4.

[246] William Meggers and Roy Ehrhardt, *American Pocket Watches*, Vol. 2. 22.

[247] *Ibid.* 23.

[248] *Ibid.*

[249] *Ibid.*

[250] *Ibid.*

[251] *Ibid.*

[252] *Ibid.* 25.

[253] *Ibid.*

[254] *Ibid.* 32.

[255] *Statement of Incorporation of the Illinois Springfield Watch Company.* Filed March 22, 1877.

[256] William Meggers and Roy Ehrhardt, *American Pocket Watches*, Vol. 2. 32.

[257] *Ibid.* 32.

[258] *State Journal Register*, August 11, 1985.

[259] Edward J. Russo, *Jacob Bunn And His Descendants*, Springfield: 1986. P. after 39, before 40.

[260] William Meggers and Roy Ehrhardt, *American Pocket Watches*, Vol. 2. 32.

[261] *History of Sangamon County Illinois*, Chicago: Inter-State Publishing Company, 1881. 574.

[262] *Ibid.* 574.

[263] *Ibid.* 574.

[264] Edward J. Russo, *Jacob Bunn And His Descendants*, Springfield: 1986. 40.

[265] *Ibid.* 40.

[266] William Meggers and Roy Ehrhardt, *American Pocket Watches*, Vol. 2. 35.

[267] Fredric Friedberg, *The Illinois Watch: The Life and Times of a Great American Watch Company*, Atglen: Schiffer Publishing Ltd., 2004. 14.

[268] *Ibid.* 14.

269 John Bartlett *Bartlett's Familiar Quotations*, Justin Kaplan, Ed. 16th ed. Boston: Little Brown, 1992. 693.

270 William Meggers and Roy Ehrhardt, *American Pocket Watches*, Vol. 2. 35.

271 *Ibid.* 35.

272 *Ibid.* 35.

273 *Ibid.* 38.

274 *State Journal Register*, August 11, 1985.

275 Sangamo Electric Company, *Yardstick For Power*, Springfield: Sangamo Electric Company, 1949. 41.

276 Alta Mae Speulda, "Men Who Made Sangamon," *Illinois State Register*, January 31, 1937.

277 *State Journal Register*, August 11, 1985.

278 "Illinois EPA's New Home Has Deep Foundations in City's Past," Illinois Environmental Protection Agency, Online. 10 Oct. 2002.

279 *State Journal Register*, August 11, 1985.

280 *Ibid.*

281 *Ibid.*

282 *Ibid.*

283 *Illinois Watches and Their Makers,* Springfield: Illinois Watch Company, 1920. 16.

284 *Ibid.*

285 Edward J. Russo, *Jacob Bunn And His Descendants*, Springfield: 1986. 40.

286 *Ibid.* 50.

287 *Ibid.*

288 *Ibid.*

289 *Ibid.* 50, 51.

290 Anonymous, *Illinois Watch Company, Springfield Illinois, History*, Undated, Circa. 1920. 1.

291 John Hoffmann, "Lincoln Essay Contests, Lincoln Medals, and the Commercialization of Lincoln," *Journal of the Abraham Lincoln Association*, Volume 24, Number 2, Summer 2003. 49.

292 *Ibid.* 36, 43.

293 *"Bunn Memorial Trust," Journal of the Illinois State Historical Society*. Vol. XVIII, No. 3, Oct. 1925. 1064.

294 *Ibid.* 1064, 1065.

295 *Ibid.* 1063, 1064, 1065.

296 *Sangamo, A History of Fifty Years. Part One: Forty Years of Sangamo* by Robert C. Lanphier, Privately Printed in 1936; *Part Two: Sangamo in Peace and War* by Benjamin P. Thomas, Springfield: Privately Printed, 1949. 3, 4.

297 *Ibid.* v.

298 *Ibid.* 26-144.

299 John Sherman Porter, Ed., *Moody's Manual Of Investments American And Foreign: Industrial Securities*, New York: Moody's, 1931.

300 *Ibid.,* 1934.

301 *Sangamo, A History of Fifty Years. Part One: Forty Years of Sangamo* by Robert C. Lanphier, Privately Printed in 1936; *Part Two: Sangamo in Peace and War* by Benjamin P. Thomas, Springfield: Privately Printed, 1949. 84.

302 *1951 Annual Report,* Sangamo Electric Company. December 31, 1951.

303 *1935 Annual Report,* Sangamo Electric Company. December 31, 1935.

304 *Sangamo, A History of Fifty Years. Part One: Forty Years of Sangamo* by Robert C. Lanphier, Privately Printed in 1936; *Part Two: Sangamo in Peace and War* by Benjamin P. Thomas, Springfield: Privately Printed, 1949. 18.

305 *Ibid.* 18.

306 *1937 Annual Report,* Sangamo Electric Company, December 31, 1937.

307 *Ibid.*

308 *1936 Annual Report,* Sangamo Electric Company, December 31, 1936.

309 *Ibid.*

310 John Sherman Porter, Ed., *Moody's Manual of Investments, American and Foreign: Industrial Securities*, New York: Moody's Investors Service, 1934. 817.

311 *Illinois State Journal,* January 29, 1939.

312 *1938 Annual Report,* Sangamo Electric Company, December 31, 1938.

313 *1945 Annual Report,* Sangamo Electric Company, December 31, 1945.

314 *1956 Annual Report,* Sangamo Electric Company, December 31, 1956.

315 Edward J. Russo, *Jacob Bunn and His Descendants*, Springfield: 1986. 104.

316 Interview with Robert H. Bunn.

317 Edward J. Russo, *Jacob Bunn and His Descendants*, Springfield: 1986. 10.

318 *Sangamo, A History of Fifty Years. Part One: Forty Years of Sangamo* by Robert C. Lanphier, Privately Printed in 1936; *Part Two: Sangamo in Peace and War* by Benjamin P. Thomas, Springfield: Privately Printed, 1949. 26-144.

[319] *1938 Annual Report,* Sangamo Electric Company, December 31, 1938.

[320] *Ibid.*

[321] *1935 Annual Report,* Sangamo Electric Company, December 31, 1935.

[322] *1942 Annual Report,* Sangamo Electric Company, December 31, 1942.

[323] *1938 Annual Report,* Sangamo Electric Company, December 31, 1938.

[324] *1954 Annual Report,* Sangamo Electric Company, December 31, 1954.

[325] *Ibid.*

[326] *Ibid.*

[327] *1958 Annual Report,* Sangamo Electric Company, December 31, 1958.

[328] *1955 Annual Report,* Sangamo Electric Company, December 31, 1955.

Bibliography

An Act to incorporate the Chicago and Alton Railroad Company. 22nd General Assembly, State of Illinois. 1861.

An Act to incorporate the Springfield and Pana Railroad Company. Private Laws of the State of Illinois, Passed At The Twentieth General Assembly, Begun and Held At The City Of Springfield, January 5, 1857. Vol. II.

An Act to incorporate the Pana, Springfield and Northwestern Railroad Company. 24th General Assembly, State of Illinois A.D. 1865. Number 8994. Box 209.

An Act to promote the construction of Horse Railways in the City of Springfield. General Assembly of Illinois. February 18, 1861.

Andreas, A. T. *History of Chicago*, Chicago: A. T. Andreas, 1884-1886. Reprint, New York: Arno Press, 1975.

Angle, Paul M. *The Marine Bank: The Story of the Oldest Bank in Illinois.* Springfield: Springfield Marine Bank, 1931.

_____, Ed. *Abraham Lincoln By Some Men Who Knew Him: Being Personal Recollections of Judge Owen T. Reeves, Hon. James S. Ewing, Col. Richard P. Morgan, Judge Franklin Blades, John W. Bunn.* 1950. Reprint, Freeport, NY: Books for Libraries Press, 1969.

Annual Report of the Chicago and Alton Railway Company, February 27, 1932.

Annual Reports for Springfield City Railway Company, 1902, 1904, 1908.

Annual Report, Sangamo Electric Company, December 31, 1935.

Annual Report, Sangamo Electric Company, December 31, 1936.

Annual Report, Sangamo Electric Company, December 31, 1937.

Annual Report, Sangamo Electric Company, December 31, 1938.
Annual Report, Sangamo Electric Company, December 31, 1942.
Annual Report, Sangamo Electric Company, December 31, 1945.
Annual Report, Sangamo Electric Company, December 31, 1949.
Annual Report, Sangamo Electric Company, December 31, 1951.
Annual Report, Sangamo Electric Company, December 31, 1954.
Annual Report, Sangamo Electric Company, December 31, 1955.
Annual Report, Sangamo Electric Company, December 31, 1956.
Annual Report, Sangamo Electric Company, December 31, 1958.
Anonymous, *Notable Men of Chicago and Their City*. Chicago: *Chicago Daily Journal*, 1910.
Anonymous, *Illinois Watch Company, Springfield, Illinois, U.S.A.*, Circa. 1913. In possession of the Sangamon Valley Collection at the Lincoln Library, Springfield, Illinois.
Anonymous, *Illinois Watch Company, Springfield Illinois, History*, Undated, Circa. 1920.
Articles of Amendment to the Articles of Incorporation of Bunn and Humphreys, Inc. Approved, October 22, 1928.
Articles of Amendment to the Articles of Incorporation of Bunn and Humphreys, Inc. Approved, January 18, 1934.
Articles of Merger of Bunn Capitol Grocery Company and Capitol Grocery Company, June 30, 1937.
Bateman, Newton and Paul Selby, Eds. *Historical Encyclopedia of Illinois and History of Livingston County,* Vol. II. Chicago: Munsell Publishing Co. 1909.
Bartlett, John. *Bartlett's Familiar Quotations*. Justin Kaplan, Ed. 16th ed. Boston: Little Brown, 1992.
Brown, Carolyn Owsley, "Springfield Society Before the Civil War." *Journal of the Illinois Historical Society*. Vol. XV, Nos. 1-2. Springfield: Illinois State Historical Society, 1922.
Bunn, George W. *The Old Chatterton: A Brief History of a Famous Old Opera House*. Springfield: Sangamon County Historical Society, 1974.

Bunn, John W. Board of Trade of the City of Chicago, Complimentary Entrance Ticket for John W. Bunn, Treasurer of the Illinois State Board of Agricultural Exhibitions. 1889.

Bunn, John Whitfield. Complimentary Entrance Ticket to World's Columbian Exposition Dedication Ceremonies. Chicago, October 11th, 12th and 13th, 1892.

Bunn, John W. Letters to Gen. R. K. Swift, *Final Report of the Military Expedition from Chicago to Cairo*, Part I. Online, Illinois In The Civil War, http://www.illinoiscivilwar.org/orders2.html.

"Bunn Memorial Trust." *Journal of the Illinois State Historical Society*. Vol. XVIII, No. 3. Springfield: Illinois State Historical Society, October, 1925.

Business Card for John W. Bunn; Illinois Board of World's Fair Commissioners. 1893.

Campbell, Bruce Alexander. *The Sangamon Saga*. Springfield: Phillips, 1976.

Cecelia Beaux and the Art of Portraiture. "John W. Bunn." Washington, DC: The National Portrait Gallery, Smithsonian Institution.

Certificate of Incorporation of Springfield Iron Company. August 18, 1871.

Chicago Daily News, June 3, 1913.

Chicago Daily News, June 4, 1913.

Clark, Victor S. *History of Manufactures in the United States: 1860 – 1914*. Washington, DC: Carnegie, 1928.

Currey, J. Seymour. *Chicago: Its History and Its Builders: A Century of Marvelous Growth*. Chicago: S. J. Clark Publishing Company, 1912.

Ellis, James Alfred. *History of the Bunn Family in America*. Chicago: Romanzo Norton Bunn, 1928.

Friedberg, Fredric J. *The Illinois Watch: The Life and Times of a Great American Watch Company*. Atglen, PA: Schiffer Publishing Ltd. 2004.

Hall, Henry, Ed., *America's Successful Men of Affairs: An Encyclopedia of Contemporaneous Biography.* Vol. I, New York: The New York Tribune, 1895-1896.

History of Sangamon County Illinois. Chicago: Inter-State Pub. Co., 1881.

Hoffmann, John. "Lincoln Essay Contests, Lincoln Medals, and the Commercialization of Lincoln." *Journal of the Abraham Lincoln Association,* Vol. 24, No. 2, Summer 2003.

Humphrey, Mary E. "Springfield Home For The Friendless." *Journal of the Illinois State Historical Society.* Vol. XX, No. 1. Springfield: Illinois State Historical Society, Apr. 1927.

"Illinois EPA's New Home Has Deep Foundations in City's Past." *Illinois Environmental Protection Agency.* Online. www.epa.state.il.us. 10 Oct. 2002.

Illinois State Journal. Springfield: May 16, 1844.

Illinois State Journal. Springfield: August 29, 1845.

Illinois State Journal. Springfield: July 6, 1847.

Illinois State Journal. Springfield: June 22, 1848.

Illinois State Journal. Springfield: August 15, 1849.

Illinois State Journal. Springfield: August 29, 1849.

Illinois State Journal. Springfield: November 28, 1849.

Illinois State Journal. Springfield: January 19, 1850.

Illinois State Journal. Springfield: May 10, 1850.

Illinois State Journal. Springfield: March 3, 1851

Illinois State Journal. Springfield: April 8, 1857.

Illinois State Journal. Springfield: August 14, 1857.

Illinois State Journal. Springfield: April 15, 1858;

Illinois State Journal. Springfield: July 29, 1858.

Illinois State Journal. Springfield: March 24, 1859.

Illinois State Journal. Springfield: January 3, 1878.

Illinois State Journal. Springfield: January 14, 1878.

Illinois State Journal. Springfield: January 29, 1939.

Illinois State Journal: Springfield in 1892, Souvenir Supplement, Springfield: 1892

Illinois State Register. Springfield: January 31, 1937.

Illinois Watches and Their Makers. Springfield: Illinois Watch Company, 1920.

Illustrated Atlas Map of Sangamon County, Ill. Carefully Compiled from Personal Examinations and Surveys. Illinois: Brink, 1874.

Illustrated Historical Atlas of Randolph Co., Illinois. Dallas: Taylor, 1990.

Insolvency Report for Jacob Bunn. The Hon. Christopher C. Brown, Esq. Reported July 14, 1890.

Inventory of the Real and Personal Estate of Jacob Bunn. July 14, 1890. The Hon. Christopher C. Brown, Assignee.

Johnson, Thomas A., and Harvey Wish. *The Oxford Companion to American History.* New York: Oxford UP, 1966.

"John W. Bunn." *Journal of the Illinois State Historical Society.* Vol. XIII, No. 1. Springfield: Illinois State Historical Society, April 1920.

Lanphier, Robert C., and Benjamin P. Thomas. *Sangamo, A History of Fifty Years. Part One: Forty Years of Sangamo* by Robert C. Lanphier, Privately Printed in 1936; *Part Two: Sangamo in Peace and War* by Benjamin P. Thomas. Springfield: Privately Printed, 1949.

Madsen, Axel. *The Marshall Fields. The Evolution of An American Business Dynasty.* Hoboken: John Wiley & Sons, Inc. 2002.

Malone, Dumas, Ed. *Dictionary of American Biography.* New York: Charles Scribner's Sons, 1932.

Mann, Curtis. *What's In A Name! The Early History of Riverton, Illinois 1837–1880. Historico.* Springfield: Sangamon County Historical Society, Oct., 2000.

Marquis, Albert Nelson, Ed. *The Book of Chicagoans: A Biographical Dictionary of Leading Living Men of the City of Chicago.* Chicago: Albert Nelson Marquis, 1911.

Meggers, William, and Roy Ehrhardt. *Volume 2: American Pocket Watches: Illinois Watch Company.* Heart of America Press, 1985.

Men of Illinois. Chicago: Halliday Witherspoon, 1902.

Moody, John. *Moody's Analyses of Investments and Security Rating Books, Part I: Railroad Investments.* New York. 1921.

Moody's Manual of Investments American And Foreign: Industrial Securities. John Sherman Porter, Ed. New York: Moody's, 1931.

Moody's Manual of Investments American And Foreign: Industrial Securities. John Sherman Porter, Ed. New York: Moody's, 1934.

Moody's Manual of Railroads and Corporation Securities. New York: Blair & Co., 1920.

Morris, Richard B., Jeffrey B. Morris, and Henry Steele Commager, Eds. *Encyclopedia of American History.* 7th ed. New York: HarperCollins, 1996.

National Cyclopaedia of American Biography, The, Vol. XIV. New York: James T. White & Company, 1910.

"Necrology." *Journal of the Illinois State Historical Society.* Vol. XVII, No. 3. Springfield: Illinois State Historical Society, October 1924.

Pontiac Sentinel, October 29, 1874.

Pontiac Sentinel, November 5, 1874.

Poor's Manual. New York: American Bank Note Company, 1890.

Poor's Railroad and Bank Section, 70th Anniversary Edition. New York: Poor's Publishing Co., 1930.

Portrait and Biographical Album of Stephenson County, Ill., Chicago: Chapman Brothers, 1888.

Power, John Carroll. *History of the Early Settlers of Sangamon County, Illinois.* Springfield: Reprinted, Phillips Brothers, Inc., 1970.

Putnam, Robert D. *Bowling Alone: The Collapse and Revival of American Community.* New York: Touchstone, 2000.

Rosenstiel, Joe (courtesy of). Genealogical documents concerning Charles Henry Rosenstiel and descendants.

Russo, Edward J. *Jacob Bunn And His Descendants*. Springfield: Privately Printed, 1986.

Sangamo, A History of Fifty Years. Part One: Forty Years of Sangamo by Robert C. Lanphier, Privately Printed in 1936; *Part Two: Sangamo in Peace and War* by Benjamin P. Thomas. Springfield: Privately Printed, 1949.

Sangamo Electric Company. *Yardstick For Power*. Springfield: Sangamo Electric Company, 1949.

Schlesinger, Arthur M., Ed. *The Almanac of American History*. New York: Barnes & Noble, 1993.

Scott, Franklin William. *Newspapers And Periodicals of Illinois: 1814–1879*. Springfield: Illinois State Historical Library, 1910.

Selby, Paul, Ed. *History of Sangamon County Illinois*, Chicago: Munsell, 1912.

Speulda, Alta Mae. "Men Who Made Sangamon." *Illinois State Register*. Springfield: Jan. 31, 1937.

Springfield City Directory and Business Mirror For 1866. Springfield: Bronson & Nixon, 1865.

Springfield, Illinois City Directory, 1855. Online. *http://www.Ancestry.com* . 2 Apr. 2003.

Springfield News, August 7, 1902.

State Journal Register, August 11, 1985.

Statement of Incorporation of the Illinois Springfield Watch Company. Filed March 22, 1877.

Stover, John F. *The Routledge Historical Atlas of the American Railroads*. New York: Routledge, 1999.

Tilden, M. H. *The History of Stephenson County, Illinois*. Chicago: Western Historical Company, 1880.

Transactions of the Illinois State Historical Society For the Year 1909 (10th Annual Meeting of ISHS). Publication No. 14. Springfield: Illinois State Historical Library, 1909.

Transactions of the Illinois State Historical Society For the Year 1921 (22nd Annual Meeting of ISHS). Publication No. 28. Springfield: Illinois State Historical Library, 1921.

Wallace, Joseph. *Past And Present of the City of Springfield and Sangamon County Illinois*. Chicago: Clarke, 1904.

Williams, C. S. *Williams' Springfield Directory: City Guidelines and Business Mirror for 1860-61*. Springfield: Johnson, 1860.

Wilson, James Harrison. *The Life of Charles A. Dana*. New York: Harper, 1907.

Index

1

1893 World's Columbian Exposition, 110
  William Douglas Richardson, superintendant of grounds and buildings for, 110
1893 World's Fair in Chicago, 110
18th century, 9, 11
19th century, xix, 1, 2, 4, 5, 11, 15, 19, 33, 81, 85, 88, 97, 119, 180, 192, 196

2

20th century, 135, 157, 170, 193, 228, 236

A

A. Collman & Co bank, 125
Abraham Lincoln By Some Men Who Knew Him: Being Personal Recollections of Judge Owen T. Reeves, Hon. James S. Ewing, Col. Richard P. Morgan, Judge Franklin Blades, John W. Bunn, 263
Abraham Lincoln essay contest award medal case, 204
Abraham Lincoln Essay Contest, 199
Abraham Lincoln Presidential Library, xv
Abraham Lincoln. *See* Bunn-Lincoln Machine
Abraham Lincoln's personal bank account, on display at [former Bunn bank] in Springfield, 70
Acker, L. F., 190, 258
Adams, John C., xiii, 180, 181, 186, 201, 220, 257
agricultural machinery
  J. I. Case, 123
Alderman Library of the University of Virginia, xv
Alexander Corn Products, 41
Alexandria, New Jersey, 9
Allied Tool and Machine Company of Chicago, 254
Alsace
  Charles H. Schwab, 135
Alton and Sangamon Railroad Company, 107. *See* Chicago and Mississippi Railroad Company
Alton and Springfield Railroad, 86, 98
Alton Railroad Company, 107. *See* Chicago and Alton Railroad Company
Alton, Illinois, 98, 99, 100, 160
American defense industry and Sangamo Electric Co., 239

American steel industry, 116
American Sugar Refining Company, 127
American watch industry, 193
ammonia-tar salvaging method. *See* Dr. Alphonse Hennin
Amundsen, Roald, 193
an architect of American empire Jacob Bunn, 246
Anderson, Brenda, xv
angle splice bars, 112. *See* Springfield Iron Company
Appleton family
  New American Encyclopedia, publishers, 128
Arkansas
  Battle of, 103
  victims of border warfare, 93
Armbruster, Julius W., 258
Armstrong, H. M., 17
Arntz, Christie, xvi
artesian well drilling, 35, 36
Arthur Young & Company, 260
"as good as wheat in the mill," 170
"as safe as J. Bunn's Bank," 170
Assistant Secretary of War Charles Anderson Dana, 128
Associated Press Franchise of the *Morning Post,* Chicago, 131
automotive industry
  Sangamo Electric Co. and, 235

B

Babcock, A. C., 128
Babcock, T. K., 23, 256
Baker, Edward L., 88
Baker, Robert, 143
Ballantyne, James F., 132, 259
Baltimore & Ohio Railroad Company, 10, 108, 146
Baltimore, Maryland, 100, 123
bank director, 3
Bank One Corporation, 151, 165
Bank One Springfield, xv, xvii
Banking House of N. H. Ridgely, 35
Banking Office of J. Bunn, 35
banking sector of Springfield, 139
bankruptcy, 118, 119, 173, 232
Barret, James A., 102
Barryman & Rippon
  and Springfield Watch Company, 181
Bates, Erastus Newton, 186, 257
Bates, George A., 258
Battle of Jackson
  Civil War, 31
Bauer, Kim, xv
Beard, William, 118
Beard-Hickox Coal Company, 113, 116
Beardstown, Illinois, 6, 14
Beaux, Cecilia
  portrait painter, John Whitfield Bunn, 150
Beckwith, Milan S., 102
beet sugar industry, 119, 122, 124, 126, 127, 228. *See* sugar beets
Bennett, R. C., 260
Berlin, Germany, 233
Bethlehem Steel, 116
Bethlehem, Pennsylvania, 116
Bettie Stuart Institute, The, 87
Big Four, the
  Case, Erskine, Baker, Bull, 143
Bigelow, John K., 181, 257
Birmingham, Alabama, 236
bituminous coal deposits, 116
Black, George N., 181
blacksmith, 16, 113
blacksmith shops, 113

Blades, Judge Franklin, 263
Bláthy, Ottó Titusz
　electrochemical engineer from Hungary, born 1860. *See* Ludwig Gutmann, who studied with him in Budapest
Bloomer Girls baseball team Illinois Watch Co., 193
Bloomington, Illinois, 24, 25, 26, 46, 73
Board of Commissioners of the 1893 Chicago World's Fair, 30
Board of Health, 17
bolt and nut works, 113
Bone, John, 103
Bon-Ton China Shop, 32. *See* crockery
Boston, Massachusetts, 236
Bowen, G. P., 95
Bowling Alone, 2
Boynton, David Bunn, xv
Brayman, Mason, 164
Breckinridge, Preston, 102, 103
brewer, 117
Brinkerhoff, George M., 111, 112, 258
British Admiralty, 251
British Sangamo, 237, 238, 250
Broadwell, Norman, 88, 103
Brown, Bettie Stuart
　wife of Christopher Brown, 88
Brown, Christopher C., 38, 39, 88, 158, 173, 174, 175
　Judge, 8
Brown, James N., 85, 99
Buchanan
　President, 79
Budapest, Hungary, 233
Buenos Aires, Argentina, 236
Bull, Stephen, 143
Bunn & Humphreys, Inc., 24, 25, 26. *See* grocery business

Bunn and Humphreys Co.
　a grocery business, 25
Bunn and Humphreys Company
　Bloomington Directors of the first Board
Howard Humphreys, Rogers Humphreys, John E. Hall, A. C. Flood, and O. W. Johnson, 25
Springfield Directors of first Board
George Wallace Bunn (son of Jacob Bunn) and Willard Bunn (son of George W. Bunn and grandson of Jacob Bunn), 25
Bunn Capitol Company, 28. *See* Bunn Capitol Grocery Company
Bunn Capitol Grocery Company, xi, 6, 24, 26, 47, 59, 245, 246. *See* grocery business
Bunn Capitol Grocery Company CoffeeCoupon, 46
Bunn Capitol, Inc., xv. *See* Bunn Capitol Grocery Company
Bunn dynasty, 187
Bunn family, 68, 95
Bunn family's legacy, 228
Bunn Memorial Trust, 230-233
"Bunn Special" Railroad pocket watch, xiv
Bunn, Alice Edwards, viii, 170, 230, 232
　daughter of Jacob Bunn, 170
Bunn, Edward, 9
Bunn, Elizabeth Ferguson, 134, 174. *See* Ferguson, Elizabeth Jane; Bunn, Mrs. Jacob; Bunn, Elizabeth J.
Bunn, Elizabeth J. *See* Bunn, Elizabeth Jane Ferguson; Bunn, Elizabeth Ferguson; Ferguson, Elizabeth J.; Ferguson, Elizabeth Jane

Bunn, Elizabeth Jane Ferguson, 32. *See* Ferguson, Elizabeth Jane
   Mrs. Jacob Bunn. *See* Mrs. Bunn p. 177
   photo, 48
Bunn, George Regan, vii, xvi, 245.
Bunn, George Regan, great-grandson of Jacob Bunn, 245
Bunn, George W., Sr., 25. *See* George Wallace Bunn
Bunn, George Wallace, xi, 54, 58, 59, 86, 109, 134, 230, 232, 243, 257
Bunn, George Wallace, Jr., 197 grandson of Jacob Bunn. *See* George Wallace Bunn [Sr.]
Bunn, Henry, 10
   father of Jacob and John Whitfield Bunn, 10
   b. 1772, 10
   married to Mary Sigler, 10
Bunn, Henry
   son of Jacob Bunn, 134, 154, 198, 230, 232, 235, 239, 243, 244, 258, 260
   born 1858, son of Jacob Bunn, 134
Bunn, J.
   Jacob, 134
Bunn, J., Grocery Company, 6
Bunn, Jacob (Grandfather of Jacob Bunn)
   b. 1736, 10
Bunn, Jacob, i, iii, ix, xi, xii, xiii, xiv, xv, xvi, xviii, xix, 1-6, 8-13, 15, 16, 18-20, 22, 23, 25, 27-35, 37-43, 45, 48, 54, 59, 70, 72, 73, 75, 76, 81, 82, 83, 85-89, 92, 94-103, 106-110, 113, 117-122, 124-129, 131-134, 139, 141, 142, 146, 149, 151, 153, 156, 158, 160, 163-165, 167-170, 172-178, 181, 184, 186-189, 193, 196-202, 219, 227, 228-230, 232, 233, 238, 239, 243, 245-247, 256-259
   and Lincoln
      a commercial associate, legal client, political ally, banker, supporter, and kingmaker, and friend, 86
   and repaying bank debts, 196
   b. 1814, 10
   death of, 1897, 197
   President of re-organized Illinois Watch Co., 1877, 188
Bunn, Jacob and Elizabeth, 95
Bunn, Jacob and John W., 68
Bunn, Jacob, Jr., 134, 198, 199, 202, 230, 232-234, 239, 243, 244, 258, 260
   portrait of, 223
   son of Jacob Bunn, 134
Bunn, Jacob, sense of duty and honor, 229
Bunn, Jacob, Sr., 232, 233, 245. *See* Jacob Bunn
Bunn, John W., 108, 109, 137. *See* Bunn, John Whitfield
Bunn, John W. Company, xi, 24, 50
Bunn, John Whitfield, xi, xii, xiv, 23, 24, 27-32, 34, 51, 60, 63, 70-80, 83, 85, 86, 90, 91, 97, 104, 108, 110-112, 115-117, 134, 135, 137-140, 147, 148, 150, 152, 168, 169, 181, 184, 199, 219, 243, 246, 256-259
   as a young businessman, 43
   as Special Messenger, Civil War, 90
   as treasurer of the Board of [the 1893] World Fair's Commissioners, 110
   brother of Jacob, 23
Bunn, Mrs.

Elizabeth Ferguson Bunn, wife of Jacob, 177
Bunn, Robert H., xv. *See* Bunn, Robert Hatcher; Bunn Capitol Grocery Company
Bunn, Robert Hatcher, 28, 47
Bunn, Ruth Regan, viii
  wristwatch, 219
Bunn, two of their sons
  Henry and Jacob Bunn, Jr., 177
Bunn, Sarah Irwin, viii
Bunn, Willard, vii, xvi, 25, 219
Bunn, Willard, III, xv
Bunn, William, Henry, George Wallace
  sons of Jacob Bunn, 177
Bunn-Lincoln, 71. *See* Bunn-Lincoln Machine
Bunn-Lincoln Machine, 53, 70, 71, 74, 77, 79, 81, 85, 86, 246
  a network of friendship and promotion, 79
Bunn-Lincoln Machine as the prototype of corporate sponsorship of a Republican Presidential candidate, 246
Bunn-O-Matic coffeebrewer, 245
Bunn-O-Matic Corporation, 245, 246
Bunn-Woods building, 168
"Bunny Brand," 27
business history, 247
Butler, William, 102
Butts, Connie, xv

C

Cadillac Motor Car Company
  Delco ampere meter, 249
Cairo, Illinois, 90
Calhoun, 17. *See* Springfield, names for
Calhoun, John, 99
California, 32, 138
Call, Matthew Baldwin, xv
campaign, 4, 72, 76, 79, 81, 83, 86
Campbell, Antrim, xii, 153, 164, 256
Campbell, Bruce Alexander, xv. *See* Campbell, Bruce A.
Canadian Stock Exchange
  Sangamo Electric Co., 236
Canedy, P. C., 95
Canfield, James, 23, 256
Canton, Illinois, 128
Cantrall, William G., 16
capitalists, 99, 101, 133
Capitol, xii,
Capitol Aviation, Inc., 254
Capitol City Band
  and Illinois Watch Co. Band, Springfield Municipal Band, 194
Capitol Grocery Company, 26
Capps, Jabez, 17
carding machine, 16
Carman, Jacob, 16
carpenter shops, 113
Carpenter, George, 38, 39
Carrier Library of James Madison University, xviii
Carter, J. T., 87
Carter, Munson, 103
Case, Jerome Increase, xii, 1 22, 123, 124, 126, 141-143, 259
Catron, B. L.
  Bunn heirs and Bunn Memorial Trust, 230
Cavanagh, Bob, xv
Champaign County, Illinois, 16
Charleston, Illinois, 23
Chase, Salmon P., 78
Chatsworth sugar factory, 121
Chatsworth, Illinois, 7, 119, 120, 127

Chatterton Jewelry Store, 37
Chatterton, George W., xvi, 205
Chatterton, George W., Jr., 258
Chestnut, John A., 88
Chicago Alton and St. Louis Railroad Company, 107
Chicago and Alton Railroad, 114, 146
   and Baltimore and Ohio Railroad, 108
Chicago and Alton Railroad Company, xii, 7, 106, 107, 108, 146, 202
Chicago and Mississippi Railroad Company, 107. *See* Alton and Sangamon Railroad Company; Chicago Alton and St. Louis Railroad Company
Chicago Board of Trade, 137
Chicago Board of Trade regiment, 130
   organized by John Villiers Farwell. *See* Civil War
Chicago Club, 137
Chicago Home for Jewish Orphans
   and Charles H. Schwab, 138
   Charles H. Schwab, 148
Chicago Papers
   newspapers and Jacob Bunn, bank closing, 176
Chicago Republican
   and Bunn. *See* newspapers newspaper, 127, 129, 133, 139, 149
Chicago Republican Company, 129, 139, 149
Chicago Republican newspaper, 7
   Jacob Bunn, principal owner of, 127
Chicago Republican Newspaper Company, 7, 127, 128
Chicago Republican printing works
   and Great Fire of 1871, 132
Chicago Stock Exchange
   Sangamo Electric Co., 236
Chicago tabernacle
   Farwell, Moody, 131
Chicago Tribune, 129, 133, 134. *See* newspapers
Chicago World's Fair, 31
Chicago, Illinois, 38, 84, 85, 90-92, 106, 110, 114, 116, 120, 127, 128, 130-132, 135, 192
Childs, Henry, 128
choral society, 17
Christian County, Illinois, 22, 102, 105
Civil War, 7, 31, 52, 53, 73, 79, 88-90, 92, 95, 117, 130, 131, 166
   Military Expedition from Chicago to Cairo, John Whitfield Bunn, messenger, 265
Civil War pensions, 79
Clark, Professor
   Chatsworth sugar factory, 121
Clarke, J. S., 191, 258
Clarke, William, 191, 258
Clear Lake Township, Illinois, 134
Cleveland Herald
   and Hanna, 82
Cleveland Opera House
   and Hanna, 82
Cleveland street railway system
   and Hanna, 82
Cleveland, Ohio, 82
coal, 7, 36, 82, 111, 113, 116-118, 179, 228
coal companies, 116
coal deposits, 36, 116, 117
coal entrepreneur, 4
coal industry, 36, 116, 117
coal mining, 117

coal rights, 7, 118. *See* coal
coal, Riverton coal mine, 118
coal, the "North Mine," at the Henry Converse farm, 118
Cohlmeyer, Jim, xv
Colorado, 194
Commissioner of Pensions of the State of Illinois, 31
Compagnie Case de France, 124. *See* J. I. Case
Company B, 114th Illinois Infantry, 31
Comptroller of the City of Chicago
    Charles H. Schwab, 138, 148
Condell, Thomas, 256
Confederacy, 91
Confederate attack, 90
Conkling, Clinton, 41
Connecticut, 55, 169, 234
Continental Illinois National Bank & Trust Company of Chicago, 260
Converse, Henry, 118
Cooley
    and Marshall Field, John Villiers Farwell, 149
Cooley, Farwell, Wadsworth and Company, 130
Cooley, Wadsworth & Company dry goods, Chicago, 130
Corn Exchange National Bank of Chicago
    J. Harry Selz, Director of, 147
corporate and political scandal [in the 20th and 21st centuries], 247
corporate landscape, 247
cotton, 16, 166
"Cotton is King"
    Senator Hammond, 166
Cox, Thomas, 16
crockery business, 32
Crockett, "Davy", 16

Crookes, Septimus, 106
Cullom Act
    Interstate Commerce Commission. *See* Cullom, Shelby Moore
Cullom, Shelby Moore, xii, 103, 140
    Congressman, Senator, and Governor of Illinois, 104
    Senator, 104
Curran, Isaac B., 79
Currier, D. G., 181

D

D. G. C. Hare Company of New Canaan, Connecticut, 255
Daily Journal, 21. *See* newspapers
Dana, Charles Anderson, 128, 129, 131-133
    Chicago Republican newspaper; Horace Greeley; Edwin Stanton, 128, 129, 259
Davis, Dr. Evan, xv
Davis, Katherine Sankey, xvi
Dean, W., 181
deep-shaft coal mine, 118
defense contracting, 239
defense sectors of the United States, 239
defense technology markets, 241
Delco-Light plants
    MS ampere hour meter, 250
Democratic city, Springfield, 75
Democratic Press, 132. *See* newspapers
Denslow, Van Buren, 132, 259
Dickerman, Watson Bradley
    employee of J. Bunn Bank, and later president of the New York Stock Exchange and president of the Norfolk & Southern

Railroad Company, and director of Long Island Loan & Trust Company, 169
Diller, Jonathan Roland, 17
distillery, 7, 16, 118
Divilbiss, Noah, 256
Dominick and Dickerman brokerage firm, 170
Dominick, W. G., 170
Douglas, Judge Stephen, 74, 75
Douglas, Lucretia (Wheeler) Johns, xi, 54
Doyle, Don Harrison, 3
druggist, 17
Drummond, Elisha, 23, 256. *See* grocery business
Dryer, John, 17
Du Page County, Illinois, 128
Dubois, Jesse K., 85, 128, 132
Duffield, W. B., 100
Dunlap, James, 98
Dunne, Governor of Illinois, 137

E

Earl Gregg Swem Library, College of William and Mary, xvi
Eastman, Asa, 103
Eastman, Asa and George, 17
Edwards, Benjamin S., 38, 39
Ehrenhart, Jane, xvi
electric meter and defense industries, 253
electric meter industry, 233, 239
Eleroy, Illinois and Rosenstiel, 123
Elgin and Waltham watch companies, 184, 193
Elgin Watch Company, xiv, 190, 201
Elgin Watch Company pocket watch, 220
Elgin, Illinois, 181
Ellis, Jacob, 16
Emmerson, Louis L. Secretary of State, of Illinois, 25
employee training program Sangamo Electric Co., 242
Enfield, England British-Sangamo plant, 238
Engineering Department Sangamo Electric Co., 242
England, 9
English British, 17
Enlow, Susan, xvi
Enos, Pascal P., 99, 100, 101
entrepreneurship, xix, 1, 32, 34, 81, 116, 119
Erskine, Massena B., 143
European markets, 171
Evey, John, 17
Ewens, W. S., 260
Ewing, Hon. James S., 263
Ewing, R. B., 100

F

Family Center of Sangamon County, 95. *See* Home For the Friendless, The Springfield
Farwell brothers, 131
Farwell, Charles Benjamin, xii, 130, 149
Farwell, Field & Company Chicago [John Villiers Farwell, Marshall Field], 130
Farwell, John V., 130
Farwell, John Villiers, xii, 128, 129, 149
Federal Treasury, 19
Ferguson, Benjamin and Alice, 197

Ferguson, Benjamin and Sarah Irwin
  parents of Elizabeth Jane, 48
Ferguson, Benjamin Hamilton, xii, 27, 28, 31, 32, 41, 134, 153, 169, 199, 246, 256, 257, 258. *See* Ferguson, Benjamin
Ferguson, Benjamin Hamilton
  bank president, 31
Ferguson, Elizabeth Jane, 31, 51, 72. *See* Bunn, Elizabeth J. *See* Bunn, Elizabeth F. *See* Bunn, Elizabeth Jane Ferguson
Ferguson, Sarah Irwin, 48, 51
  mother of Elizabeth Jane Ferguson Bunn, 48
Ferguson, William, 32, 134. *See* Elizabeth Ferguson Bunn
Field, Marshall, 130, 149
  Farwell, Chicago companies, 130
Finley, Thomas, 102
Fire Insurance Company, 139
First Methodist Episcopal Church of Springfield
  construction project of William D. Richardson, 110
first-mover advantage, 124
First National Bank, 37
First National Bank of Chicago, 260
First Presbyterian Church, Springfield, 51
  Presbyterian church of the Bunns and Fergusons, 51
Flood, A. C., 25
Fondey, William B., 35, 102, 163
food service corporations, 24. *See* Bunn Capitol. *See* Bunn Capitol Grocery Company
Forrest, J. K. C., 128
fossil fuel, 36
Fowler, Roger, 91

France, 233
Frankford Arsenal at Philadelphia
  mechanical time fuses, 251
"Franklin House," 95
Freeport Opera House, 121, 122
Freeport Public Library, xviii
Freeport Sugar Company, 122, 124, 125, 141, 259
Freeport Triumvirate, The, xii, 122, 127, 142
Freeport, Illinois, 120, 128
  and Charles Henry Rosenstiel, 122
French, A. W., 88
French, Dr., 167
French, Mason, 102
Friedberg, Fredric J., xvi, 190
Frink, William S., 102, 103
frontier region, xix, 1
Funk, Donald S., 239, 240, 241, 242, 244, 260
Furry, Dr. William, xvi

G

G. A. Colby & Co, 125
Galena, Illinois, 160
Garvert, Linda, xvi
Gassler, Charles, 258
Gaulard and Gibbs
  engineers in France, 233
Gay, Farrell, xvi
general store, 17
General Time Instruments Company, 239
General Time Instruments Corporation
  Robert Carr Lanphier, director of, 222
Gennert and Bunn partnership
  sugar industry, 120
Gennert, Ernst T., 121
Gennert, Gottlieb, 121

and Ernest T. Gennert, 119
George Pasfield House, The, xvii
German and Japanese submarines
   Sangamo Electric Co. apparatus and destruction of, 241
German immigrants, 119, 135, 138
German language newspaper, 73
German population, 73
Germania Sugar Company, 7, 119, 120, 121, 125
Gilbert, E. M., 106
Gilder, Richard Watson
   author of book on Lincoln, 150
Glassler, Charles, 190
global industry
   watch company, 180
Globe newspaper, 23. *See* newspapers
"Golden Age," 27
Good, G. W., 260
Goodrich, William A., 102, 103
Gothard Manufacturing Company of Springfield, 254
Goudy, Calvin, 102, 103
Grabarek, Dave, xvi
Grand Army of the Republic, 31. *See* Civil War
Grant, Ulysses S., viii, 130
Great Britain, 238
Great Fire of Chicago, 8, 132. *See* Chicago
Great Western Railroad, 109
Greeley, Horace, 12, 128. *New York Tribune. See* John Babsone Lane Soule
Greene, H. E., Jr., 260
Greer, Elizabeth Taylor, xvi
Greer, T. Keister, xvi
grist mills, 16
grocery, 20, 21, 30, 82, 245

grocery business, 6, 14, 19, 21-34, 97
grocery store, 18
Gutmann meter, 244
Gutmann, Ludwig, 238, 239, 244, 260
   electric meter, 233
   Gutmann meter, 234
   invention, 233

H

Haendle, G. J., 190, 258
Hall, Frederick H., 129
Hall, John E., 25
Hall, William B., 102, 103
Hamilton & White
   dry goods, Chicago, 130
   dry goods, John Villiers Farwell, 149
Hamilton Watch Company
   and Sangamo Electric Co. in Springfield, 237
   Springfield Division, 237
Hamilton Watch Company of Lancaster, Pennsylvania, 236
Hamilton Watch Company of Pennsylvania, 220
Hamlin & Day
   dry goods, Chicago, 130
   dry goods, John Villiers Farwell, 149
Hampden-Sydney College, xv
Hammond, Senator James H. of South Carolina, 166
Hanna, Marcus, 81, 82, 85
   grocery business, 82
Hanna-McKinley Machine, 81
Hanna-McKinley Political Machine. *See* Hanna-McKinley Machine; Bunn-Lincoln-Machine
Harlew, George N.
   Secretary of State, 185

Harner, Jo Anna Lynn
   factory conditions, Illinois Watch Co., 194
Harris, Kathryn M., xvi
Harrison, Peyton, 103
Harrison, President Benjamin
   for whom F. K. Whittemore served as Acting Asst. Treasurer of the United States, 169
hat manufacturer, 17
Havemeyer, Henry Osborne
   sugar, 127
Hawley, E. B., 88
Hay, Charles E., 112
Hayes, H. B., 112
Hazard, J. G.
   Charles Anderson Dana, editors, 128
Hennin, Dr. Alphonse, 259
   ammonia-tar salvaging method, 114
   The Hennin Method. *See* Springfield Iron Company (and p. 114)
Herndon, Archer, 16
Herndon, Elliott, 103
Herndon, William H., 87
Hibbard, H. N., 132
Hibbs, William H., 190, 258
Hickox, Virgil, xvi, 100, 101, 102, 113
Hieronymus, Dennis, xvii
Higgins, I. Newton, 259
historical impact of the watchmaking industry on the railroad industry, 191
Hodde, J. Henry "Dutch," 260
Hoffmann, Dr. John, xvii
Hohenstein, Dr. Kurt, xvii
Holbrook, J. H., 230, 260
Holtz, F. C., 260
Home For the Friendless, The Springfield, 94, 95, 246
   photo, 52
honorable repayment of the debts
   Bunn family and, 174
Horrell, C. R., 260
Horse Railways in the City of Springfield, 263
Hough, J. A., 164
Houmes, Barry, xvii
Howlett, Parley L., 117, 118
   coal seam in town, 117
Hoyt, Otis, 181, 184, 257
Humphreys, Howard, 25
Humphreys, J. F. & Co.. *See* grocery business
Humphreys, Rogers, 25
Hunterdon County, New Jersey, ix, 9, 10, 13, 28. *See* Bunn home in New Jersey
Hurst & Taylor, 17
Hurst, Charles R., 35

I

ICC, 104. *See* Cullom; Interstate Commerce Commission
Iles Junction, Illinois
   coal seam, Jacob Loose, 117
Iles, Elijah, 15, 16, 37. *See* Kentucky
Illinois & Pacific Telegraph Company, 37
Illinois and Mississippi Telegraph Company, 37
Illinois Athletic Club, 147
Illinois Board of World's Fair Commissioners, 137
Illinois Centennial Commission, 137
Illinois Central Railroad, 90
Illinois coal industry, 116
Illinois College, 239
Illinois farmland, 134
Illinois iron and steel industry, 116

- 293 -

Illinois Journal, 162
    newspaper. *See* newspapers
Illinois River, 13, 16, 98, 104
"(Illinois) Springfield Watch Company"
    label for watches made by Springfield Watch Company in Illinois for a time, 185
Illinois Springfield Watch Company, xiii, 8, 185, 186, 187, 207
    new name, in 1877, of Springfield Watch Company to distinguish it from the New York Watch Company's "Springfield" watches, 185
Illinois State Archives, xv, xvii, xviii
Illinois State Board of Agricultural Exhibitions
    John W. Bunn, Treasurer of, 137
Illinois State Capitol, xi, xii
Illinois State Historical Library, xv, xvi, xvii, xviii
Illinois State Journal, 97, 98
Illinois State Register, 35, 37, 192. *See* newspapers
Illinois State Senator, 19
Illinois steel industry, 116
Illinois Watch
    The Life and Times of a Great American Watch Company, xvi
Illinois Watch. *See* Illinois Watch Company.
Illinois Watch Co. Band, 193
Illinois Watch Company, xi, xii, xiii, xiv, 8, 29, 31, 32, 49, 50, 59, 153, 154, 186-193, 195-199, 201-203, 205, 206, 208, 213-217, 220, 223, 234, 236, 245, 246

advertisement in *The American Magazine,* 212
advertisment, *Saturday Evening Post,* 209, 210
portrait of Lincoln, 49
Women's Club, xiv
Illinois Watch Company wireless station, 195
Illinois Watch Company Wireless Station
    photo, 216
Illinois Watch factory, xiv. *See* Illinois Watch Company
Illinois Watch: The Life and Times of A Great American Watch Company, The
    the authoritative book on vintage Illinois Watch Co. wristwatches. *See* Fredric J. Friedberg
Indian Commissioner
    John Villiers Farwell, 130
Indian Queen Tavern, 16
Indiana, 99, 100, 175
Indians, 16
indicating instruments, 238
industrial pioneer, 246
integrity, vii, xix, 1, 2, 5, 11, 23, 33, 71, 77, 80, 138, 164, 177, 232, 236, 241, 243-247
International Order of Odd Fellows, 168
Inter-Ocean
    newspaper, 132. *See Chicago Republican* newspaper
Interstate Commerce Commission, 104, 108, 140. *See* ICC; Shelby Cullom
Iowa, 175
iron and steel industry, 113
iron company, 228
iron making, 115
Irwin, Robert, xiii, 153, 163, 164, 165, 256
"A. Lincoln's" signature for

new bank account, 165
Iselin, Adrian, 106

J

J. and J. W. Bunn Company, 24. *See* grocery business
J. Bunn
   grocery, 20
J. Bunn Bank, xiii, 7, 8, 82, 89, 110, 119, 139, 156, 159, 167-170, 172-175, 177, 178, 188, 229, 230, 232
J. Bunn Grocery, ix, xi, 22
J. Bunn Grocery Company, ix, xi, 19-23, 27, 31, 32, 33, 45, 46, 256. *See* grocery
J. F. Humphreys & Co., 24, 25. *See* grocery business
J. I. Case & Company, 143
J. I. Case Company
   offices in US, Europe, and South America, 124
J. I. Case Threshing Machine Company, 123
J. P. Morgan and Company, 165
J. V. Farwell Company. *See* John V. Farwell Company
Jackson, Mississippi, 236
Jacksonville, Illinois, 98, 160, 239
Jacob Bunn legacy, 30, 232
Jay Cooke & Company (bank in Philadelphia)
   failure of, 1873, 171
John V. Farwell. *See* John Villiers Farwell
John V. Farwell Company, 149
John W. Bunn. *See* Bunn, John Whitfield
John W. Bunn & Company, xi, 44
John W. Bunn and Company, 25. *See* grocery business
John W. Bunn And Company
   and J. F. Humphreys & Co., 25
John Whitfield Bunn
   photo as elderly man, 218
Johnson, George F., 191, 258
Johnson, George Penn, 32
Johnson, Mr.
   wireless operator, Illinois Watch Co., 195
Johnson, O. W., 25
Jones, Frank Hatch, viii
Jones, Melinda, viii
Journal of the Illinois State Historical Society, 29, 272

K

Kankakee, Illinois, 128
Karwowski, Gerald, xvii
Keefer, William E., 35
Keen, B. L., 259
Kelley, Elisha, 15. *See* Springfield, name of. *See* North Carolina
Kentucky, 15
Kett, Dr. Joseph F., Corcoran Professor of History, University of Virginia, xvii
Keyes, Charles A., 88
king-makers
   Bunn, Hanna, 82
Koerner, Governor Gustavus, 85
Kollsman Instrument Division of the Square D Company and Sangamo Electric Co., 251
Konkling, W. J., 184
Kullberg, Professor William, 121

L

La Salle, Illinois, 239
labor environment
   Illinois Watch Co., 194

laborers, female
    at Illinois Watch Co., 194
Lamb, James L., 85, 164
Lamb, John C., 163
Lanphier Eulogy, 240, 243
Lanphier, Charles, 260
Lanphier, Charles H., 88, 102, 242, 244
    older son of Robert Carr Lanphier, 239
Lanphier, Robert Carr, 222, 223, 234, 235, 237, 238, 239, 240, 244, 260
    photo, xiv,
    portrait of, 222
Lanphier, Robert Carr, Sr. *See* Robert Carr Lanphier, Robert C. Lanphier
Latin America, 254
law, 103
Lawrence, George Wellesley, 254, 260
Lawrenceville School, The, 59
Lee, David, xvii
legacies
    Jacob Bunn, 30, 198, 200
legacy, 1, 2, 5, 11, 19, 23, 27, 28, 30, 32, 85, 104, 138, 168, 178, 197, 198, 200, 228, 236, 241, 243-246
Lehmann, Prof. Louis
    conductor of Illinois Watch Co. Band, 194
Leiter, Levi
    Chicago, 130
Leland Hotel, The, xii, 144, 145
Leone, Anthony J., Jr., xvii
Lexington Genealogical & Historical Society, Inc., Lexington, Illinois, The, xvii
library association of Springfield, 87
Library of Virginia (Richmond, Virginia), The, xvi, xvii

Lincoln Essay Medal, 204
Lincoln Illinois Times
    newspaper. *See* newspapers
Lincoln Library, xii, 152
Lincoln Library in Springfield
    John W. Bunn, an organizer of, 152
Lincoln Meter Company of Springfield, 254
Lincoln Monument, xii, 68, 85, 110, 228
Lincoln presidency
    and Jacob Bunn, 200
Lincoln presidential campaign, 7, 72, 78
Lincoln, Abraham, xi, xiii, xv, xvi, xvii, xviii, 7, 37, 41, 48, 49, 50, 53, 60, 63, 66-68, 70-81, 83, 85, 86, 96, 131, 155, 243, 246
    bank account at Springfield Marine and Fire Insurance Company, 153
    comments to J. W. Bunn about Stephen Douglas' speech, 74
    discussion with John W. Bunn about Salmon P. Chase of Ohio and Lincoln's cabinet, 78
    Essay Award Medal, xiii
    influence and John Whitfield Bunn's position as city treasurer in Springfield, 76
    J. W. Bunn, 150
    leading lawyer in central Illinois, 80
    political mentor to John Whitfield Bunn, 74
    question for J. W. Bunn about votes for Bunn, 76
Lincoln, Abraham presidential campaign, 228
Lincoln, Abraham, and Alton and Springfield Railroad, 99

Lincoln, Abraham's signature on bank ledger, 165
Lincoln, Illinois, 176
Lincoln's death, 85
Lincoln's funeral, 85
Lincoln-Bunn friendship, 73
liquor company, 228
Livingston County, Illinois, 119
Locher, Barry J., xvii
Logan County, Illinois, 22
Logan, Stephen T., 38, 39, 85, 164
London Stock Exchange, 237
    Sangamo Electric Co., 236
London, England, 235, 238
Long Island Loan & Trust Company, 170
"long wave" depression, 171
Loose, Jacob, 117, 118, 164
    coal seam and Sangamon River. *See* Howlett, Parley L.
Los Angeles, 235
Lynn, Scott, 254, 260

M

M. Selz and Company
    shoes and boots, Chicago, 135, 137, 138, 147
machine shops, 113
Mack, A. W. *See* Mack, Alonzo W.
Mack, Alonzo W., 128, 131, 133, 259
Mack, W. E., 259
Macoupin County, Illinois, 16
Madison and Franklin Streets in Chicago
    M. Selz and Company, 135
Mann, Curtis, xvii
Manners, Charles A., 103
Marshall Field, 130
    in Chicago dry goods companies, 130
Marshall Field & Co., 130, 149
Mason County, Illinois, 22
Mason, Charles E., 181, 186, 257
Massachusetts, 9, 56, 121, 185
Massachusetts Bay Colony, 56
Matheny, Charles W., 85, 103
Matheny, Mrs
    benefactor to war refugess, 94
Matheny, N. W., 88
Mather, Thomas, 87, 98
Mather, Thomas S., 38, 39
Matthew Bunn, 9. *See* Edward Bunn
McClernand, John A., 103
    Major General, 103
McConnel, 6, 19, 20. *See* McConnel, Bunn & Van Syckel
McConnel, Andrew B., 103
McConnel, Bunn & Van Syckel, 6, 19, 20
McCoy, Joseph G., 103
McCullagh, Joseph B., 132
McElwain, Benjamin, 16
McKinley Tariff Act, 84
McKinley, William, 82, 84, 85
McLean County, Illinois, 24
Mechanical Innovations of the Sangamo Electric Company. *See* Appendix I
Men of Illinois, 43, 65, 140, 147, 149, 156, 158
merchant steel and plates, 113
Meredith, George W., 190, 258
Meredosia, Illinois, 98
Merriweather, John H., 23, 256
metallurgy, 115
meter and electrical instrument industries, 238
Mexican War, 166
Meyer, Lewis H., 106
Meyer, Max A., 135
Midwest Stock Exchange
    Sangamo Electric Co., 236

Midwestern railroads, 107
miles of railroad track
   statistics, 1890 and 1900, 171
Milford, New Jersey, 29
mill, 113, 123
mill, Blooming, 113
mill, Merchant, 113
mill, rail, 113
Miller, Mr.
   Secretary, Springfield Watch Company, 182
Miller, W. B., 257
Miller, William B., 181
Miner, Orlin H., xii, 111, 112, 140
Mississippi River, 13, 14, 98, 99, 100, 101
Mississippi, Upper and Lower, 100
Missouri, 16
Mitchell, J. J., 106
Monnett, Jacob, 258
Monroe and Franklin Streets
   M. Selz and Company, 135
Montreal, 235
Montreal Curb Market
   Sangamo Electric Co., 236
Moody, Dwight Lyman, 131
   North Market Mission, 130
Moran, Charles, 106
Moran, John, 23, 256
Morgan County, Illinois, 13, 15, 98
Morgan, Col. Richard P., 263
Morgan, Frederic W., 258
Morrison, C. L., 88
Morrow, J. M., 257
   NYC office of Springfield Watch Company, 182
Moultrie County, Illinois, 22
Mrs. Bunn
   Elizabeth Ferguson Bunn, wife of Jacob Bunn, 94, 174, 177
Mt. Morris Seminary, 130
Muir, J. A., 260
Mumford, Lewis
   author of *Technics and Civilization*, 1934, 191
municipal utilities, 3
municipal water facility, 34
Munn, Ira Y., 128
musical society, 17

N

Naples, Illinois, 6, 13, 14, 98, 99
National Association of Watch and Clock Collectors, The, xvii
National Business Hall of Fame, xvi, 309
National Cordage Company
   failure of in 1893, 171
National Observatory in Washington, D.C.
   and a watch competition, 193
nationwide panic
   economic, 172
Navy Ordinance
   timing mechanisms, Sangamo Electric Co., 252
Nebraska, 134, 175
Nehls, Herbert, 260
Nennett, Jacob, 190
New American Encyclopedia, The
   Charles Anderson Dana, 128
New Jersey, 9, 10, 11, 12, 13, 28, 29, 30, 59, 76, 238, 246
New Lisbon, Ohio, 82
New Orleans, Louisiana, 14, 21
New York Canton Tea Company, 21
New York City, 21, 129, 132, 166, 169, 192, 235
New York Produce Exchange, 137
New York Stock Exchange, 108,

169, 170
Sangamo Electric Co., 236
New York Tribune, 12, 129
   Horace Greeley and Charles A. Dana, 128
New York Watch Company in Springfield, Mass., 185
New Zealand, 254
Newberry Library, The, xvii
newspapers, 3, 7, 12, 21, 22, 23, 34, 37, 82, 83, 102, 127, 129, 161, 172, 173, 176, 183, 186
Nichols, Charles, 190, 258
Nickerson, John, 181, 257
Nicolay, John G., 132, 259
Norfolk & Southern Railroad Company, 170
North Carolina, 15. *See* Elisha Kelley
North Grand Avenue, 182
North Market Mission Moody, Chicago, 131
North, the, 166
Northern Cross Railroad, 98
Northern Pacfic Railroad, 171
Norwegian explorer Roald Amundsen. *See* Amundsen, Roald; and the Bunn Special watch, Illinois Watch Co.

O

Oak Clearing Museum, Union Grove, Wisconsin, xvii, 142, 143
Oak Ridge Cemetery, xii, 39, 68, 86
   Bunn family plot, 261
Oelheim, Linda, xvii
Ogden, William B., 106
Ohio, 78, 81, 82, 100, 116
Ohio Life Insurance Company, 166
Ohio River, 124
Old Capitol Square, 33

Old Chatterton and Jacob Bunn. *See* Rudolph's Opera House
Old Northwest, 11, 246
Oneida County, New York, 56
Opdycke, S. B., 99
Open Board of Brokers Watson Bradley Dickerman, 169
Osaka, Japan, 235
Owen, T. J. V., 88

P

Pana, Illinois, 102, 103, 105
Pana, Springfield and Northwestern Railroad Company, 7, 103, 104, 105
Panic of 1837, 160
Panic of 1854, 166
Panic of 1857, 166
Panic of 1873, 8, 126, 135, 170, 172, 177, 178, 183, 229
Panics, 27. *See* 1873
Paris, France, 235
Pasfield, Dr. George, 17, 94, 110, 112, 181
pattern shops, 113
Pearson, 168
Peck, Nathan, 106
Perone, Jan, xvii
period of panic and cyclical depression, 170
Philadelphia, 100, 171, 236
Philadelphia and Reading Railroad
   failure of in 1893, 171
philanthropy, 2, 52, 87, 93, 138, 232
Phillips, Judge Isaac N., 73
Piatt County, Illinois, 22
Pickens Realty Corporation, 255
Pickrell, William, 99
pioneer region, 5

Pittsburgh, Pennsylvania, 84, 100, 116
pocket watch, 219, 220, 221
Polk, Ted, xvii
Poor's Railroad Manual, 64, 112
Pope, Captain John
   US Army, 92
Post, Stephenson, 31. *See* Civil War
pot manufacturer, 17
Poughkeepsie, N. Y., 194
Prairie Archives, Springfield, Illinois, The, xvii
Presbyterian, xi, 9, 17
Priest, John W., 35
Principle of Visionary Succession, 243
printer, 16
puddle mill, 112
puddle works, 113
Pulliam, Robert, 16
Pullman railroad cars
   ampere hour meter, 249
Putnam, Robert D., 2

Q

Quincy, Illinois, 99, 100, 128

R

Racine, Wisconsin, 122, 123
   and Jerome Increase Case, 122
Radio News
   and Illinois Watch Co., dependable source of keeping track of time accurately, 195
Ragsdale, 77
rail manufacturing, 110
rail mill, 112
railroad companies, 10, 101, 106, 227
railroad industry, 10, 22, 83, 96, 97, 98, 99, 108, 110, 191, 198, 201, 221, 234
   and Sangamo Electric Co., 235
railroad timepiece market
   Illinois Watch Co., 191
Railroads, 22, 70, 98, 108, 109
Railroads, Southern Pacific, 192
Railroads, Maine Central, 192
railroads, principal [ones] in the west, 113
rails and fastenings, 113
Randolph County, Illinois, 134
Range recorder or SONAR equipment
   for British Admiralty through Sangamo Limited, 251
Raymond, Walter J. and Marianne S., xvii
Red Cross, The, 239
Reed, Cathy, xvi
Reeves, Judge Owen T., 263
refuge for war victims
   and Elizabeth Ferguson Bunn, 92
Regan, Ruth. *See* Bunn, Ruth Regan
Reinhardt, John, xvii
Republic Steel and Iron Company, 116
Republic Steel and Iron Company of Chicago
   bought the Springfield Iron Company in 1900, 115
Republican, 53, 59, 85, 89, 134, 246, 259
Republican Senator
   Charles Benjamin Farwell, 149
Republican campaign, 4
Republican candidate, 71
Republican city convention, 75
Republican Party, 71, 72, 80, 81,

85, 86, 96, 138, 139, 243
Republican Party in Illinois, 131
Republican Party platform, 73
Republican Party presidential
   supporter
   a Bunn legacy, 85
   Jacob Bunn, prototype for, 81
Republican politics, different
   styles of support and image
   (Bunn's and Hanna's), 83
Republican presidential
   candidate, 80
   Bunn-Lincoln Machine, 86
Republican State Committee,
   137
Republican supporter
   Jacob and John Bunn
      (Lincoln) 86, 246, 84
   Marcus Hanna (McKinley),
      84
Reynolds, H. G., 88
Rhodes, John T., 182
Richardson & Latham, 61
   an insurance and real estate
      partnership, 110
   estate and insurance
      company, 61
Richardson Construction
   Company, 62. *See*
   Richardson, William Douglas
Richardson, Ada Willard, xi, 54-56, 58, 59, 86, 109, 168
Richardson, Betsey Elizabeth
   (Johns), xi, 55
Richardson, Charles, xii, xviii
   brother of William Douglas
      Richardson, 144
Richardson, Henry Earle, 55.
   See Betsey Elizabeth Johns
   Richardson
Richardson, Lucy (Willard), xi,
   56
Richardson, William D., 110,
   134. *See* Richardson, William
   Douglas

Richardson, William Douglas, xi,
   54-58, 61-63, 68, 86, 109, 111,
   112, 116, 140, 144
   construction projects
      included: Lincoln
      Monument, Illinois State
      Capitol, First Methodist
      Episcopal Church of
      Springfield, 110
Ridgely, Charles, 75, 103, 110,
   111, 112, 115, 258
Ridgely, Franklin, 259
Ridgely, N. H., 35, 89
Ridgely, Nicholas, 98
Ridgely, Nicholas H., 168
   store building, 168
Ridgely, William Barret, 115, 259
Riverton mining enterprise, 118
   Western Coal and Mining
      Company, 118
Riverton, Illinois, 7, 117, 118, 119
Robb, James, 106
Roll, Jacob, 16
rolling bars, 113
Rosenstiel, Bunn & Case, 8
Rosenstiel, Charles Henry, xii,
   xvii, 119, 121, 122, 123, 126,
   141, 142, 259
   C. H. Rosenstiel, 123
Rosenstiel, Heinrich Christian
   Carl
   Charles Henry, 122
Rosenstiel, Joe
   Charles Henry Rosenstiel, 267
Rosenwald, Samuel
   Sears & Roebuck, 40
   Springfield Board of Trade, 40
Rudolph's Opera House
   and Jacob Bunn, 83
Russo, Edward J., xvii
Ruth, R. F., 256
Rutherford, Matt, xvii
Rutter, Joseph O., 135

S

saddler, 16
Saint Louis Post-Dispatch, 172
San Francisco, 32, 192, 235
Sangamo, x, xiv
Sangamo, 17. *See* Springfield, names for
Sangamo Company Limited (Canada), 260
Sangamo Company Limited (Toronto), 253
Sangamo Electric Clock, 225
Sangamo Electric Co., some products
    meters, flash devices, sonar devices for US Navy, electric clock motors, refrigeration apparatus. *See* Appendix I
Sangamo Electric Company, x, xiv, 154, 222-224, 226, 233-238, 240, 245, 246, 249, 252, 253, 260, 274
    1931, offices in Springfield, NYC, Chicago, San Francisco, Los Angeles, Toronto, Montreal, Paris, London, Osaka, Buenos Aires, Boston, Philadelphia, Birmingham (AL), Jackson, MS and 25 other cities in the US and Canada, 236
Sangamo Generators, Inc., 254
Sangamo Insurance Company, 35
Sangamo International, Inc., 254
Sangamo Limited
    Canadian subsidiary of Sangamo Electric Co., 251
Sangamo Spectator, 16. *See* Newspapers
Sangamon, xix, 145, 152, 214
Sangamon and Morgan Railroad, 98, 100
Sangamon Company, the
    a Riverton distillery, 119
Sangamon County Agricultural Board, 134
Sangamon County Historical Society, The, xvii
Sangamon County, Illinois, 1, 16, 36, 78, 227, 264, 266, 280
Sangamon Distilling Company, 7
Sangamon River, 117
Sangamon Valley Collection of the Lincoln Library, The, xvii
Sangamon-Weston Limited, 253
Sartoris, Nellie Grant, viii
Saunderson, William, 118
Savings Bank, 173
Scammon, J. Y., 128, 132
Scharf, Louis, 190, 258
Schimenz, J. A., 260
Schnell, Christopher, xvii
Schnirring, Cheryl, xviii
Schuyler, William H., 132
Schwab, Charles H., xii, 135, 137, 138, 147, 148, 259
Scotland, 132
Sears & Roebuck, 40. *See* Samuel Rosenwald
Second Presbyterian Church and the choral society, the Springfield Harmonic Society, 1835, 17
Secretary of State, Louis L. Emmerson, 25
Selz and Schwab, 135
Selz, J. Harry, xii
    son of Morris Selz, 147, 259
Selz, Manuel F., 136, 259
Selz, Morris, xii, 135-138, 147, 148, 259
Selz, Morris, funeral for, 138
Selz, Schwab and Company, 135, 137, 138, 139, 147, 148, 259
Selz, Schwab Shoe Company.

See Selz, Schwab and
Company
senator, 19
Senator Ferguson. *See* Ferguson,
William
Seth Thomas Clock Company of
Thomaston, Connecticut, 239
Shaffer, J. Wilson, 128
Sheppard, James and Joseph, 16
Sheridan, Tom, 233
    master mechanic for Illinois
Watch, 233
Shinkle, Cyrus, 190, 258
shoe machinery industry, 136
shoemaker, 17
Shumway, D. D., 102, 103
Siemens gas furnace, 113, 114
Siemens-Martin, or open hearth
process
    steel, 112
Signal Corps
    and Sangamo Electric Co., 252
Sigler, Mary, viii, 10
Silva, Joseph, 190, 258
Smith, Caleb B.
    Secretary of the Interior, 80
Smith, Henry M., 132, 259
Smith, La Fayette, xii, 65, 111, 112
Smithsonian Institution, 150
Smorowski, Charles
    Secretary of re-organized
Illinois Watch Co. in 1877, 188, 258
social capital, 3
social capitalist, 2, 138
Solomon, Ruth, xviii
Sondal, T. A., 190, 258
Soule, John Babsone Lane, 12.
    See "Go West, young man."
South Carolina, 166, 255
South Pole
    expedition of Roald
Amundsen and the Bunn

Special watches, 193
South, the, 166
Spreckels Sugar Refining
Company, 127
Spreckels, Claus
    sugar, 127
Spreckels, Rudolph
    sugar, 127
Sprigg, John C., 164, 256
Springer, Francis, 93
    Lutheran minister, 93
Springer, Mary
    wife of Francis, 93
Springer, William, 103
"Springfield"
    name of watches made by the
New York Watch Company
in Springfield, Mass., 185
Springfield & Pana Railroad
Company, 7, 102
Springfield and Pana Railroad
Company, 102, 103, 113
Springfield Board of Trade, 7, 40, 41
Springfield City Railway
Company, 7, 38, 39, 40
Springfield City Treasurer
    John W. Bunn, 83
Springfield Harmonic Society, 17
Springfield Home for the
Friendless, xi
Springfield Iron Company, xii,
62, 63, 64, 65, 66, 67, 111-117,
137, 140, 246, 258
Springfield legacy of Jacob Bunn,
178, 228
Springfield Library Association,
246
Springfield Marine and Fire
Insurance Company, xii, 6, 37,
83, 139, 151, 153, 160, 162-165,
167, 256
Springfield Marine Bank, xii, xiii,
31, 59, 70, 151, 153-155, 157,

159, 167, 198, 239, 246, 257
Springfield Municipal Band
and Illinois Watch Co. Band,
Capitol City Band, 194
Springfield Refrigeration
Company
a subsidiary of Sangamo
Electric Co., 250
Springfield Rope Company, 6,
40
Springfield Rotary Club, 239
Springfield Telegraph, 6
Springfield Town Square, 46
Springfield Watch Company,
xiii, 41, 180, 181, 182, 183,
184, 185
New York City office at 11
Maiden Lane, 1873, 182
stock certificate, 207
Springfield Waterworks
Company, 7, 35, 36
Springfield Woolen Mills, 41
Springfield, names for
(considered) Calhoun,
Sangamo, 17
Springfield, new state capitol
building, 228
Springfield-Terre Haute
correspondences, 99
about a connecting railroad,
101
St. Louis, 114
St. Louis, Missouri, 14, 99, 106,
162
stagecoach, 37
Standard Club
of Chicago, 138, 147, 148
standard railroad time, 234
standard railroad timekeeping,
200
standard time, 191
standardization of American
railroad time
Illinois Watch Co., 196
Stanton, Edwin

Civil War, 128
Starne, Alexander, 103, 112
State Agricultural Board of
Illinois
Charles Henry Rosenstiel,
served on, 123
State Bank of Illinois, 160, 161,
162, 164
state capital, 15, 19, 28, 56
State Capitol, construction of
the new. *See* William Douglas
Richardson
State House Square, 17
State Journal Register, The, xvii
State National Bank, 168
State Treasurer of Illinois
F. K. Whittemore, 169
steam mill, 17
steel conversion factory, 113
steel corporations, 116
Steel, Bethlehem, 116
Steel, U.S., 116
steel-making process, 113
Stephenson County
Genealogical Society,
Freeport, Illinois, The, xviii
Stewart, Julia, xviii
strategies of antisubmarine
operations
Attack Teacher mechanism,
Sangamo Electric Co., 251
Stratton, William J.
Secretary of State of Illinois,
26
Strawbridge, Thomas, 16
Stuart and Edwards
law firm, 167
Stuart and Edwards, office of, 35
Stuart, John Todd, xiii. *See*
Stuart, John T.
"Stuart" Grade
watch movement, 15 jewels,
183
Stuart, John T., 35, 38, 39, 85,

86, 88, 99
Stuart, John Todd, 180, 183, 201, 257
submarine defense technology Sangamo Electric Co., 241
sugar factory, 123
sugar refining, 119, 127
Sugar Trust, the, 127
Sullivan, Illinois, 99
Swift, Gen. R. K., 90, 92

T

tachograph, xiv
   photo (see book cover), 226
tavern keeper, 16
Taylor, Elizabeth Bunn, xviii
Taylorville, Illinois, 102, 103, 104, 105
Tazewell County, Illinois, 16
telegraph, 6, 36, 37, 38, 228
Terre Haute, Indiana, 99, 100, 101
Texas State House, 130
Third District Republican Congressional Committeeman Chicago, Morris Selz, 147
Thomas G. Plant Shoe Machinery Company, 136
Thomas, Dr. Mark, xviii
Thompson, Lewis E., 103
timepiece company, 180
timepiece industry, 191
timepiece technology, 200
Tinsley, S. M., 164
Toledo, Peoria and Western Railway Company, 108
Toronto, 235, 253
Toronto Stock Exchange Sangamo Electric Co., 236
Tracy, Frank W., 257
transportation, 10, 13, 28, 34, 38, 39, 102, 108, 109, 146

transportation industry, 38
Treat, Judge Samuel H., 85, 94

U

U.S. Steel, 116
Underwater Sound Section of the United States Bureau of Ships.
   contract with Sangamo Electric Co., 241
Union League Club, 137, 138, 147, 148
   (of Chicago) Morris Selz, John W. Bunn, Charles H. Schwab all members of, 137
Union National Bank Hanna, Ohio, 82
United Shoe Machinery Company, 136
United States and the British military
   and Sangamo Electric Co., 235
United States Navy, 235, 251
United States Senator from California, 32
University of Illinois, xvii, 30, 137
   John Whitfield Bunn, first Treasurer of, 137
University of Virginia, xvii, xviii
utilities, 34, 36

V

Van Ness & Company
   china and home furnishings, 167
Van Syckel, 6, 19, 20
Vandalia, 15. *See* State capitals
Vandalia, Illinois, 13, 160
Vandever, Horatio M., 102, 103
Veiller, Jayne & Co. of New

York, 125
Vicksburg
   Battle of, 31, 103. *See* Civil War
violent economic disasters, 170
Von Hoffman, Louis, 106
von Siemens, Dr., 233

W

Wabash Avenue
   Chicago, 135
Wabash, Illinois Central, Chicago & Alton, Northwestern Railroads, among the principal ones in the west, 113
Wadsworth & Phelps
   dry goods, Chicago, 130
   dry goods, John Villiers Farwell, 149
Wallace, Dr. William S., 17
Walsh, John R., 132
Waltham and Elgin products watches, 184
Waltham Watch Company, 220
war efforts, British, US, Canadian and Sangamo Electric Co., 242
war refugees, 93, 95
Warren, Hooper, 16
Washington Park in Springfield coal mining, 117
Washington, D.C., 193
watch companies, 8
watch industry, 191
watch making, 179, 196
watch manufacturing industry, 180
watch markets and timepiece industry, 191
watch movement production rate, 183
watches, *Beau Royale*
   Illinois Watch wristwatch for men, 209
watches, Bunn Special
   Illinois Watch Co. *See* Amundsen, Roald
watches, children's timepiece market
   Illinois Watch Co., 190
watches, first nickel watch movement
   Illinois Watch Co., 1879, 190
watches, jeweled timepiece movement industry, 220
watches, ladies' watch market, 190
watches, manufacturing specialties and personnel, 1918
   Illinois Watch Co., timing and adjusting; finishing; train; jeweling; screw; machine; escape; plate; dial; damaskeening; punch; engraving; balance staff; gilding, 190
watches, men's watch market
   Illinois Watch Co. and Elgin Watch Co., 190
watches, national standard for timepiece accuracy, 192
watches, open-face stem-winding watch in America first, Illinois Watch Company, 186
watches, pocket watch
   Bunn Special railroad pocket watch
   photo, 221
watches, smallest in America, 1886
   Illinois Watch Co., 190
watches, Swiss, 193
watches, *The Bar Harbor*
   Illinois Watch strap watch,

211
watches, *The Beau Brummel* Illinois Watch strap watch, 212
watches, *The Claudette* Illinois wristwatch for women, 209
watches, *The Dean* Illinois Watch pocket watch for men, 210
watches, *The Del Monte* Watch Illinois Watch strap watch, 211
watches, *The Edgewater* Illinois Watch strap watch, 211
watches, *The Ensign* Illinois Watch strap watch, 212
watches, *The Glenna* Illinois Watch wristwatch for women, 209
watches, *The Marquis-Autocrat* Illinois Watch, 212
watches, *The Miami* Illinois Watch strap watch, 211
watches, *The New Yorker* Illinois Watch strap watch for men, 210
watches, *The Newport* Illinois Watch strap watch, 211
watches, *The Vanity Fair* Illinois Watch ribbon watch for ladies, 210
Waterworks Company, 36, 117, 118
Watson, B. A., 88
Webster, B. C., 99
Webster, J. D., 91
Weiss, Debra, xvi
Western Clock Company, 239
Western Coal & Mining Company, 7, 118

Weston Electrical Instrument Company Ltd. of Great Britain, 253
and Sangamo Electric Co., 238
Weston Electrical Instrument Corporation of New Jersey, 253
Weston Electrical Instrument Corporation, a New Jersey corporation, 238
"Wheelbarrow Dialogue" between Jacob Bunn and his younger brother John Whitfield Bunn in NJ, 30, 243
Wheeler and Schebler Carburetor Company permanent magnet, 249
Wheeling, Virginia [now West Virginia], 100
White, George, 181
White, Joseph B., 106
White, Otis, 260
Whittemore, F. K., xiii, 156, 168, 169, 246
wholesale and retail, 21, 22, 27
wholesale and retail commerce, 21
wholesale and retail goods, 20
wholesale house, 19, 31
Wickersham, C. I., 259
Wieties, Ilert, 191, 258
Will, Grundy, and Kankakee counties
A. W. Mack, Senator of. *See* counties
Willard & Zimmerman, 56. *See* paint and wallpaper company contractors. *See* Richardson, Ada Willard.
Willard, Alexander Perry, 56, 168. *See* Lucy Willard Richardson

Willard, Lucy, 62. *See* Lucy Willard Richardson wife of William Douglas Richardson, 58
Willard, Major Simon, 56
Williams, John, 35-37, 85, 86, 93, 99, 100, 101, 103, 111, 112, 160, 163, 164, 181, 201
Williams, Melinda, xviii
Williston Academy, 177
Williston Seminary in Easthampton, NY, 169
Williston, George D., 132, 259
Wilson, James, 103, 133
Wilson, James Harrison, 132
wireless operators, amateur during WWI, 195
"Wishbone," 27
"Wishbone Coffee," xi
"Wishbone Coffee" label, 47
"Wishbone Coffee" tin, 47
Women's Clubs
　Illinois Watch Co. employees, 214
Wood, John, 128
Woods & Henkle clothing enterprise, 167
Woods, George, 167
woolen mills, 17
World War II, 241
World's Columbian Exposition 1893, 110, 137, 148
Worthington pump, 113
Wright, Erastus, 85
Württemberg
　Morris Selz, 135

Y

Yale University, 177, 234, 235, 244
　Robert Carr Lanphier, 222
Yates, Richard, xi, 53, 90
　as Commander in Chief, Civil War, 90
　Republican Governor, 89
Yelich, Hope, xvi
Young Men's Christian Association of Chicago
　John Villiers Farwell and, 131
Youngstown, Ohio, 116

Z

Zimmerman, Robert, 56

Note of Interest

On March 18, 2005, Jacob Bunn was accepted into the National Business Hall of Fame and the Illinois Business Hall of Fame.

March 18 is also the birthday of both Jacob Bunn, the subject of this book, and Andrew Taylor Call, the author of this book.